Second Edition

The Sociology of Law

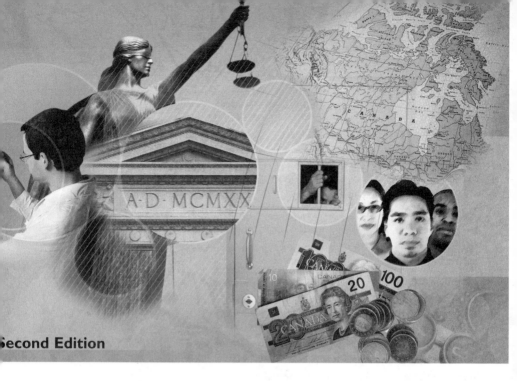

Second Edition

The Sociology of Law

critical approaches
to social control

Brian Burtch

Simon Fraser University

THOMSON
—⋆—™
NELSON

Australia   Canada   Mexico   Singapore   Spain   United Kingdom   United States

THOMSON

NELSON

The Sociology of Law: Critical Approaches to Social Control
Second Edition
By Brian Burtch

Editorial Director and Publisher:
Evelyn Veitch

Executive Editor:
Joanna Cotton

Acquisitions Editor:
Brad Lambertus

Marketing Manager:
Lenore Taylor

Developmental Editor:
Shefali Mehta

Production Editor:
Carrie Withers

Production Coordinator:
Helen Jager Locsin

Copy Editor and Proofreader:
Erin Moore

Creative Director:
Angela Cluer

Interior Design:
Sonya Thursby

Interior Design Modifications:
Peter Papayanakis

Cover Design:
Angela Cluer

Cover Image:
Created and designed by Greg
Holoboff, Graphic Designer/Illustrat
Centre for Distance Education, Simc
Fraser University. Permission for use
granted by the Centre for Distance
Education/Simon Fraser University

Compositor:
W.G. Graphics

Indexer:
Edwin Durbin

Printer:
Transcontinental

**National Library of Canada
Cataloguing in Publication Data**

Main entry under title:
Burtch, Brian E., 1949 –
   The sociology of law: critical
approaches to social control

Includes bibliographical references
and index.

ISBN 0-17-622392-4

1. Sociological jurisprudence I. Title

K370.B87 2003   340.115
C2002-902905-8

For my family, friends, and colleagues

TABLE OF CONTENTS

PREFACE

An appreciation of the origins of law, and how modern laws function, is essential in the study of social sciences and jurisprudence. Courses in law and society help students to express and reassess their assumptions of law and political and social relations. As I developed lectures and worked with students in the smaller setting of tutorials, it became important to breathe life into the sociology of law and to come to terms with contemporary issues. Issues include the growth of feminism and feminist jurisprudence; struggles for human rights and an end to some of the more blatant forms of discrimination; national and international forces that contributed to systems of injustice (or movement toward justice); changes in the nature of the family, as well as family law and divorce law; and the politics of criminal law.

This second edition of *The Sociology of Law* presents a selective overview of theory and research in the broad areas of law, social control, and social change. The study of lawmaking and legal processes has its roots in classical social thought and historical research. Historical examples are used in many chapters to complement contemporary law and society research. Attention is also drawn to *contemporary* social science research and theorizing on the state, social class, gender, and social inequality. Canadian material is featured, along with international evidence. This new edition, designed primarily for undergraduate courses, concentrates on emerging perspectives in law and society research, including new social movements, social justice initiatives, restorative justice, globalization, and postmodern approaches.

I have accepted a colleague's suggestion that students are eager to discuss and rethink competing theories of law and society. Theoretical approaches are introduced early in this text, and are applied as we cover particular topics. Hopefully, this book will underscore the limits of law, and its potential for realizing justice. Each chapter concludes with a set of *study questions* to assist you in reviewing key themes from the chapter. An *author/subject index* is found at the end of the book to help you locate particular topics. Instructors and students may wish to use supplementary resources along with this text.

The first chapter covers various ways in which law is defined and different meanings attached to the concept of law. Law reflects profoundly different, and often antagonistic, ways of interpreting the world. Conservative, liberal, and radical versions of law and society are briefly reviewed. Chapter Two reviews some aspects of the European-based, classical writings of Durkheim, Weber, and Marx.

Chapter Three gives particular emphasis to the historical origins of law in Canada and in England. Chapter Four introduces issues of gender, including feminist-based research on law and society. Chapter Five addresses First Nations and their experiences with law. A specific case—the wrongful conviction of Donald Marshall, Jr.—is covered with respect to criminal justice and Native people. This is followed, in Chapter Six, by a wider discussion of discrimination in law, using a variety of studies of racial discrimination in society, legal aspects of racial and ethnic discrimination, and efforts to reverse long-established patterns of racial imbalance.

Chapter Seven provides a critical look at the legal profession and the judiciary. Race, class, and gender are explored in the context of women in the legal profession, and the nature of sentencing decisions. Chapter Eight outlines issues in the use of the criminal sanction in Canada. Chapter Nine brings forward conflicting interpretations of the role of the law in human reproduction. This includes separation and divorce (child custody, child support, and the broader question of spouses' equality before the law), abortion, and midwifery. Finally, Chapter Ten reviews a number of key themes, especially the implications of reforming legal structures, and the role of law in facilitating or resisting social change.

I've tried to present ideas as clearly as possible, to minimize what William Zinser calls "clotted language" (2001, 6)[1]. I have also tried to present both positive and negative examples of legal regulation, hopefully avoiding an undeservedly bleak analysis of law in society, and preserving a sense of hope in the face of massive forces such as globalization and various kinds of discrimination.

The sociology of law is a complex multidisciplinary area, covering such vast approaches as philosophy of law, case law and jurisprudence, economics, politics, anthropology, sociology, and linguistics. This text is clearly a selective work, given the complex issues that it introduces. This text is best used with other sources—readers, custom courseware, Internet sites, reserve readings—depending on the needs and outlook of the instructor and students. Selected references are provided at the end of this chapter for students who wish to pursue this subject in greater detail.

Brian Burtch
April 2002

---

[1] Zinsser, W. (2001) *On Writing Well.* New York: HarperCollins.

Acknowledgements

I am grateful to faculty, staff, and students in the School of Criminology and the Department of Women's Studies at Simon Fraser University. John Whatley and his colleagues in The Centre for Distance Education at SFU were very helpful in fostering an on-line version of a Sociology of Law course. As always, Jack Corse and his peers in the Reference Division, SFU Library, were especially helpful in locating materials. My favourite book-seller—Mary Trentadue of North Vancouver's 32 Books—kindly helped with missing references. I am thankful for the camaraderie of The Writers' Union of Canada, including Nadeem Parmar and Bill Schermbrucker. The University of Hull, England, provided a hospitable environment for research and writing in December 2001.

The staff at Nelson Thomson has been very helpful in this project. Brad Lambertus has been a stalwart Acquisitions Editor and catalyst for redeveloping this book. Shefali Mehta, as Developmental Editor, Carrie Withers, as Production Editor and Erin Moore as copy editor, have been very professional and helpful. Six anonymous reviewers provided essential, and at times quite pointed suggestions for improving the first edition of this book. My spouse, Carol Hird, has been very supportive as has my daughter, Leora. Special thanks to my parents, my two brothers, and my sister for their support over the years.

1

Introduction to the Sociology of Law

At the present as well as at any other time, the centre of gravity of legal development lies not in legislation, nor in juristic science, nor in judicial decision, but in society itself.

(*Eugen Ehrlich,* Fundamental Principles of the Sociology of Law*)*

INTRODUCTION

Law and legal obligations seem to be everywhere. Law covers the spectrum of our lives, ranging from trivial matters to profound, life-and-death issues. The morning newspaper is full of crime news, labour-management disputes, international law, land claims and self-government initiatives by First Nations people, and immigration. Terrorism and counter-terrorism are in the news, including the attacks of September 11, 2001, the escalating conflicts in the Middle East, and the aftermath of the sarin gas attack that killed and injured thousands of people in the Tokyo subway system in 1995 (Murakami 2001). From municipal governments to international bodies, political authority and law are pervasive, contested areas worldwide.

Law is not a monopoly of legal practitioners and scholars, but also an institution that stems from historical senses of justice and dispute-resolution. The sociology of law offers a way of looking at law not merely as a natural force for resolving disputes, but as a socially constructed institution that attracts opposition and criticism from all quarters. In a sense, law is an "open book," contested and explained in countless ways for many issues. These include censorship and sexually explicit materials, First Nations land claims and self-determination, the issue of Québec sovereignty *vis-à-vis* Canadian nationalism (federalism), and legal claims associated with the gay and lesbian movement.

SOCIOLOGICAL PERSPECTIVES ON LAW AND SOCIETY

Sociology is remarkably diverse in its theoretical outlook and methodological approaches (Clark 1999). For some, sociology is a scientific discipline that produces a growing "body of interrelated scientific positions, or generalizations, that explain social behaviour" (Theodorson and Theodorson 1979, 401). Sociologists also seek to predict and provide empirical verification for human behaviour. In practice, however, many sociologists routinely lament the gulf between theoretical statements and empirical proof of these statements. One key concern is how law emerged from previous customary arrangements in "pre-law" societies as well as law's role in contemporary societies. The nature of authority in pre-law societies has attracted great interest in the social scientists. Anthropologists, for example, contrast formal state law with use of custom in earlier and contemporary societies. Pre-law societies are often associated with collective dispute-resolution and often draw on spiritual, religious, and even "heroic" sources in resolving conflicts (see Treviño 1996, 3). Custom is thus an integral part of dispute-resolution processes in earlier societies. Olivia Harris sees custom as many-headed; that is, sometimes taking the form of oppression of minority groups, and other times serving as a form of resistance to "an alien and imposing state" (1996, 9). Dembour, in a similar vein, points out that human rights in non-Western societies may be more than an imposition of Western authority and values. Asserting traditional or modern forms of human rights can check the power of "ruling classes" (Dembour 1996, 22–23).

The sociology of law is a central tradition within classical and contemporary sociology. Sociologists who study law place specific legal cases, laws, regulations, and the general administration of justice into a social context. To this end, sociologists have used materials from other disciplines—history, anthropology, political science, and economics, among others—to explain patterns of legal control within this broader, social context. Much of this work is of a *scholarly* nature and is meant to increase our general knowledge of the social underpinnings and influences on legal process, and how legal process influences social values and behaviour. Other work in this field may be of a more *applied* nature, in that the researcher seeks to evaluate outcomes of particular legal strategies, for example, or to provide practical suggestions with respect to legal policy. The former approach is referred to as the sociology *of* law; the latter as sociology *in* law. Incorporation of theory and practice is critical for many scholars and practitioners, whether they are seeking liberal reform of laws and policies or a more fundamental transformation.

In recent years, the study of sociological factors in law has been challenged by critical theorists, most notably as a result of a resurgence of interest in Marxist-derived theories of law (referred to as neo-Marxist theories) and a strong interest in decentralized, less formal strategies of social justice. These Marxist-based theories seek to explain social inequality and legal equality with reference to economic factors and the creation of social classes. Feminist scholarship, particularly feminist jurisprudence, has also challenged conventional assumptions about the nature of law, especially its claims of equality of women and men before the law, and about the representation of all citizens within the social contract. These critical theorists have generally emphasized the importance of placing legal and social control in historical context, as a process that cannot be reduced to abstract principles or limited ideologies in support of existing authority relations. These critical studies of law and social control underscore the power of certain ideologies—for example, "white, patriarchial prescriptions" (Backhouse 1991, 7)—used to define patterns of dominance and subordination within societies. There has also been substantial criticism of legal positivism, which is a tendency to treat jurisprudence as an exact science, a rational process that consists of identifiable data and rules (Cotterrell 1984, 10). Such an approach to law is questionable, since "it assumes a certainty and clarity in rules that is by no means apparent..." (Cotterrell 1984, 11). The spirit of legal positivism, i.e., "... the proper resolution of a legal dispute can typically be determined by the morally unbiased application of authoritative legal rules ..." has certainly been attacked and widely discredited by many scholars (Waluchow 1998, 387–88). One danger in this attack on positivism is the oversimplification of positivism, as if it is nothing but a misguided monolithic practice, rather than a multifaceted set of philosophies and approaches (see Waluchow 1998).

Postmodernists are suspicious of modern beliefs in scientific rationality and the grand political ideologies of liberalism and Marxism. Baum (1990) refers to dynamic "new associative patterns," with complex affiliations and cross-affiliations of people in social movements such as ecology, peace, and the women's movement. Baum (1990) adds that postmodernists emphasize "solidarity, community, conviviality, and spirituality," but not in the more doctrinaire forms of traditional political ideologies. Hunt (1991, 80) notes that at a very general level, postmodernism stands as a "critique of the rationalism of Enlightenment thought," and has often been directed at various forms of socialism and Marxism. Hunt (1991) is critical of some strands of postmodernism, as well as its tendency toward a fragmented approach to politics, and its end-point (as Hunt sees it) of pessimism.

Along with a renewed interest in critical theories of law and social control, there has been a movement by conservative lobbyists to influence various aspects of law. These include reforms to family law, efforts to restrict or outlaw access to therapeutic abortions, more severe penalties for juvenile and adult offenders, and restrictions on freedom of expression and speech, to name a few. The more conservative emphasis on increased powers of state surveillance and arrest, cutbacks in the welfare state (together with a free-market ideology), and various punitive dispositions underscores the extent to which the legitimacy of law in modern, complex societies is contested. The conservative nature of many forms of modern law, however, is increasingly under attack from emerging social movements that challenge dominant ideologies and practices that exclude a variety of citizens from greater participation in law and social opportunities (Melucci 1988; Young 1990).

FORMAL EQUALITY AND SUBSTANTIVE INEQUALITY

A central theme in this book is the disparity between the *formal equality* promised under the doctrine of rule of law, and the *substantive inequality* that exists within the social order. For Ehrlich (1975, 497), the "living law" reflected that substantial portion of law that groups or individuals adhered to, distinct from the technical rules of conduct set out in law. Cotterrell (1984, 29) defines the *living law* as "rules that are actually followed in social life," and that serve to deactivate disputes that might be dealt with by state authorities. The living law has been assessed by a number of theorists as falling far short of idealized formal law.

There is no single, uncontested definition of or approach to the sociological study of law. Milovanovic (1988) places the sociology of law in a general framework, in which descriptions of case law and legal processes, and the logic of legal principles are explored through the social sciences. The origins of law and the factors that influence the making and application of laws are of central importance. The concepts of *social order* and *social conflict* are crucial, inasmuch as there is great disagreement over the extent to which law actually reflects a widely shared moral consensus or is, conversely, the site of profound conflicts and differing interests. The related concept of "public interest" or "public opinion" has also been criticized. Diverse opinions and interpretations about law and morality have led many to discuss such broad conceptions of the public as glorified artifacts; rather, there are many "publics" within a given constituency (see Cotterrell, 1984, 149).

Milovanovic (1988) identifies two broad approaches to the study of law: jurisprudence and the sociology of law. The first, *jurisprudence*, begins with definitions of law and legal rules as set out by the state and proceeds on the assumption that legal decision-making is rational and that legal processes are legitimate, and indeed essential to social order. Certain conflicts are thus subject to the abstract application of legal principles to "factual situations" (Milovanovic 1988, 4), keeping in mind the doctrine of *stare decisis* (whereby current legal cases are decided with reference to preexisting decisions, or precedents). The logic underlying decisions in legal cases, while intricate and considered (ideally), is seen as relatively unproblematic as far as the value of legal decisions is concerned.

The second approach identified by Milovanovic is the *sociology of law*. Rather than beginning with legal definitions as codified by the state, or a description of various legal decisions and principles, the sociology of law centres on the social aspects of legal control. The interests served by law, and the dimensions of coercion and domination through law, are important questions in this approach. The sociology of law is more closely linked with social science methodology and theory than with professional legal training or legal practice. These two approaches are not wholly distinct— there is overlap in theory, research, and practice—and Hunt (1980) has written of a movement away from jurisprudence as such, toward a "sociological movement" in the study of law. Jurisprudence is nonetheless more closely associated with the logic of law and the interpretation of legal decisions, while the sociology of law serves to explore central themes of social order, social conflict, and power relations expressed through law.

DEFINITIONS OF LAW

Definitions of law range from fairly straightforward definitions of the limits and scope of law, and the roles played by legislators, administrators, and pressure groups in forming and changing law, to more critical interpretations of legal powers. The dominant ideology in support of Western legal systems values the rule of law as a hallmark of freedom, widely supported by the public. For others, this equation of modern law and freedom is mistaken, a chimera. They see law as a powerful means of maintaining social order, including the preservation and widening of social and legal inequalities (Ericson 1983).

Following his extensive review of different conceptualizations of law, Cotterrell (1984, 46) concludes that state law must be the main focus for the study of law in contemporary Western societies. He defines state law as "that category of social rules for which the processes and institutions of creation, interpretation and enforcement are most visible, formal and elaborate." He adds that law thus refers to doctrines and social rules as they are interpreted and enforced by state agencies, within a politically organized society. Max Weber has established a classic definition of law as a more organized system of sanctions used to ensure compliance or "avenge violation" (Milovanovic 1988, 41).

Not all reactions to deviant conduct are greeted with legal sanctions. The vast majority may be tolerated or treated, not as violations of law as such, but as infractions of a social norm. Hoebel defines a *social norm* as follows: "A social norm is legal if its neglect or infraction is regularly met, in threat or in fact, by the application of physical force by an individual or group possessing the socially recognized privilege of so acting" (cited in Milovanovic 1988, 5).

Timasheff (1974, 23–24) believed that law fulfilled the social function of "imposing norms of conduct or patterns of social behavior on the individual will." The issue of what is socially recognized is also significant. Not all legal powers are demonstrably based in public consensus, and some may clearly be unpopular. The mythical figures of Robin Hood or Jean Valjean (in Victor Hugo's *Les Misérables*) are two examples of people fighting against social and legal injustice. Civil disobedience and "direct action" justify the use of force or violence as a political strategy against forms of injustice. In 1990, the well-publicized release of Nelson Mandela ended 26 years of political imprisonment for a man who fought against South Africa's policy of apartheid. In Canada, Native people have increasingly relied on acts of civil disobedience to protest government insensitivity to their plight. In considering this motif of conflicting definitions and perspectives on the social context of law, we should bear in mind that there have been significant breaks from conventional approaches to law. Smart (1989, 4) challenges conventional definitions of law when she writes that law is inherently contradictory, with "conflicting principles" and contradictory effects wherever law is applied. Thus, while law *claims* a fundamental unity in theory and practice, this supposed unity is continually being challenged. The issue is thus not only how we define law, but how we sustain the integrity of alternative approaches in the face of legal powers that seek to co-opt and undermine these social movements.

PURPOSES AND FUNCTIONS OF LAW

> They [the poor] have to labour in the face of the majestic equality of the law, which forbids the rich as well as the poor alike to sleep under bridges, to beg in the streets, and to steal bread.
>
> (Anatole France, Le Lys Rouge, 1894, quoted in Partington 1997)

Law can be seen as a leavening force in modern political life, easing conflicts or short-circuiting possible conflicts through an elaborate process of public education, surveillance, arrest, mediation, and so forth. There is considerable disagreement, however, over the functions that law serves. Much of this disagreement centres on the relationship between legal ordering and social power. Law can be seen as a dynamic force that relies on a wide range of resources, used in complex ways to ensure the survival of political power despite conflicts within a given political or social order.

Critical theorists, especially those developing a Marxist-based approach to law, identify three central functions of law in capitalist societies: the repressive function, the facilitative function, and the ideological function. The *repressive* function of law is arguably the most visible and dramatic. This function rests on the coercive powers of the state, as assured by law. Some regimes may rely more heavily on direct uses of force, via the police and military troops, while others use incentives and strategies to promote compliance with the law. Powers of arrest, incarceration, and detention are a few examples of the use of direct force by the state. The use of "deadly force"—killing civilians—is an extreme example of the repressive powers of the state. In Canada, police shootings of visible minority citizens generated protests in Winnipeg, Toronto, and Montreal (McMahon and Ericson 1987, 38–39). The killing of Indian leader John Joseph (J.J.) Harper in Winnipeg in March 1988 prompted charges of racist policing policies, and the formation of an inquiry into aboriginal justice in Manitoba (Sinclair Jr. 1999).

Repressive powers are vital to state rule, but must be accompanied over time by the other two functions: the facilitative function and the ideological function of law. The *facilitative* function of law represents "the degree to which law aids in assuring predictability and certainty in behavioral expectations" (Milovanovic 1988, 9). The contract-like structure of law thus seeks to provide greater stability and regularity in modern, complex societies. Milovanovic (1988) discusses how this facilitative function has been interpreted in different ways. Thus, as discussed in Chapter Two, Max Weber provided a more favourable outlook on the value of legal rationality as a feature of capitalist development, while Karl Marx provided a powerful critique of capitalism and emphasized the need to replace bourgeois legality with a socialist order that was not dependent on the artifices of state control, including its legal apparatus.

The *ideological* function in law pertains to belief systems, specifically, the way in which legal ideology helps promote domination, legitimation, and hegemony. The concept of hegemony can be used in its broadest sense of "leadership, esp[ecially] of one State of a confederacy" (*Concise Oxford English Dictionary*). In a more positive sense, it stands as an overarching kind of power associated with continued governance and decision-making. Hegemony is also widely used in critical approaches. One definition of hegemony draws attention to its role in generating mistaken, or "falsely conscious," beliefs or misrepresenting actual forms of domination and power in given societies (Sumner 1979, 4–5). This element of consent and compliance in oppression is embodied in the Gramscian approach to hegemony. Antonio Gramsci envisioned hegemony as rooted in historically specific blocs consisting of various allies and coalitions. "This bloc represents a basis of consent for a certain social order, in which the hegemony of a dominant class is created and re-created in a web of institutions, social relations, and ideas" (Sassoon 1983, 201). Hegemony is a means whereby the state and its agents can justify social and legal inequality. This kind of social order assumes that individuals are responsible for their own fate, that there are ample economic and social opportunities within the social structure, or that encroachment on specific civil liberties is tolerable or even desirable. Hegemonic power is seen as a dominant, but not exclusive, power within modern societies. It predominates, but does not monopolize, social thought or action in specific societies. Hegemony can thus be faced with opposing, or counter-hegemonic, values surrounding law and the social order.

KEY THEORETICAL MODELS OF LAW AND SOCIETY

Disenchantment with consensually rooted theories of law and society has generated several competing theories, which constitute the conflict perspective. Conflict theorists outline persistent controversies, such as the failure of federal and provincial governments to resolve Native land claims in British Columbia and other jurisdictions within Canada. There have also been numerous criticisms of blatantly racially-motivated legislation such as internment of Japanese-Canadians during World War II. For conflict theorists, the legal apparatus does not automatically or naturally operate in the interests of a shared morality. Law may ameliorate or resolve certain conflicts, but the overwhelming influence of powerful political and economic interests may steer lawmakers and legal authorities to serve the interests of particular groups.

There has been a longstanding, conventional distinction between theories of law that assume a general consensus of values and norms within societies (structural-functional approaches) and those theories that assume substantial disagreements and conflicts over the nature of law and society. The consensus-conflict debate is exhausted and oversimplified. New theories of justice and social control challenge stock versions of consensus and conflict theory. Nevertheless, some discussion of the two perspectives is important, as current theories retain some elements of conflict and consensus. At this point, it is helpful to review some key models (see Comack 1999). We begin with structural-functionalism.

Functionalism

There are many variations within the social-consensus perspective. An American jurist, Roscoe Pound, regarded law as an institution that serves to maintain "social cohesion" through its management of competing interests and claims (Cotterrell 1984, 76–77). This process serves to contain potentially destructive conflicts and to preserve a sense of order as societies change (Cotterrell 1984, 76–77). The assumption of a shared consensus, and the view of the state (including law) as a catalyst, ensuring orderly change in the public interest, is criticized for overlooking persistent inequalities and exclusion in lawmaking and law enforcement. Even so, proponents of consensual theories argue that the law, for all its faults, is central and indispensable in ensuring some measure of regularity in social life, political life, and economic transactions.

Functionalist perspectives are an important legacy in studies of law and society. A key feature in the functionalist approaches of Emile Durkheim and of Talcott Parsons is the metaphor of society-as-organism. The "health" of the organism requires that certain needs are made, and this is applied to societies which can be functional or dysfunctional. In reality, all societies are a mixture of the two—functions and dysfunctions. For functionalists, key social institutions need to operate effectively for the society to survive. These key institutions are often described as the economy, family, religion, schools, law, and government. For functionalists, law serves to resolve myriad social conflicts through the civil or criminal courts, for example. The point here is that law is seen as based on a general social consensus.

There are many criticisms of functionalist theories of law and society. First, few would now argue that social values are uniform, that law rests on some general social consensus, given the complexity of modern societies. Disagreements abound, seemingly everywhere we turn there is a dispute or contest, and court challenges and political debates underscore how a consensual society may reflect earlier, essentially homogenous societies, but not modern societies. The possibility of achieving uniformity of values is also vain, given a wide number of ideological differences in complex, post-industrial societies. Second, functionalist theories lack a dynamic quality of explaining how social change develops, and how specific groups or social forces may instigate or block social change. It may take something of a status quo approach to society, focusing on interrelationships of key institutions but without the dynamic quality of Marxism, feminism, and other more critical frameworks. Third, there is an apolitical quality to functionalist theories. More critical theorists draw on such themes as globalization, capitalism and social inequality, patriarchy, gender disadvantage, and homophobia. These critical approaches rest on an appreciation of ways in which social structures, including legal institutions, have been used against specific groups, limiting their involvement in society, or in extreme cases, leading to slavery and genocide.

In legal scholarship, Roscoe Pound is frequently used as an example of the functionalist approach. Pound envisioned society as essentially harmonious, with law serving to reconcile conflicting interests. Vago (1994, 18) sees this approach resting on "social compromise" in complex, "pluralistic" societies. For Pound "... the purpose of law is to maintain and to ensure those values and needs essential to social order, not by imposing one group's will on others, but by controlling, reconciling, and mediating the diverse and conflicting interests of individuals and groups within society ... the purpose of law is to control interests and to maintain harmony and social integration" (Vago 1994, 18). Talcott Parsons was also a prominent functionalist. For Parsons, law is one of several social institutions that can work in concert to increase harmony within society. The emphasis here is on accord not discord, on social order over conflict even within very complex societies (Vago 1997).

Many social science scholars regard structural-functionalism as an anachronism. They dismiss the fiction of an assumption of general consensus in societies. Structural-functionalists have faced scathing criticisms for what some see as a fanciful model of social relationships, one which downplays deeply-rooted social antagonisms manifested as sexism, hatred of minority groups, and social class warfare, for example. Nevertheless, concepts of social solidarity, social harmony, shared values and expectations, and the interlocking of various social institutions within a given society have been essential in the sociological tradition.

In this consensual model, law serves a general consensus of opinion about proper conduct in society. In criminal law, a system of punishments is ostensibly made in the general interest to deal with crimes that offend public safety and the public interest in social order. Likewise, complex systems of civil law are built, replacing earlier structures that were based on social customs. The interlocking nature of modern social institutions such as the family, work, education, economy, and so forth is seen as requiring regulatory structures to co-ordinate social needs. In this respect, government powers, including various forms of law, lend coherence to a social system that would otherwise not be viable. Early functionalist outlooks have been followed by neo-functionalist sociological approaches that retain such concepts as regulation, reproduction of the social system, and "functional differentiation" (see Treviño 1996, 323–24).

The law is also linked with a conservative outlook. Emphasis on family stability, religiosity, punishment of criminals, protection of private property and capital is undertaken not only through social policy but through legislation and application of the law. Conservative outlooks on law and society are often referred to as traditional outlooks and, in the law and society literature, it is increasingly difficult to find social scientists who articulate a distinctively conservative outlook on social issues. Conservatives highlight the importance of citizens' activities—"thrift, industriousness, deferral of gratification"—and decry excessive litigation and unjustified "social provision" for people who cannot manage for themselves (Will 1998, 21).

Jerry Muller, after providing several examples of the range of conservative thought and principles, concludes that conservatism is not a distinct theoretical approach, but rather a "positional ideology" (Muller 1997, 3; citing Huntingdon). This ideology often takes the shape of defending established institutions and social practices, and an ongoing argument that such institutions serve a tangible social good. Put simply, such institutions work, and the onus is on critics to show how weakening such institutions is desirable (1997, 8). Conservatism is not a simple, monolithic outlook, even though it may be caricatured as such. There is a common core of concern over threatened institutions such as government, family, or religion, but the intensity of concern varies dramatically among conservatives. We can contrast this preservationist outlook with the change-oriented ideologies associated with Marxism, Feminism, Postmodernism, for example. As Muller notes, Liberals are often skeptical of institutional limitations on individual freedom, where conservatives are more likely to support the legitimate authority of certain institutions over individuals (1997, 11).

Muller identifies several fundamental "themes" in conservative thought: the need to instill manners "in shaping character and restraining the passions," the importance of authority and the dubious value of individual liberation, and the inevitability of inequalities and "cultural, political, and economic" elites. Moreover, the state is vital in ensuring property rights and "the rule of law" (Muller 1997, 18). Conservatism is clearly an important part of legislation and law enforcement, and as will be discussed, is very much alive in our current experience of neo-liberalist politics and economic globalization.

Liberal-Pluralism

Liberal-pluralisists emphasize individual rights and the importance of protecting minority populations from unjust control by a majority of the population. Emphasis is placed on the rule of law, as distinct from arbitrary measures that the citizens must endure. The legal sphere is of course not the only source of justice or social progress. Social institutions and interactions are also valued by liberal-pluralists. It is assumed that there is a plurality of interests in political, cultural, and social life, rather than a uniform, monolithic power bloc. Comack and Brickey (1991, 19) distinguish liberal-pluralists from functionalists, in the sense that liberal-pluralists do not adhere to the society-wide image of social consensus. Instead, liberal-pluralists acknowledge that there are many (plural) value-systems and competing interests in complex societies. They add that power is not evenly distributed, but varies with the "stratification order of society" (Comack and Brickey 1991, 19). This means that liberal-pluralists can offer a more dynamic account of the evolution of law, especially how special-interest groups can use law to apply sanctions against less powerful groups. Consider, for example, how the use of Prohibition was employed to criminalize consumption of alcohol in Canada and the United States in the early twentieth century (Ajzenstadt and Burtch 1994). This pluralistic approach identifies differences among various social groups on such issues as religion, politics, and cultural beliefs. The differences are not necessarily seen as stark and unresolvable, but rather, as amenable to discussion, compromise, and mutual respect

Michael Walzer has created a prolific body of work on liberalism in legal and political philosophy. He builds on the concept of *distributive justice,* which involves sharing and exchanging not only of tangible goods but of identities and other aspects: "... power, honor, physical security, work and leisure ..." (Walzer 1984, 3). In *On Toleration* (1997), Walzer discusses "... the peaceful coexistence of groups of people with different histories, cultures, and identities, which is what toleration makes possible" (1997, 2). Walzer regards the practice of toleration and of promoting a democratic society as difficult work, in part because the work is complex and often unappreciated. Far from decrying differences, Walzer states "I prefer the many to the one" (1997, xii).

Marxism and Neo-Marxism

A Marxist-based perspective on law and society clashes quite directly with its more liberal counterpart. For Marxists, social conflicts in society flow from artificial divisions of social class, conflicting economic interests, and the overarching influence of capitalist relations. Some of the strongest work in the sociology of law has used Marxist principles, sometimes in conjunction with revised (neo-Marxist) theories and research. Marxist approaches to law challenge the reform-oriented approaches of liberals, and the image of social consensus advanced by functionalists. Instead, the economic stratification of capitalist societies is at the centre of Marxist analyses. No doubt you will be exposed to classical Marxist concepts, and modifications of his concepts as you continue in university.

Frequently discredited in virtually all spheres of contemporary North American society, Marxist and neo-Marxist approaches are nonetheless valuable in exploring the shortfall between law's promises of equality and human betterment, and people's lived experiences of discrimination, violence, and injustice. Marx' writings are also very useful in exploring ways in which legal structures are mystified, thus distorting sources of bias and unfairness through an image of progressive, balanced decision-making.

Feminism

The women's movement has been one of the most influential, and far-reaching developments in the twentieth century and into the new millennium. This general perspective rests on the assumption that women are often treated unequally in society at large, and in legal processes. There is also considerable agreement among feminists that oppression of girls and women is often embedded in social structures, not simply the actions of a small minority of misogynists. Nevertheless, there are many different approaches within feminism, and many differences among feminists when it comes to theorizing law and society, or exploring specific social policies and events.

We begin with liberal feminism, a moderate approach that seeks to change women's status within established institutions of law, private property, and individual rights. Many hard-won rights such as the right to vote (suffrage), to divorce, and expanded definitions of what constitutes sexual assault have their roots in liberal activism. While liberal feminists have been criticized for being too moderate, it can be argued that the focus on individual rights and removing barriers to women's participation in society is valuable, and enjoys considerable public support. Labels such as liberal-feminist, or socialist-feminist, while useful in distinguishing specific interpretations of law and society, are somewhat artificial. Not all feminists stick to hard-and-fast conclusions on particular issues, and there is considerable overlap among these somewhat artificial frameworks. Work in the social sciences is increasingly concerned with overlapping categories, keying in on such categories as race, class, and gender. An example of this is Zillah Eisenstein's book, *The Color of Gender: Reimaging Democracy* (1994). Her wide-ranging discussion touches on limits of democratic reforms in various countries, including the former Soviet Union, Eastern European democracies, the United States, and developing countries. Eisenstein exemplifies this trend to not treat specific variables as airtight and isolated, but to bring them together as an integrated whole.

Feminist theories of law reflect a shared insight into myriad ways in which women are treated differently than men, usually as their inferiors. It is important to note that there are many strands of feminist thought, and it is misleading to speak of feminism as if it is a monolithic framework, a sort of "groupthink" among women critical of the social order. Rather, there are profound differences of opinion within the general rubric of feminism, something we will explore in greater depth in Chapter Four.

Postmodernism

Elizabeth Comack (1999, 61) speaks of the "postmodern challenge" which rejects a number of truth claims associated with earlier perspectives on society and law. Postmodernists have, among other things, reconceptualized power and authority relations, critiquing many forms of institutionalized power such as medicine, government, education, and law. At the same time, postmodernists resist a "totalizing" conceptualization of society, power, or other structures (Comack 1999, 66). The search for all-encompassing theoretical explanations of social behaviour is seen as futile; instead, postmodernists tend to open up inquiry to diverse outlooks.

Postmodernists debunk the impossible promises of earlier, presumably enlightened perspectives on society and justice. Carol Smart says "Modernity has now become associated with some of the most deep-seated intellectual problems at the end of the twentieth century. It is seen as synonymous with racism, sexism, Euro-centredness and the attempt to reduce cultural and sexual differences to one dominant set of values and knowledge" (1995, 37). She characterizes modernity as an outlook that promotes belief in "certainty in progress" (1995a, 213).

Postmodern discourse includes law, but extends to all spheres of social life, including art, music, literature, architecture, and, of course, politics. Postmodernism rests on a key assumption that many "givens" such as rationality and the ideal of progress in Western societies are very problematic. Affirmative postmodernists often associate with social movements opposing some established power relations, while skeptical postmodernists tend to be more negative about reconstructing society (Rosenau 1992, 174). Regardless, the spirit of deconstruction "... seeks to destabilize dominant or privileged interpretations" (Handler 1992, 698). Rejecting massive theories such as liberalism and Marxism, many postmodernists concentrate on local initiatives. "Change will be brought about through small-scale transformation ... The goals of postmodern politics are stated in terms of a *radical* and *plural* democracy. The contemporary state, reflecting the logic of modernity, is characterized by extremely centralizing tendencies; it is colonizing, totalizing, bureaucratic. In contrast, the postmodern state is minimalist because radical democracy depends on the proliferation of public spaces where social agents become increasingly capable of self-management..." (Handler 1992, 701). One difficulty with the "minimalist state" argument above is that contemporary capitalist states are now "downsizing" personnel, privatizing some agencies, and for some critics, this promotes social injustices (Armstrong 1998).

Michel Foucault's theorizing of power and resistance departs from a Marxist framework in that class struggle is not seen as the primary form of resistance to power. Barry Smart puts it this way: "What Foucault meant ... is that resistance is present everywhere power is exercised, that the network of power relations is paralleled by a multiplicity of forms of resistance" (Smart 1985, 133). Relations of power and authority thus extend well beyond the state and into the much wider fabric of society. There is a deepening interest in Foucault's conceptualization of *governance* that goes beyond state regulation and into myriad forms of social regulation. Hunt and Wickham define governance as "any attempt to control or manage any known object. A 'known object' is an event, a relationship, an animate object, an inanimate object, in fact any phenomenon which human beings try to control or manage" (1995, 78). There has also been a shift away from parochial jurisdictions to international forces, including globalization. Smart (1993, 125–26) writes of the profound impact of globalization in weakening the hegemony of nation-states and national economies. He adds that the central importance of European and American "master narratives" has been challenged from other parts of the world, including the economic influence of Asia and the "resurgence of Islam" (Smart, 25, 150).

Postmodernism is often associated with new social movements. Recent social movements include the women's movement, environmental action groups, the gay and lesbian movement, anti-poverty movement, Aboriginal/First Nations movement, the persons with disabilities movement, and the peace movement (see Young 1990, 7). Postmodern social movements generally reject grand political traditions such as liberalism, feminism, and Marxism. The new left social movements, as Young terms them, are distinguished from earlier social movements. Specifically, Young draws attention to their perception of oppression, "not because a tyrannical power coerces them, but because of the everyday practices of a well-intentioned liberal society" (1990, 41). These new social movements act as a counterpoint to liberal and conservative policies affecting relatively powerless individuals and groups.

Handler (1992, 721) credits some of these movements for successfully contesting development projects, for example, thus preserving liveable neighbourhoods and protecting the interests of the poor. In his book, *Law and the Search for Community* (1990), Handler explores possibilities for transcending liberalism's focus on the individual and the vexing problem of social inequality, establishing a more trusting, egalitarian community. Alan Hunt (1993, 227) notes that many critics are concerned with the implications of using law to promote the aims of "progressive social movements."

Some are skeptical of the time and resources devoted to attempts to reform dominant structures, and the danger of co-optation of radical initiatives. Hunt (1993, 237) points out that many critics of rights struggles confuse rights and litigation. Hunt clarifies that taking an issue to court, litigating in other words, is but one "tactic" in what he presents as "an essentially political, rather than legal, strategy" (ibid). He offers another important insight, that apparent failures can propel social movements rather than discourage their members. He gives the concrete example of offensive legal decisions against battered women that galvanize people against the decision, and generate "a new and emergent discourse or rights and autonomy" (1995, 240).

David Lyon (1999, 5) sees the origins of postmodernism as rooted in the Enlightenment's search for universal laws and the "forward movement" of history. Lyon acknowledges that these lofty ideals were questioned and challenged later in the twentieth century, prompted in part by environmental concerns, the peace movement, and generally the rise of "new social movements" (Lyon 1994, 6).

Postmodernism has been hailed as a profound improvement on more doctrinal approaches of liberalism, Marxism, feminism, and other established political and cultural outlooks. Postmodernists tend to favour decentralization of power, with resources and decision-making shifted from paternalistic power-centres such as politics, media, and medicine—to name only a few—to a grassroots level where people shape their destinies.

In *Post-modernism and the Social Sciences* (1992), Pauline Rosenau outlines various strands of postmodernism and its critics. Rosenau outlines two key approaches by postmodernists: skepticism and affirmation. *Skeptical postmodernists* "question the value of a unified, coherent subject such as a human being, a person, as a concrete reference point … They consider the subject to be a fossil relic of the past, of modernity, an invention of liberal humanism, the source of the unacceptable object-subject dichotomy" (Rosenau 1992, 42). *Affirmative posmodernists* on the other hand encourage a renewal of the concept of the subject. This renewed subject is perhaps the motor for the new social movements. These social movements provide a way in which atomized individuals can work for social justice through ecology, the women's movement, and peacemaking. For Dallmayr, this emergent subject will not dominate human relations, but will seek "communalism, association, community, anticipatory-emancipatory practice" (see Rosenau 1992, 58).

The power of law is clearly one area in which people have been deemed subversive, criminal, and deemed. Postmodernist deconstruction challenges the very bedrock on which legal institutions rest. Rosenau cites objections of postmodernists to legal theory and practice: "[Postmodernists] argue that there is no definitive meaning in law and question the possibility of any truth claims based on reason in the field of law. For the affirmative postmodernists, law is political, subjective, controversial, mere personal interpretation. The skeptics, going even further in the direction of radical indeterminacy, state that no interpretation of any law is ever really legitimate" (1992, 125).

Some advocate a postmodern legality to uncover damaging effects of existing laws. They see postmodern law as aiding the powerless in their struggles against privilege and state powers. In Bonaventura Santos' words, this means moving toward a "radical democratisation of social and personal life" (p. 127). Rosenau concludes her book with a cautious assessment of postmodernism. She suspects that more orthodox left-wing thinkers who turn to postmodernism will continue to have reservations about the merging of postmodernism with feminist, Marxism, and socialism (Rosenau 1992, 182). She believes that some of the more absurd claims of the skeptics will draw further criticism (and perhaps, no attention whatsoever in the future). If international developments move toward a more peaceful, more democratic world, arguably the more moderate, affirmative post-modernists will find a niche for their vision of "self-fulfillment, tolerance, and humanizing technology" (Rosenau 1992, 183).

In his 1992 Presidential address to the Law and Society Association, Joel Handler spoke to the issue of postmodern politics and its ability to transform society and legal relations. For Handler, the main direction of postmodernism is toward subversion. This subversive tendency challenges established, mainstream discourse and spotlights "the inherent instability of seemingly hegemonic structures, that power is diffused throughout society, and that there are multiple possibilities for resistance by oppressed people" (1992, 697–98). These possibilities hinge largely on a rejection of entrenched institutions and promotion of "small-scale transformation" (Handler 1992, 701). Such transformation requires greater participation of citizens in the interests of a "democratic plurality" (ibid). As many critics have noted, this radical-pluralist democratic vision may be fanciful, since without a clearer foundation for action, postmodernism can deteriorate to "unbridled relativism" (Handler 1992, 702) where no vision is privileged, no knowledge is established in an enduring way. The potential for excitement and invention may thus founder on a welter of conflicting outlooks and strategies. Handler notes how postmodernists often reject "essentialist" categories such as "women" and the stark juxtaposition of men versus women. As Handler states (1992, 706): "Such talk masks the heterogeneity of women and perpetuates the privileged position and domination of white middle-class feminists. There is a difference between sex and gender, and it is an error to focus on gender in isolation from identity. *Identity is constructed by race, ethnicity, class, community, nation; it is both multiple and unstable*" (italics added). Here again some feminist writers contest this premise, arguing that local initiatives and deconstruction/subversion are far too weak to tackle colossal structures such as patriarchy and capitalism.

Silbey (1997) recognized the disenchantment of many critics of globalization and social injustice. She traces how postmodern colonialism has shifted its character and its targets: "In postmodern colonialism, control of land or political organization or nation-states is less important than power over consciousness and consumption, which are much more efficient forms of domination" (1996, 219). Silbey is concerned with the unequal exchanges of symbols and products in this globalized world, marked by the exporting of American franchises and culture worldwide (p. 223). Speaking directly to contemporary university offerings, Paul Delany (2000) calls attention to globalization and market pressures on university administrators, and a culture of competition "from wall to wall and from ceiling to floor"; nevertheless, he insists that many humanities programs survive despite these drives for prestige and cost recovery more so than teaching or otherwise fostering students.

Young (1990, 96–99) contests the liberal model of rights and justice. She pictures this model as "adopting an impartial and impersonal point of view on a situation, detached from any particular interests at stake, weighing all interests equally, and arriving at a conclusion which conforms to general principles of justice and rights, impartially applied to the case at hand" (1990, 96). Young outlines a postmodern account of this liberal model. Critics hold that the "logic of identity" which seeks a universal principle or essence in justice is not only impossible, but obscures or ignores "difference" (1990, 98). Rather than being absorbed as fragments of a liberal-pluralist whole, then, postmodernists cling to the importance of difference, and the dangers of vesting power in such centralized institutions as the state.

Neo-liberalism is often linked with economic globalization. Neo-liberalism, as ideology and practice, stands as a return to relatively unencumbered market forces. Martinez and Garcia (2001) list key facets of neo-liberalism. First, there is an emphasis on international trade agreements such as NAFTA (North American Free Trade Agreement) and faith in market forces, with less governmental oversight. Second, cutbacks in social welfare and social services are implemented. Third, deregulation of government activities is used to reduce state expenditures, e.g., workers' safety provisions and environmental protection. Fourth, formerly state-run or "state-owned" activities are privatized, giving a higher priority to "individual responsibility," with less emphasis on concepts of "community" or "the public good" (see Martinez and Garcia 2001).

We began by discussing legal ideology: the role of jurisprudence as an ideology, and sociological approaches that explore various social patterns, ideologies, and instances of legal power. Social justice is sought through politically correct strategies of empowerment. For others, political correctness is totalitarianism with no long-term memory. It suffers from a political agenda that caricatures both the powerless and the powerful, and oversimplifies a sense of common cause in society, and celebrates various forms of "tribalism" at the expense of individuality and fundamental freedoms. Robert Hughes foresees a deserved end to the PC debate: "When the waters of PC recede—as they presently will, leaving the predictable scum of dead words on the social beach—it will be, in part, because young people get turned off by all the carping about verbal proprieties on campus. The radical impulses of youth are generous, romantic and instinctive, and are easily chilled by an atmosphere of prim, obsessive correction"[1] (Hughes 1993, 25).

CRITICAL LEGAL STUDIES

The critical legal studies (CLS) perspective is set against mainstream notions of law and social order. The critical legal studies perspective first emerged in the late 1970s, highlighting what Kelman (1987, 1) identifies as the sterility of existing legal socialization and legal education. Kelman (1987, 1) sees CLS as bridging the wide gap between "actual social life" and the artificial, stratified atmosphere of law schools. Opposed to mainstream liberal doctrines of law, CLS theorists address the *contradictions* of liberalism, including the gap between respect for individual decisions and beliefs (subjectivity, individual rights) and the ostensibly objective, factually-based sphere of legal reasoning. Kelman (1987, 4–6) adds that liberalism actually takes on a "right-wing" character, ironically becoming quite illiberal, and resisting progressive innovations in the nature of legal services, for example, activist courts.

Critical legal studies help provide a structure for applying a variety of critical theoretical perspectives on law and social control. These studies challenge the hegemonic, or dominant, status of particular legal ideologies. CLS poses a challenge to structural-functionalist perspectives of the social order, including the premise that laws reflect and adapt to evolving social needs (Kelman 1987, 242). The CLS perspective also outlines regressive developments in contemporary law and legal structures. Kelman (1987, 243) mentions the erosion of community ties that occurs as societies undergo modernization. This process promotes a culture based, in part, on opportunism and isolationism rather than collectivism. Laws may thus serve to obstruct efforts to forge alternative social structures, for example, those designed to resolve neighbourhood conflicts and to promote a more authentic sense of community (Handler 1990). The modern edifice of law can be seen as a blight, disguised as a blessing. CLS theorists demystify this negative side of formal legal structures and, as noted above, the "privileged" discourse of liberal progression and general social harmony. CLS theorists thus challenge utopian portraits of modern law that misrepresent legal relations as rooted in fairness, and serving a supposed public interest. The critical legal studies perspective draws our attention to law as politics, and rather than adhering to a false assumption of wide social consensus, seeks to empower embattled groups by demystifying legal ideology and developing strategies to counter legal dominance. Tomasic (1985, 17–24) regards the critical legal studies movement as a diverse and dynamic enterprise. The work within this CLS tradition warrants considerable attention, and Tomasic (1985, 18) cautions that it is premature to dismiss Marxist-influenced theories of law and society, given the valuable work by critical legal scholars.

As outlined above, the concept of social consensus has guided some sociologists' theories of law and society. The concept of the *social contract* is worth exploring, as it endures in various forms in several modern legal ideologies. Formulated by Hobbes, Locke, and Rousseau, among others, the general premise of social contract theory is that agreement among citizens forms the legitimate basis for stable government. The legitimacy of government thus properly rests on a wide consensus among citizens on the desirability or inevitability of the rule of law and the necessity of preserving the modern state. Social contract theory presents a world view in which citizens voluntarily relinquish some freedoms in order that the general interest is secured. Barker (1970, xii–xiii) outlines two cardinal ideas guiding social contract doctrine. First, there is a "contract of government" in which the rulers (government) and the subjects (citizenry) agree to the terms of lawful government; and second, there is a contract established to preserve the society itself.

In his treatise *The Social Contract*, first published in France in 1762, the philosopher Jean-Jacques Rousseau presented a strong argument against the automatic legitimacy of any government. People are obliged to obey only "the legitimate powers of the State" (cited in Barker 1970, 173). He added that states based on the adage "might is right"—that is, that the most powerful members could rightfully subordinate weaker members—were undesirable. Agreement was thus the sole legitimate foundation for political authority. As such, in Rousseau's formulation, if the state departs markedly from its obligation to govern fairly—to represent public not sectarian interests—it may lose its legitimate support and be removed from office. Rousseau emphasized that in eighteenth century societies, people were not free in general terms, but were often enslaved.

History required that people surrender certain freedoms to allow "the whole strength of the community" to be used as a protector of each citizen's property and freedoms (Rousseau, cited in Barker 1970, 180). Rousseau was not an apologist for unfettered state powers; indeed, *The Social Contract* can be seen as a critique of ways in which private property is treated like a fetish, with an acquisitive spirit leading to sumptuous wealth for a few, and starvation or subsistence living for many others. In this respect, Rousseau argued that each individual must restrict his or her claims to property that is rightfully his or hers, and not make claims on property that rightfully belongs to the community (Barker 1970, 186). Rousseau's critique of the distribution of property, and other forms of wealth, was accompanied by his recognition of the potential for tyranny in government and law. He thus argued for a "code of laws" authored by the people. While Rousseau did not resolve this paradox of substantial state authority, justice, and public authorship of proper laws, he argued forcefully against unjust laws that would promote the suffering of "just men" (Barker 1970, 201–03). Rousseau was wary of placing too much power with the people, as evidenced by his concerns over the "blind multitude" or the "vulgar herd," his terms for those citizens who were not enlightened about their true interests (see Barker 1970, 204 and 207).

Rousseau's *The Social Contract* was influential in re-establishing a political foundation for governments and was a major influence in the social thought that preceded the American Revolution of 1776. Critics of social contract theory have pointed to groups that have been excluded from the social contract. Some criticize Rousseau for passages that support the subordination of women to men, for example, in family relations. Eisenstein (1981) is critical of the explicit patriarchial values expressed in Rousseau's treatise, including his assumption that fathers or husbands were the natural rulers within families and marriage, while wives were responsible for the nurturance and stabilization of families and households.

One question that I pose to students is whether they believe they are part of a social contract. Many respond that they support the overall political structure of democracy, that injustices are gradually being removed, and that, taken as a whole, life is improving in many ways. A general belief—taken from classical social contract theory—is that we have to forfeit some actions in order for the society to operate more fairly and efficiently. The example of rules of the road is frequently offered: if drivers didn't obey red lights, stop signs, and speed limits, then life would become more hazardous for drivers and pedestrians alike. Beyond this example, however, social issues become very problematic as students seek to apply the premise of the social contract to their own lives. Specifically, do women feel they are protected by a social contract? Most female students indicate that they are uncomfortable walking alone at night. Some say that they will not travel for groceries after dark, unless the store is a secure place, or if they have an escort for protection. On the other hand, all students understand that men enjoy much greater freedom of movement than women. Other students express concerns over lack of protection for their own interests. Contemporary environmental policies and laws are seen by some as too lax, with little regulation of ongoing pollution and relatively ineffective fines for the polluting companies. Still other students see little influence of affirmative action programs on creating more access to employment for groups that have traditionally been excluded or subordinated in the work force (people of colour, the disabled, women). One can also point to groups that have been denied access to the social contract. In Canada, for example, Native people were denied the vote until 1960, and many argue that the current political and social order often undermines First Nations interests.

SEXUALITIES AND THE LAW

For less visible minorities, legal or social discrimination can also have profound effects. The contemporary gay liberation movement, in conjunction with general efforts to realize civil rights for male and female homosexuals, can be set against a legacy of legal repression against homosexuals and current obstacles including conservative judicial decisions and ongoing homophobia (Cain 2000). There are some signs that social tolerance of homosexuals has increased in recent years, underscoring the dynamic quality of social movements and public attitudes. An Environics public-opinion poll of 2,035 adult Canadians in April 2001 revealed that 55 percent supported a right to same-sex marriage, while 40 percent were opposed. The same poll found that 44 percent approved of homosexuality (twice that of a poll taken five years earlier), 37 percent disapproved, and 16 percent neither approved nor disapproved. Québec and B.C. residents were most likely to support gay weddings (69 percent and 60 percent respectively) while respondents in Alberta and Saskatchewan were least likely to support this (43 percent). Respondents approving homosexuality tended to be more highly educated, with higher incomes, women, and younger than those disapproving (Arnold 2001). Rayside and Bowler (1998) noted this liberalizing trend in Canada, but added that there is still considerable condemnation of homosexuality. They highlight the clash between support for individual rights and choices on the one hand, and the enduring power of heterosexism and "traditional family" ideologies. American researchers have noted a similar trend toward increased public support for gay and lesbian rights in "employment and housing" (Cain 2000, 287).

Even here, categories are contested and everchanging. The social construction of gayness and straightness has been critiqued for an either/or approach to sexuality and gender identity. Some contemporary scholars and activists have deconstructed gender and sexuality. For instance, as opposed to a polarized female/male outlook—or gay/straight—some commentators argue for a more nuanced approach where such labels are not fixed (Colker 1995, 250). Deconstruction of identities can take many forms, challenging not only traditional concepts associated with heterosexism, but also alternative concepts of sexuality. The binary assumption of being either heterosexual or homosexual, for example, helps to eradicate bisexuality. Kenji Yoshino (2000) maintains that such erasure is promoted by those lobbying for traditional family values of heterosexual marriage and families, and by those aligned with gay and lesbian social movements. Bisexuals have resisted such erasure and destabilized the "gay/straight" dichotomy. Interestingly, Yoshino notes that asexuals—those who express no desire for other people–are almost entirely removed from legal or social discourse, even though such people are hardly a rarity (2000, 357). Here again, we confront an ongoing debate over the meaning of gender. Whereas some writers such as Kate Bornstein (1994) actively promote transgenderism, others are dismissive of the value of transgenderism which is presented as more style than substance. For example, Janice Raymond, even while recognizing hate directed to some people who cross gender roles—such as Brandon Teena, murdered for trying to pass as a man—is largely unsupportive of transgender politics. She criticizes the eclipsing of "collective political challenges to power" with what she terms "expressive individualism" (1996, 223). In a caustic and, in my view, simplistic argument, she claims "... transgenderism reduces gender resistance to wardrobes, hormones, surgery, and posturing—anything but real sexual equality" (ibid). While respecting her insistence on separating the frivolous from more serious strategies of transforming society, there is cause for concern over her view of what constitutes a "real sexual equality" since many transgendered people express alienation not only from mainstream society but from more "progressive" social movements as well.

Professor Mossman (1994) tackles the fundamental question of whether feminist perspectives are compatible with "legal method." She points out that legal method is self-limiting, in the sense that some issues are deemed irrelevant and out-of-bounds. Moreover, it is not uncommon for legal decision-makers to reach conclusions without evidence. Even so, proponents of legal method tend to regard such decisions as relevant, informed, and impartial (1995, 332–33). Feminist legal practitioners and feminist legal scholars may face a quandary, working within the straitjacket of legal method as well as a more open feminist conceptual and activist framework. She puts this bluntly: "Feminist legal scholars are expected to think and write using the approaches of legal method: defining the issues, analyzing relevant precedents, and recommending conclusions according to defined and accepted standards of legal method. A feminist scholar who chooses instead to ask different questions or to conceptualize the problem in different ways risks a reputation for incompetence in her legal method as well as lack of recognition for her scholarly (feminist) accomplishment" (Mossman 1994, 333).

A standpoint research approach can be used to address the "lack of voice" of people subject to law and social control. Christie Barron (2000, Chapter Two) argues that youth violence is often (mis)represented in mass media, with the construction of violence youth largely determined by "professional discourse" not through the voices of youths themselves. Listening to young people is not only useful as a critique of established institutions, but can also help to generate alternative approaches for youth (Barron 2000, 62) and the homeless (Allen 2000).

SUMMARY

This exercise of analyzing one's place inside or outside the social contract brings us closer to an understanding of the politics of law. Unlike the idealized view of jurisprudence as a neutral force that acts in an impartial and logical manner, sociological studies of law are based on a clearer emphasis on the impact of economic pressures and political interests in the formulation of specific laws.

Sociological perspectives on law centre on the importance of legal structures in resisting or producing social change. This book provides a review of these sociological perspectives, with special emphasis on critical social theory, including feminist jurisprudence and theories that derive from Marxist principles of political economy. It is worth noting, however, that, while the discussions to follow are based on such critical literature, none of us speaks *ex cathedra* on these issues. In particular, the debate over whether legal structures can ever serve the purposes of justice remains very much an open question in these times. The chapters that follow provide several footholds for reconsidering law in its wider social context.

STUDY QUESTIONS

1. While the law is ostensibly designed to protect individuals and protect certain liberties, the application of law—the "living law"—may undermine individual freedoms in Western societies. Discuss briefly.

2. Elaborate on the three functions of law: repressive, facilitative, and ideological. Briefly give two contemporary examples of your own choosing to illustrate how these three functions of law may influence legal processes. Indicate how these legal functions might be used to repress social action, to effect reforms, or to legitimate the powers of law.

3. Review the elements of social contract theory. What criticisms have been made of the premise that a social contract (or covenant) is possible, or desirable, within a democratic political framework? To what extent do you believe you are part of a social contract? To what extent are you excluded from this contract?

NOTES

1. Robert Hughes, *Culture of Complaint: The Fraying of America.* New York: Oxford University Press, 1993, p. 25. Used by permission of Oxford University Press.

REFERENCES

Ajzenstadt, M. and B. Burtch (1994) "The Idea of Alcoholism: Changing Perceptions of Alcoholism and Treatment in British Columbia, 1870–1988." *Health and Canadian Society* 2(1): 9–34.

Allen, T. (2000) *Someone To Talk To: Care and Control of the Homeless.* Halifax: Fernwood Books.

Armstrong, P. (1998) "Missing Women: A Feminist Perspective on *The Vertical Mosaic.*" In *The Vertical*

Mosaic Revisited, edited by R. Helmes-Hayes and J. Curtis, 116–44. Toronto: University of Toronto Press.

Arnold, T. (2001) "Support for homosexuality doubles over five years: poll." *National Post*, May 10, p. A1.

Backhouse, Constance (1991) *Petticoats and Prejudice: Women and Law in Nineteenth-Century Canada.* Toronto: The Women's Press.

Barker, E. (1970) *Social Contract: Essays by Locke, Hume, and Rousseau.* London: Oxford University Press.

Barron, C. (2000) *Giving Youth a Voice: A Basis for Rethinking Adolescent Violence.* Halifax: Fernwood Books.

Baum, G. (1990) "The Postmodern Age." *The Canadian Forum* 69 (789): 5–7.

Bornstein, K. (1994) *Gender Outlaw: On Men, Women and the Rest of Us.* London: Routledge.

Brickey, S., and E. Comack (1989) "The Role of Law in Social Transformation: Is a Jurisprudence of Insurgency Possible?" *Canadian Journal of Law and Society* 2: 97–119.

Cain, P. (2000) *Rainbow Rights: The Role of Lawyers and Courts in the Lesbian and Gay Civil Rights Movement.* Boulder: Westview Press.

Clark, R. (1999) "Diversity in Sociology: Problem or Solution." *The American Sociologist* 30(3): 22–41.

Colker, R. (1995) "Disembodiment: Abortion and Gay Rights." In *Radical Philosophy of Law: Contemporary Challenges to Mainstream Legal Theory and Practice*, edited by D. Caudill and S. Gold, 234–54. New Jersey: Humanities Press.

Comack, E. (1999) "Theoretical Excursions." in *Locating Law: Race/Class/Gender Connections.* Halifax: Fernwood Books, 19–68.

Cotterrell, R. (1984) *The Sociology of Law: An Introduction.* London: Butterworths.

Delany, P. (2000) "The University in Pieces: Bill Readings and the Fate of the Humanities." In *Profession 2000*, edited by P. Franklin, 89–96. New York: Modern Languages Association.

Dembour, Marie-Bénédicte (1996) "Human rights talk and anthropological ambivalence: The particular contexts of universal claims." In *Inside and Outside the Law: Anthropological studies of authority and ambiguity*, edited by O. Harris, 19–40. London: Routledge.

Ehrlich, E. (1975) *Fundamental Principles of the Sociology of Law*, translated by W. Moll. New York: Arno Press. First published in 1913.

Eisenstein, Z. (1981) *The Radical Future of Liberal Feminism.* New York: Longman.

Ericson, R. (1983) "The Constitution of Legal Inequality." John Porter Memorial Address. Ottawa: Carleton University Press.

Handler, J. (1990) *Law and the Search for Community.* Philadelphia: University of Pennsylvania Press.

——. (1992) "Postmodernism, Protest, and the New Social Movements." *Law and Society Review* 26(4): 697–731.

Harris, O. (1996) "Introduction: Inside and outside the law." In *Inside and Outside the Law: Anthropological studies of authority and ambiguity*, edited by O. Harris, 1–15. London: Routledge.

Hughes, R. (1993) *Culture of Complaint: The Fraying of America.* New York: Oxford University Press.

Hunt, A. (1980) *The Sociological Movement in Law.* London: Macmillan.

Hunt, A. (1991) "Postmodernism and Critical Criminology." In *New*

Directions in Critical Criminology, edited by B. MacLean and D. Milovanovic, 79–85. Vancouver: The Collective Press.

———. and G. Wickham (1995) *Foucault and Law: Towards a Sociology of Law as Governance.* London: Pluto Press.

Kelman, M. (1987) *A Guide to Critical Legal Studies.* Cambridge: Harvard University Press.

Lyon, D. (1999) *Postmodernity.* Buckingham: Open University Press (2nd edition).

Martinez, E., and A. Garcia (2001) "What is 'Neo-liberalism'? A brief definition for activists." *The Keele Guide to Political Thought and Ideology on the Internet* (http://www.ac.uk/depts/por/ptbase .htm).

McMahon, M., and R. Ericson (1987) "Reforming the Police and Policing Reform." In *State Control: Criminal Justice Politics in Canada,* edited by R.S. Ratner and J.L. McMullan, 38–68. Vancouver: University of British Columbia Press.

Melucci, A. (1988) *Nomads of the Present: Social Movements and Individual Needs in Contemporary Society.* Edited by J. Keane and P. Mier. Philadelphia: Temple University Press.

Milovanovic, D. (1988) *A Primer in the Sociology of Law.* New York: Harrow and Heston.

Mossman, M.J. (1994) "Feminism and Legal Method: The Difference It Makes." In *Historical Perspectives on Law and Society in Canada,* edited by T. Loo and L. McLean, 321–37. Mississauga: Copp Clark Longman.

Muller, J. (1997) "Introduction." In *Conservatism: An Anthology of Social and Political Thought from David Hume to the Present,* edited by J. Muller, 3–31. Princeton: Princeton University Press.

Murakami, H. (2001) *Underground: The Tokyo Gas Attack and the Japanese Psyche.* Toronto: Vintage Canada.

Partington, A. [ed.] (1997) *The Concise Oxford Dictionary of Quotations* [revised 3rd edition]. Oxford: Oxford University Press.

Raymond, J. (1996) "The Politics of Transgenderism." In *Blending Genders: Social Aspects of Cross-Dressing and Sex-Changing,* edited by R. Elkins and D. King, 215–23. London: Routledge.

Rayside, D. and S. Bowler (1998) "Public Opinion and Gay Rights." *Canadian Review of Sociology and Anthropology* 25(4): 649–60.

Rosenau, P. (1992) *Post-modernism and the Social Science: Insights, Inroads, and Intrusions.* Princeton: Princeton University Press.

Sassoon, A. (1983) "Hegemony." In *A Dictionary of Marxist Thought,* edited by T. Bottomore, L. Harris, V. Kiernan, and R. Miliband, 201–03. Cambridge: Harvard University Press.

Silbey, S. (1997). "'Let Them Eat Cake': Globalization, Postmodern Colonialism, and the Possibilities of Justice." *Law and Society Review* 31(2): 207–35.

Sinclair Jr., G. (1999) *Cowboys and Indians: The Shooting of J.J. Harper.* Toronto: McClelland and Stewart.

Smart, B. (1985) *Michel Foucault.* London: Tavistock.

———. (1993). Postmodernity. London: Routledge.

Smart, C. (1989) *Feminism and the Power of Law.* London: Routledge and Kegan Paul.

———. (1995) "Feminist Approaches to Criminology, or Postmodern Woman meets Atavistic Man." In C. Smart, *Law, Crime and Sexuality: Essays in Feminism,* 32–48. Thousand Oaks (Calif.): Sage Publications.

———. (1995a) "Proscription, Prescription and the Desire for Certainty? Feminist Theory in the Field of Law." In C. Smart, *Law, Crime and Sexuality: Essays in Feminism*, 203–20. Thousand Oaks (Calif.): Sage Publications.

Sumner, C. (1979) *Reading Ideologies: An Investigation into the Marxist Theory of Ideology and Law*. London: Academic Press.

Theodorson, G., and A. Theodorson (1979) *A Modern Dictionary of Sociology*. New York: Barnes and Noble.

Timasheff, N. (1974) *An Introduction to the Sociology of Law*. Westport, Connecticut: Greenwood Press.

Tomasic, R. (1985) *The Sociology of Law*. London: Sage Publications.

Treviño, A. (1996) *The Sociology of Law: Classical and Contemporary Perspectives*. New York: St. Martin's Press.

Vago, S. (1994) *Law and Society* (4th edition). Upper Saddle River, NJ: Prentice Hall.

Waluchow, W. (1998) "The Many Faces of Legal Positivism." *University of Toronto Law Journal* 48: 387–449.

Will, G. (1998) *The Woven Figure: Conservatism and America's Fabric*. New York: Touchstone.

Yoshino, K. (2000) "The Epistemic Contract of Bisexual Erasure." *Stanford Law Review* 52: 353–461.

Young, I. (1990) *Justice and the Politics of Difference*. Princeton: Princeton University Press.

2
The Classical Theorists: Durkheim, Weber, and Marx

INTRODUCTION

Our understanding of modern legal systems is rooted in the classical work of three European scholars of the late nineteenth century. This chapter provides an overview of the writings of Emile Durkheim, Max Weber, and Karl Marx. The three writers share an interest in explaining the relationships among law, economy, society, and politics. There are substantial differences among the three, including their theoretical perspectives on politics and the social order. The French sociologist Emile Durkheim is considered an "order theorist" (Horton 1966), ideologically committed to preserving the general contours of the social system. Nevertheless, Durkheim was not merely an apologist for the status quo in late nineteenth and early twentieth century politics. His work covered such diverse issues as sociological method (*The Rules of Sociological Method*), social cohesion, economics, and legal systems (*The Division of Labour in Society* and *Suicide*).

In contrast, the German scholar Max Weber developed a comprehensive theoretical approach that accentuated a multiplicity of social conflicts in modern societies. A proponent of rationalized capitalist economic systems, Weber argued against several elements of Marxist-based doctrines of economic materialism and class conflict. He provided a complex approach to such issues as religion, economics, quantitative and qualitative methodology in the social sciences, the ubiquitousness of social conflicts, variations in legal systems and kinds of domination, and the centralization of bureaucratic administration in government and other spheres. Karl Marx was a revolutionary nineteenth century thinker who is credited with reformulating the nature of principles of political economy, drawing attention to the exploitation that he believed was inherent in capitalist economic systems. Marx promoted controversial and influential theories on the origins of capitalism—its tremendous disparities of wealth and political power—and predicted the replacement of capitalism with socialism, and eventually communism. Marx was forced to leave Germany, and did much of his greatest work as a private scholar in London. His approach to law, while secondary to his interest in political economy and the revolutionary transformation of capitalist-based economies and societies, remains very influential in current studies of law and state control.

This chapter offers a selective review of the outlooks of Durkheim, Weber, and Marx on law and society. Particular attention is given to the various ways in which these writers conceptualized law, not only as a system of control, but as a vehicle for social stability or social change. The three writers also differed on the purposes of law and the extent to which legal regulation is desirable or even necessary.

EMILE DURKHEIM (1858–1917)

Biography

Emile Durkheim was born and raised in the Jewish community of France's Alsace-Lorraine district. Durkheim's father was a chief rabbi, and his mother operated an embroidery shop as a cottage industry. The family, according to Lukes (1977, 39), was far from wealthy. Durkheim was a superlative student, completing his school studies easily and proceeding to advanced studies at the École Normale Supérieure in Paris (Lukes 1977, 41–42). Durkheim was appointed to the Faculty of Letters at the University of Bordeaux in 1887, and to the Sorbonne in Paris in 1902. Durkheim's accomplishments included four major studies covering such topics as work, religion, the phenomenon of suicide (and how suicide was best explained by sociological factors), and his *Rules of Sociological Method*. His work attracted considerable acclaim as well as sharp criticism. Durkheim was a prolific writer, producing literally hundreds of essays and other publications between 1885 and 1917 (Lukes 1977, 562–90).

Introduction

Durkheim was concerned with religious influences in social life and studied various religious systems around the world. Milovanovic (1988, 22–23) observes that, although Durkheim was influenced by an eminent psychologist (Wilhelm Wundt), he was opposed to psychological explanations of social behaviour and favoured a scientific approach in which collective life largely defined and determined individual conduct. Durkheim's famous assertion that individual life is born of collective life, not vice versa, underscores this emphasis on social factors. It would be misleading, however, to suggest that Durkheim was concerned only with larger structures of society and their functioning. He was also concerned with issues of justice, and he supported the protection of human rights at national and international levels. The question of how societies survived, the regulatory purposes of various kinds of laws and customs, and the differing forms of *social* solidarity were of direct interest to Durkheim.

It is important to appreciate that Durkheim believed in the *scientific* approach to social life. To this end, he utilized the available statistics on various aspects of society, and insisted on the importance of logic in investigating sociological phenomena. He opposed the more speculative approaches of metaphysics, preferring an empirically-based science of society. For Durkheim, measurement and statistical analysis were essential to the scientific development of sociology. Critics of Durkheim have argued that psychological approaches to law and society can also build on rigorous scientific methodologies. Durkheim was regarded as a proponent of "conservative democracy," who had faith in the scientific redirection of industry and in the development of intellectual and moral thought among the public. In addition, Durkheim advocated greater justice in economic relations. Lacking the intense commitment to socialism espoused by Marx and Engels, Durkheim nevertheless adopted a scientific outlook that was "strongly reformist and revisionist" (Lukes 1977, 320 and 323).

Politically, Durkheim discounted the notion that intellectuals should be above politics. Rather, he believed they could serve to advise and enlighten politicians with respect to social policy. Lukes (1977, 330–32) interprets Durkheim's approach to politics as largely reserved: while Durkheim felt that academics had an obligation to speak out on significant social issues, he generally believed that academics were ill-suited to statecraft. Nevertheless, he became deeply involved in some of the political issues of his day, including the First World War[1] and the Dreyfus scandal. Durkheim, along with the French novelist Emile Zola, protested the conviction for treason of the French captain Alfred Dreyfus. Dreyfus was incarcerated on Devil's Island in 1884 and, despite substantial protests against his conviction, was not exonerated until 1906. The Dreyfus affair is widely regarded as an outrageous example of scapegoating and official corruption. The overtones of anti-Semitism and government abuses make the Dreyfus affair far more than a case of malicious and wrongful prosecution.

Durkheim saw the Dreyfus affair as a scandal that consisted of "gross illegalities." He also regarded the affair as an opportunity for the public to participate in a wider movement to forge a higher moral consciousness and renewed involvement in the affairs of France (Lukes 1977, 333). Reproached by many quarters of French society, and braving considerable expressions of anti-Semitic sentiment, Durkheim joined other *Dreyfusards* (intellectuals, artists, and others mobilized against the corruption of the Dreyfus affair) in seeking to reverse Dreyfus's conviction. In his participation in this movement, Durkheim emerged from his customary role of detached intellectual. He provided direct replies against the anti-Dreyfusard historian Ferdinand Brunetière. In his rebuttal of Brunetière, Durkheim defended the *Dreyfusards'* decision to prize "logic" over the official opposition of the authorities. He was unbending in this insistence upon putting "reason above authority" and holding that individual rights ought not to be ignored (see Lukes 1977, 338). Durkheim's efforts in the

Dreyfus case underscore his interest in social justice and his awareness of the ways in which minorities could be used for political purposes. Pearce (1989, 72) notes that Durkheim was critical of the gap between formal constitutional protections in France and the ease with which Jews were scapegoated. The cohesion of many Jewish communities was set against a backdrop of "this need of resisting a general hostility, the very impossibility of all communication with the rest of the population" (Durkheim, cited in Pearce 1989, 71).

Pearce (1989) offers a fresh look at Durkheim's writings, suggesting that the almost "universal consensus" that Durkheim is a political conservative and positivist thinker is too simplistic. Pearce argues instead that Durkheim's work reveals some elements of socialism and can also serve as a corrective to some of the more extreme or overstated versions of Marxism (Pearce 1989, xiii–xiv). Overlaps appear between Durkheim's politics and those of more critical works in the Marxist and neo-Marxist traditions. Pearce (1989, 183) remarks that Durkheim was concerned about the power that could be exercised by the state. Accordingly, Durkheim believed that the state would not necessarily adhere to checks on its power or measures to ensure that the state and its officials were subject to the rule of law. Durkheim was not, however, wholly opposed to state powers, suggesting instead that with the proper development of the state, greater liberty could be realized (Pearce 1989, 187). This vision of an orderly and just society can be derived from Durkheim's contributions to the sociology of law. As Pearce (1989, 193) puts it: "For Durkheim, the rationality of the human subject is produced and sustained by society. Society ... provides individuals with the capacity to follow its rules and the ability to engage in meaningful and orderly social interaction."

Law and Social Cohesion

There are many dimensions to the general concept of society: social, economic, and political dimensions, for example. For Durkheim, society represented a "moral phenomenon" in which the individual was inescapably bound and influenced by a moral milieu (Cotterrell 1984, 79). In its ideal form, society stood as a crystallization of widely shared social values.[2] These shared values were not completely established, especially in more complex, modernized societies. Thus, law served as an index of particular kinds of social solidarity, and as a key regulatory device in more complex societies, it served to reinforce important social values. The concept of social solidarity is fundamental to Durkheim's thought. Durkheim postulated that two kinds of social solidarity characterized social development: mechanical and organic solidarity. First, *mechanical solidarity* was evident in earlier, "simpler" societies in which the division of labour was rudimentary. In keeping with Durkheim's argument that collective life determined individual life, the *collective con-*

science (or "conscience collective") was seen as an external force, independent of individual will, that acted as a "social fact."[3] Durkheim saw religion as the origin of the modern collective conscience. In earlier times, religion served an important function of giving coherence to structures and providing a general form of social stability. Nonetheless, the initially cohesive character of religious regulation became, in Durkheim's view, more divisive than unifying in modern societies (Lukes 1977, 518). Lukes notes that Durkheim believed that social institutions, rather than religious institutions, could be most useful in producing "social cohesion" in modernizing societies (Lukes 1977, 518).

In societies where mechanical solidarity was established, individual differentiation in terms of personality was very limited. Cotterrell (1984, 78) notes that in conditions of mechanical solidarity, religion and law often work together and are not easily differentiated. They serve to uphold common values and to offer mechanisms to react to or regulate deviation from social values. Under the force of the collective conscience, individual identity as we know it becomes subordinated to the moral milieu. The collective conscience, according to Durkheim (1966, 96), acted as a source of "general vitality" for the sake of the society as a whole. Durkheim regarded mechanical solidarity as a means of social integration, but an integration that was characterized by vengeance and often harsh punishments against those who offended the collective conscience. Indeed, for Durkheim (1966, 70), crime was defined as those acts that generated punitive reactions. These crimes, with very few exceptions, were "universally disapproved of" by members of a given society (Durkheim 1966, 70). Durkheim (1966, 87–89) did not discount the repressive sanctions that he thought characterized these earlier societies; rather, while he viewed them as a crude means of social survival and as insufficient for modern societies, he admitted that they served their societies in their need for moral expressions of outrage or disapproval.

In more complex societies, mechanical solidarity evolved into *organic solidarity*. Organic solidarity corresponded to a more complex, *inter*dependent division of labour, as well as a weakening of the collective conscience. Organic solidarity is thus associated with the onset of a more co-operative society, in which restitutive law and co-operative law might be used synonymously (see Lukes 1977, 155). Increased division of labour reflected massive social changes, including population density in cities and developments in communication and transportation (Milovanovic 1988, 26). Specialized knowledge and specific occupational groups were essential in these complex societies, where people were increasingly reliant on others. Criminal law, and other forms of legal regulation, could bolster social cohesion in these new, more variegated societies. Durkheim realized, however, that legal regulation and other normative systems could fail. Industrial conflicts as well as conflicts in social life led to severe tensions and breakdowns in the moral order. Durkheim conceptualized such breakdowns as *anomie*, in which social integration lacked adequate regulatory mechanisms (see Cotterrell 1984, 79).

In conditions of organic solidarity, as societies became more populous and complex, punishment became less the property of a group and was administered in a less "haphazard" manner under the aegis of state tribunals (Durkheim 1966, 87). The modern character of punishment served the methodical purpose of "social defence." It emerged as a form of moral denunciation; however, it took on the character of "a passionate reaction of graduated intensity that society exercises through the medium of a body acting upon those of its members who have violated certain rules of conduct" (Durkheim 1966, 96). The transition from mechanical solidarity to organic solidarity—from repressive law to restitutive law—and the emergence of many new forms of social regulation are vital aspects of Durkheim's theorizing. It is important, however, to bear in mind that the transition from mechanical to organic solidarity did not represent a complete break in norms. Giddens (1971, 77) outlines this transition:

> *The progression of organic solidarity is necessarily dependent upon the declining significance of the* conscience collective. *But commonly held beliefs and sentiments do not disappear altogether in complex societies; nor is it the case that the formation of contractual relations becomes amoral and simply the result of each individual following "his best interest." ... a society in which each individual solely pursues his own interest would disintegrate within a short space of time.... "There is nothing less constant than interest. Today, it unites me to you; tomorrow, it will make me your enemy."*

The increasing social density of these new societies and the erosion of a "common morality" (Milovanovic 1988, 26) meant that an ethos of individualism began to eclipse the collective life. As the collective conscience weakened, law became transformed. The transformation of law was envisioned as a movement away from repressive, harsher sanctions toward restitutive sanctions. *Repressive law* is exemplified by penal law, which inflicts suffering and punishment on rule breakers. Modern forms of repressive law include the systematization of criminal law and its various agencies of punishment, including incarceration. Giddens (1971, 74) defines crime as "an act which violates sentiments which are 'universally approved of' by the members of society." Crime thus involves actions that transgress these universally shared and understood beliefs. For Durkheim, the collective conscience appears as an external, *reified* (or enlarged) force, whose integrity depends on collective reactions against a variety of rule infractions. In simpler societies, the collective conscience is conventionally established through religious systems, which bring coherence to expected behaviours and penalties for violations of these expected behaviours (Giddens 1971, 75).

Restitutive law is a second type of law, one that Durkheim associated with more complex societies. In contrast to criminal law, restitutive forms of law appear in civil law, commercial law, and a variety of procedural laws (Milovanovic 1988, 27). Restitutive law was vested within the framework of the modern, centralized state. As these modernizing societies developed, there was less emphasis on the religious system as a regulatory mechanism. In this secular modern state, legal processes were not as informed by the standard meanings and the sense of shame associated with offences against the collective conscience. Weakening of traditional restrictions thus freed individuals from the ever-present constraints of local life. Ideally, these disappearing forms of constraint would be eclipsed by other, more secular, forms of regulation. Giddens (1971, 74) observes that restitutive sanctions serve not so much to punish wrongdoers as to restore relationships: "If one man claims damages from another, the object of the legal process is to recompense the claimant, if his claim is upheld, for some sort of loss which he has incurred as an individual. There is little or no social disgrace attaching to the individual who loses a case of this sort. This is typical of most areas of civil, commercial and constitutional law."

Durkheim subdivides restitutive law into *negative relations* (the relations of individuals and things, including property and tort law) and *positive relations* (which are less conflictual and emphasize co-operation between individuals). At this point we should mention the premise that occupational moralities developed alongside restitutive laws (Milovanovic 1988, 27). Certainly, a variety of professional bodies (i.e., the medical, nursing, and legal disciplines) have outlined guidelines for practice and research, and have the power to "discipline" their members by suspension, probation, or barring them from practice. Be critical, however, of the assumption that there exists a "common ideological outlook" within these professional bodies (Milovanovic 1988, 77). As we will discuss in Chapter Nine, there are some schisms and disagreements evident among the memberships of professional bodies such as the medical profession, particularly in addressing such controversial issues as the midwifery movement or the abortion debate.

Some researchers challenge Durkheim's premise that simpler societies were essentially "repressive" in their methods of resolving disputes. On the basis of anthropological studies, Clarke (1976) contends that Durkheim erred in his theory of a repressive-restitutive dichotomy. There is evidence that less complex societies were not necessarily so reliant on repressive sanctions. It is also noteworthy that, as Western societies have evolved, many societies still rely on extensive systems of criminal justice, including penal systems. Thus, one can argue that, while there has been a tendency to institutionalize "restitutive" mechanisms in modern law, the repressive function of penal law is still quite evident. In fact, studies show that, in the early 1980s, the United States saw a dramatic increase in the number of people admitted to federal and state prisons (Lowman and Menzies 1986, 101). Keep in mind, however, that there have also been cycles of contraction of prison populations (Lowman and Menzies 1986, 101), and that some industrialized countries such as Japan and the Netherlands have very low rates of imprisonment (Rutherford 1986).

Social Consensus and Social Development

A key feature of Durkheim's theory of social development is the premise that social inequality will be reduced as societies move toward greater division of labour. However, Durkheim allowed for exceptions to this theory of normal social development. Milovanovic (1988, 29–30) refers to "pathological" forms of social development noted by Durkheim. One pathological form emerges in the form of anomie. The concept of anomie is pertinent to an understanding of Durkheim's approach to social pathology. Anomie is said to reflect a state of normlessness, in which previous rules and regulations are in flux, and social life becomes more ambiguous. Taken to its extreme form, anomie would threaten social life as such, as social relations fall into disequilibrium. Anomie is contrasted with Durkheim's assumption that ordinarily societies will develop in such a way that all elements of society adjust to social change. We might conceptualize this as a dynamic process, but one that takes place within a generally stable framework.

Critics of Durkheim argue that he is not attentive to the *divisive* results of social stratification, social inequality, and economic exploitation. This critical view rests on a less optimistic view of social solidarity and the myriad regulations of modern social life. For some critics, then, deviations from orderly social development might reflect deeper, structural aspects of economic and political arrangements. Durkheim also foresaw that a second abnormal form could emerge if the division of labour was forced (Milovanovic 1988, 29). Class conflicts could become more extensive and threaten social harmony if contractual relations between individuals came to rest on coercion, rather than a more natural relation between the person's position in the economy and the demands and rewards associated with that position. Clearly, such a *forced division of labour* undermined Durkheim's preference for an orderly, meritocratic division of labour.[4]

Durkheim generally favoured the introduction of the *contract* as a partial replacement for status (Milovanovic 1988, 30). In earlier societies, contracts appeared primarily as *real*, or *solemn*, contracts. Divine authority became the guarantor to the contractual undertaking, which consisted of words, sometimes combined with specific rituals or rites. In modern societies, the demands and complexities of trade and commerce rendered these earlier forms of contract obsolete. Thus, the *consensual contract* emerged as the standard form of contractual relations. Durkheim observed, however, that the promissory aspects of the earlier contracts remained with the newer forms of contractual obligations (see Milovanovic 1988, 32). Indeed, it is clear that Durkheim believed that the older norms and expectations were often incorporated into evolving societies (Giddens 1971).

Durkheim's epistemological emphasis on objectivity reappeared in his formulation of *contracts of equity* (Milovanovic 1988, 32). According to Durkheim, contracts freely entered into are not necessarily equitable contracts; that is, some contractual arrangements may be accompanied by extortion, and this would vitiate the apparent fairness of the agreed-upon contract.

Durkheim's approach to social development has been linked with his general support for political liberalism. Lukes (1977, 338–40) criticizes some of Durkheim's critics for misreading Durkheim and incorrectly caricaturing him as politically conservative and essentially hostile to an ethos of individualism. Lukes (1977, 338–40) believes that a more careful reading confirms Durkheim's insistence on the importance of the collective conscience in modernizing societies. Furthermore, for all the elements of structural constraint in his writing, Durkheim was opposed to oversimplified, mechanistic analyses that set individuals within a largely predetermined system of "production and exchange." Certainly, in one of his major works—*Suicide*, published in 1897—Durkheim allowed for the ways in which a society might engulf individuals and produce suffering; nevertheless, for Durkheim, the emerging societies offered opportunities for new thought and expressions. These emerging societies required "a system of different and specialized functions united by definite relations" (Lukes 1977, 153) and a more variegated economic and social structure that rested on bonds of organic solidarity.

Durkheim favoured individualism, but not its manifestations of egoism and narrow self-interest. Durkheim wrote of individualism as a means of establishing a "sympathy for all that is human, a wider pity for all sufferings, for all human miseries, a more ardent desire to combat and alleviate them, a greater thirst for justice" (Lukes 1977, 340–41). To this end, Durkheim was not only committed to peace over war, and to the efforts of the *Dreyfusards*, but also served as a member of the *Ligue des Droits de l'Homme* (League of Human Rights) in France.

Durkheim's contributions to the sociology of law included the formulation of the repressive and restitutive character of law as it evolved in civil society and under the aegis of various agencies, including the modern state. While actively critical of some aspects of state tyranny—as evidenced in the Dreyfus affair—he viewed the centralized state body as indispensable in modernizing societies. His scientific approach was useful in combatting much of the speculation and dogmatism associated with some forms of metaphysics. His broad-based approach to religion, economics, social relations, politics, statistical methods, and ethics provided much of the groundwork for what stands as modern sociology.

MAX WEBER (1864–1920)

Biography

Max Weber was born in Erfurt, Germany, in 1864. He studied law and economics in university, and taught law at the University of Berlin, and later at the University of Freiburg. His doctoral dissertation concerned trading companies in medieval times, and his subsequent work included a study of Roman agrarian history (Parkin 1982, 13). His brilliant career was not without difficulties; in 1898 he suffered a nervous breakdown, which lasted for several years, during which time he neither wrote nor taught (Parkin 1982, 14). Weber was a prolific writer, and his legacy of works is still debated, including the "encyclopedic," two-volume work, *Economy and Society* (1921). Parkin (1982, 14) notes that Weber's scholarly output is "unsurpassed," and reflects a comprehensive grasp of such complex areas as law, the social sciences, history, and religion. Weber was renowned as a conflict theorist. His theoretical approach is critical of Marx's emphasis on the importance of materialist, economic forces on social development.

Capitalism and Law

For many readers, the development of capitalist economic systems appears natural, perhaps almost as a "given." But for Weber, the reasons underlying the rise of capitalism were the subject of intense scholarly interest. The institution of law was a considerable force behind the rise of capitalism. Weber defined law as follows:

> An order will be called law *if it is externally guaranteed by the probability that coercion (physical or psychological), to bring about conformity or avenge violation, will be applied by a* staff *of people holding themselves specially ready for that purpose (cited in Milovanovic 1988, 41; emphasis in original).*

For Weber, the legal order was a reciprocal part of the wider social order. Weber's holistic approach to law and society was based on the complex influences among law, religious institutions, society, and forms of domination (Käsler 1988, 144). The extent to which people conformed to legal order—perhaps through fear of repressive forms of law or through a belief in the correctness of legal order—was a central concern for Weber.

Weber was strongly opposed to simplistic models of law. He viewed economic factors as important, but not singular, influences on legal development. According to Weber, law is best understood within a *matrix* of forces; therefore, a scientific, multicausal approach to legal order is essential if one is to truly understand the complex evolution and purposes of specific legal systems (see Milovanovic 1988, 42). This approach posed a challenge to the more materialistically oriented and deterministic forces postulated by Marx. The capitalistic economic system rested on *calculation* and *stability*

(Milovanovic 1988, 42), and was not simply a means of exploitation and profit maximization.

Kronman (1983) devotes a chapter of his book on Weber to the topic of law and capitalism. For Weber, the capitalist system of production stood as "the most fateful force" in his time (Kronman 1983, 118). Rather than establishing a simple relationship between these forces of capitalism and the growth of formal legal rationality, Weber envisioned the two as "reciprocal" forces (Kronman 1983, 118). Although the two conditions could not be reduced to a simple relationship, Weber attributed great importance to the role of formally rational structures of law and administration in promoting economic calculability (Kronman 1983, 120).

Weber had a keen eye for exceptions to general rules; as such, his theoretical work used historical instances and cross-cultural studies which served to identify patterns of social and economic life that could be qualified by specific variations and influences within particular legal, social, and economic systems. Weber's general approach to the links between the promotion of capitalist transactions and the systematization of formally rational legal structures is a case in point. Weber noted that the English common law was, for the most part, formally irrational. Nevertheless, predictable "market transactions" were fostered in England, despite the lack of university-based, formal legal training (Kronman 1983, 120). Weber noted that English lawyers were oriented to commercial life in their training, and this fact facilitated a reshaping of laws favourable to business interests (Kronman 1983, 121). Thus, apprenticing in law served as a practical training, akin to learning a craft. This, in turn, corresponded with concrete legal training, which was largely congruent with the practical needs of business clients (Kronman 1983, 121).

For Weber, the causal relationships among law, economy, and society were complex. Historically, the absence of a systematized legal order—for instance, classical forms of early Roman law—served to impede the rationalistic process that was essential to modernized economic life. Kronman (1983, 126) adds:

> *In the absence of a law of agency or corporations or legal recognition of the principle of free negotiability, commerce can be rationalized only to a limited degree. According to Weber, without these particular legal devices, a stable and continuous system of capitalist production is inconceivable.*

For Weber, bureaucratic structures were essential, given the nature of developing capitalist economies. Weber noted that the increasing complexity of bureaucratic operations generated a need for greater precision, reliability, and efficiency in bureaucratic procedures. This combination of needs was imposed on modernizing bureaucratic systems of administration (Runciman 1980, 350). Weber's ideal of a fully rationalized administrative and legal structure was tied with the increasing division of labour and ever-specialized work tasks being undertaken in complex economies. Weber believed that bureaucratization allowed labour to be designed along "purely objective criteria"; for example, "individual parts of the work may be allotted to functionaries who have had specialist training and will continually improve their skills by practical experience" (Runciman 1980, 351).

Bureaucratization was linked with society-wide demands for a "stable and absolute peace for order and protection" (Runciman 1980, 239). Weber traced the growth of modern police forces to earlier structures of kinship, in which an individual's kin would be expected to resolve disputes or avenge injuries. Bureaucratization also stemmed from the growing range of "social policy" activities required of the state (under pressure from certain interest groups) or undertaken by the state. For Weber, such motivations were "economically determined in the highest degree" (Runciman 1980, 239).

Weber was clearly aware of some of the excesses of early capitalism. These excesses included difficult situations for workers and the development of factories where workers faced "bondage to the machine and a common work discipline" (Runciman 1980, 252). Weber disagreed with Marx's prediction of increasing emmiseration of workers[5] and intensified class conflict between workers and the bourgeoisie. Instead, he argued that, with a tendency to "cartelization" (rather than cutthroat competition) by capitalist entrepreneurs and greater stability with respect to banking and credit, many of these predicted "crises" had not materialized (Runciman 1980, 259). Weber also foresaw a continued increase in the number of employees whose interests were aligned more with capitalist and government sectors than with a manual, labouring class. He noted a "rapid increase" in the number of office workers—an increase that exceeded any increase in proletarian workers (Runciman 1980, 258). In addition, Weber envisioned a generation of myriad "interest groups" whose competing interests would prevent them from forming a clear, workable alliance against the bourgeois economic system.

Forms of Law and Legal Thought

Weber formulated two key dimensions of law: formality and rationality. *Formality* referred to "the employment of criteria, standards, and logic" (Milovanovic 1988, 43) in the legal system. Ideally, in *formal* legal systems, legal rules and procedures would be confined within the legal system and not be influenced by external factors. Conversely, *substantive* legal systems would be swayed or directed by political or ideological criteria. Weber believed that no legal system was entirely formal or substantive; rather, a system could be positioned on a continuum between the two pure forms of formal and substantive systems.

The second dimension, *rationality*, is a key concept to the subject of justice. Rationality refers to the use of criteria such that decisions that are made apply to all like cases (see Milovanovic 1988, 44). When similar legal cases are dealt with differently, the process would become "irrational": similar cases would receive dissimilar decisions, and the predictability of legal decisions would be weakened. The purest form of law—formally rational law—is attained only when five criteria are established: application, derivation, "gapless" character of legal propositions, legal irrelevance of that which is not rendered in legal terms, and the all-inclusive legal ordering of social conduct via the legal system (Milovanovic 1988, 46–47). This ideal type of law overcomes elements of ambiguity in rule-making and rule-application, and safeguards the importance of logic and neutrality in deciding particular cases.

Weber added that laws become fully rational when legal rules are applied fairly to equally situated persons, and when legal rules are clearly stated and administered without preferential treatment.

Domination and Law

In Weber's approach, *domination* refers to the probability that a particular group of people will obey certain commands (Milovanovic 1988, 47). Weber formulated three fundamental kinds of domination, which he presented as "ideal types," or pure forms, of domination[6]—traditional domination, charismatic domination, and legal domination.

Traditional domination is summarized as a custom or habit that is determined by longstanding obedience to particular rules. Weber used the example of kadi justice in Islam, in which established conventions of sacred tradition governed decisions. Although kadi-based justice was commonly associated with more charismatic forms of justice (discussed below), Weber indicated that it was in fact regulated by "extremely formalistic" interpretations of sacred traditions (Runciman 1980, 230).

Charismatic domination is linked with *personal* qualities of leadership, not with the highly co-ordinated, impersonal character of rational-legal domination. Weber emphasized that charismatic leaders are restricted by "the mission and power" of their characters, not by external regulations. The properties of "submission" to and "faith" in the power of charismatic rules preclude recourse to objective standards of dispute resolution. For Weber, the actions of charismatic rulers had an absolute quality, against which citizens had no means to appeal to other authorities or safeguards. It was an "intensely personal" form of leadership, with a quality of divine authority vested in the bearer of charismatic authority (Runciman 1980, 230). Charismatic domination posed a challenge to the traditional patriarchal structure of societies. The traditional elements of obedience, reverence of traditional obligations, and "bonds of personal loyalty" were often challenged by what Weber saw as the "revolutionary role" of charismatic authority (Runciman 1980, 233).

The essential character of charismatic domination is unstable.[7] Weber pointed out that the tremendous devotion and enthusiasm typical of the initial stages of a charismatic movement rarely maintain their original force. Instead, the original impetus is compromised and overtaken by "the conditions of everyday life":

> *The charismatically ruled . . . usually become tax-paying "subjects," contributing members of the church, sect, party or club, soldiers conscripted, drilled and disciplined according to the rules and regulations, or law-abiding "citizens" (Runciman 1980, 237).*

The unstable quality of charismatic domination is reflected in legal decisions. In its pure form, charismatic justice is entirely free of rules and the weight of tradition, and remains tied to the subjective powers of the ruler, or the "bearer" of charisma. "Trial by ordeal" is one example of charismatic justice that remains largely free of regular rules (Runciman 1980, 230–31).

Legal domination, in contrast, rests not on the weight of custom or on the personal qualities of a leader, but on the belief that existing laws and regulations are constructed rationally and fairly, and administered impersonally (see Milovanovic 1988, 47). Certainly, Weber was well aware of the limitations of the new rational order being ushered in together with intensified capitalist relations of production.[8] There is, however, an emancipatory quality that can be read into much of Weber's writing. Weber was clearly aware of the profound impact of class structures, including the gap between legal rights and the inability of many individuals to exercise such rights. The ideal type of rational-legal domination could be undermined if inordinately powerful economic interests capitalized on legal resources. For example, Weber was conscious of the limits of the legal dictum that "everyone 'without respect of person' may establish a business corporation"; he felt that "the propertied classes as such obtain a kind of factual 'autonomy,' since they alone are able to utilize or take advantage of these powers" (cited in Käsler 1988, 147). Weber went further, arguing that the reciprocal relationship between law and the economic order of capitalism rested on economic (material) power. Weber wrote that "economic interests are among the strongest factors influencing the creation of law: inasmuch as the authority underlying the legal order relied largely upon 'constellations of material interests'" (Lachmann 1970, 131–32).

Among the criticisms of Weber's theoretical approach, it has been suggested that Weber's view of capitalism appears largely static over time. Binnie (1988, 35) thus notes that, for Weber, capitalism appears to be "an unchanging concept in relation to law." She adds (1988, 35) that he paid insufficient attention to capitalism with respect to *political forms*, concentrating instead on its relationship to economic factors. Binnie (1988) observes that Weber's approach is largely bereft of the ideological aspects of law under capitalism, and is thus too narrow to appreciate the implications of these largely noneconomic features of capitalist relations and corresponding forms of law. Lachmann (1970, 131–33) notes Weber's emphasis on the "plasticity" of social institutions and relationships—a source of the flux and, to some extent, unpredictability of politics, economics, culture, and society. Lachmann points out, however, that Weber's dislike of overgeneralization led him to limit his appreciation of "wider problems" within the larger institutional structures.

KARL MARX (1818–1883)

Biography

Karl Marx was born in Trier, Germany, in 1818. His father, Heinrich Marx, was a practising notary and lawyer. At age twelve, Karl Marx enrolled in the Friedrich-Wilhelm-Gymnasium, a first-class school with a liberal direction. Marx graduated in 1835. In 1836 he was engaged to Jenny Westphalen, and they were married, despite family opposition, in 1843. Marx entered the University of Bonn in 1835, studying jurisprudence. In 1836, however, Marx transferred to the University of Berlin, where he studied history, philosophy, and law. Marx completed his dissertation in 1841, but did not obtain a university appointment (partly due to his reputation as a young Hegelian critic). For a short period of time, he edited a newspaper, but was forced to resign. In 1843, he and his wife began "what was virtually a lifelong exile from Germany" (Kamenka 1988, xvi). Marx worked in Paris, producing the *Economic and Philosophical Manuscripts of 1844*, a critique of modern society.

Marx was, however, expelled from France at the instigation of the Prussian government. He visited London briefly, then settled in Brussels, where he and Engels wrote the famous polemic, *The Communist Manifesto*, published in 1848. Marx was expelled from Brussels shortly thereafter, following a suspicion that he was supplying arms to revolutionaries. Marx returned to Paris briefly and then travelled to Cologne (where he was tried for and acquitted of sedition). From 1849 on, he lived most of his life in London, often in dire poverty. His great work, *Das Kapital*, was never finished, although the first volume appeared in 1867. By 1873, Marx was suffering severe health problems and, while he read extensively, he "was incapable of further serious creative work" (Kamenka 1988, xxii). His wife died of liver cancer in 1881; Marx died in London in 1883.[9]

Introduction

The writings of Karl Marx have had a profound influence on intellectual thought and political practice. In the early 1980s, Karl Marx was the most widely cited political philosopher discussed in social science references. His critique of capitalism and its institutions has influenced social, economic, and political policies throughout the world. Kamenka (1988, xxxviii) describes Marx as "the greatest of the socialist ideologists," while Tucker (1972, vii) comments that "no other intellectual influence has so powerfully shaped the mind of modern left-wing radicalism in most parts of the world." Marxist-based principles remain very much alive, influencing, for example, the development of a critically based criminology (Taylor, Walton, and Young 1973), and the attempts to combine feminist and Marxist analyses of oppression in capitalist societies.

A central concern of our discussion is how Marx (and his successors) viewed law and the state. An important dimension of Marxist approaches to law is the difference between law as it appears and law as it is; that is, the extent to which law under capitalism reflects the specific interests of a dominant class rather than the general interests of all citizens. For Marx, the power of law was essentially oriented toward bourgeois interests. The phrase *bourgeois legality* reflects this partisan quality of law. It is also important to note that Marx saw law as a mystifying force that deliberately misrepresented its true nature. As we shall see, Marx's approach to law under capitalism stands in fairly sharp contrast to those of Durkheim and Weber.

Studies of Law and Political Economy

It is well-established that, for Marx, the study of law was, at most, a secondary interest. References to law in Marx's writings are sporadic and not developed in a comprehensive way; rather, his emphasis was on understanding the *material* forces in history, especially how differing class formations and modes of production influence social and political life.

A complete understanding of the historical development of capitalism required a focus on the material elements of history, along with an appreciation of law and justice. Wood (1980, 3–4) contends that Marx did not explicitly view capitalism as unjust, despite Marx's clear outline of the reality of exploitation of workers, and the misappropriation by the few of the wealth produced by the labouring classes. Rather, Marx rejected the valorization of justice and the assumption that the best possible society could be realized through state-mediated justice (Wood 1980, 5). Wood (1980, 14) assesses Marx's neglect of juridical ideals as deliberate, and not as an oversight:

> Because Marx regarded juridical institutions as playing only a supporting role in social life, he attached considerably less importance to juridical conceptions as measures of social rationality than most previous social thinkers were inclined to do.

The genius of capitalism is that patterns of inequality can be excused, denied, or justified in large part through its ideology of private property and individual acquisition. Marx objected to capitalism as a system not because it was inherently unjust but, as Wood (1980, 37) contends, because "it is a form of *concealed dominion* over the worker" (italics added). A Marxist-based critique of bourgeois law emphasizes the importance of this concealment of economic power and legal advantage as they are actually exercised in capitalist societies.

Although Marx did not provide a systematic basis for the sociology of law, his critique of the rule of law is a major contribution to an understanding of the nature of class rule in industrial societies. Collins (1987, 1) states that the rule of law is viewed by Marxists as a "pervasive legitimating ideology" in these societies. As such, the task for Marxists is to demystify the tenets of liberal political philosophy so as to revolutionize existing political, economic, and social institutions. Part of this demystification, for Marx, was to place analysis of the modern state in the context of political economy. In *The German Ideology*, published in 1846, Marx and Engels linked economic production with changing forms of human consciousness. Growing contradictions and conflicts in society led to the development of the modern state, a locus for class-related struggles (see Knuttila 1987, 94–95). The state appeared as an "independent form" in which

> the struggle between democracy, aristocracy, and monarchy, the struggle
> for the franchise ... are merely the illusory forms in which the real strug-
> gles of the different classes are fought out among one another (from The
> German Ideology, cited in Knuttila 1987, 95).

Given this critical emphasis and the unsystematic nature of Marx's contributions to legal philosophy, we might think it odd that Marx figures so prominently beside the classical writings of Durkheim and Weber or modern contributors to the sociology of law. Nevertheless, Marxism remains a vital area of legal scholarship. As noted earlier, in the early 1980s, the Institute for Scientific Information found that Marx was the most widely cited scholar in the social sciences and humanities. There has also been a renaissance of interest by Marxists in the nature of modern legal systems (Cain and Hunt 1979; Beirne and Quinney 1982; Collins 1987, 1). This renewal of interest is particularly impressive, since Marxism has in many respects been discouraged, even vilified, as a desirable form of Western scholarship. As outlined in this section, there are numerous arguments for and against a Marxist, or Marxist-derived, perspective in understanding law, class, and power.

Of the several neo-Marxist approaches to state, law, and economy (see Ratner, McMullan, and Burtch 1987), instrumental Marxism and structural Marxism stand as two core approaches in critically understanding the nature of domination and social change in capitalist societies.[10] *Instrumental Marxism* begins from the premise that the state (including its legal component) serves the general interests of the ruling class, not the general interests of all citizens. As set out in *The Communist Manifesto*, "The executive of the modern State is but a committee for managing the common affairs of the whole bourgeoisie" (Marx and Engels 1979, 82). This instrumentalist approach means that state officials have *very little autonomy* in setting policies, and that their primary role is to assist the bourgeoisie in accumulating surplus value[11] and consolidating their dominant position over the mass of workers.

Milovanovic (1988, 64) discusses some aspects of Marx's *A Contribution to the Critique of Political Economy*. A key point is that, for Marx, people become involved in relationships that are *independent* of their will. These relationships are determined in large measure by the fundamental economic structure of a particular society. This economic *base* underlies and shapes the *superstructure* of social thought, law, politics, and culture. Marx adds: "It is not the consciousness of people that determines their existence, but their social existence that determines their consciousness" (see Milovanovic 1988, 64). This statement reveals the strength and weakness of Marx's writing. Its strength lies in the boldness of his attack on an uncritical acceptance of social contract theory and the essential validity of law; its weakness appears in his tendency to overstate such points or to write in contradictory ways. Specifically, his statement that material forces determine consciousness is contradicted by other passages in which he sees human consciousness and material structures as dialectically interrelated.

Marx's historical perspective is evident in his typology of modes of production: slavery, feudalism, capitalism, and communism (with socialism an interstitial mode of production that precedes true communism). Under capitalism, goods that were previously used for subsistence and for barter become transformed into commodities sold for profit (Milovanovic 1988, 64–65). It is essential to appreciate that for Marx, and others working within the Marxist tradition, law was seen as a dynamic force, altering legislation and legal practices in order to resolve crises and contradictions in particular societies at certain periods of time. This *dialectical* approach is often used to argue against instrumentalist theories of law, and provides an understanding of law as a form of struggle that includes workers (Chambliss 1986, 30 and 49).

Milovanovic (1988, 66–67) brings forward two general strands of Marxist theory. The first strand is portrayed as *superstructure as determined by the (economic) base*. The interests of the more powerful class are realized, in part, through the repressive and ideological functions of law. Hence, police and army forces may be mobilized to extend the interests of capital, through warfare at one extreme and by quelling domestic struggles, such as unionization, at the other extreme. An ideology favourable to social stratification, private property, and the accumulation of wealth may also be seen as essentially favourable to the dominant economic class.

Structural Marxists shift attention to the "internal dynamics" (Milovanovic 1988, 69) of capitalism as a complex formation that not only works toward consolidating the dominance of capitalism but also must address challenges and pressures that would weaken this dominant status. They discount Weber's premise that the legal order attains an autonomous status as it moves toward "formal rationality" (Milovanovic 1988, 69). Structural Marxists claim that the capitalist state achieves only a relative autonomy. In this relative-autonomy approach, then, the state is not conceptualized as an instrument that is alternately concealed, misrepresented, and brandished on behalf of capital. Nor are economic forces presented as the essential determinants of social life, since the state assumes greater autonomy in addressing the diverse (sometimes opposed) interests of various constituencies, including social classes.[12]

Instead of adhering to the base-superstructure distinction, this strand of Marxist theory argues that the economic, political, and ideological spheres interact to produce particular "conjunctures" in a given social formation. Taken to its extreme, it sees human agency—the importance of ideas, consciousness, and personal actions—as disappearing from the matrix of factors that affect social life. A less stringent interpretation would allow for the influence of social movements, resistance, and class struggle in reshaping the social formation.

Milovanovic (1988, 68) continues his discussion of *domination*, noting that instrumental Marxists view media, family, and educational institutions as transmitters of values favourable to capital accumulation. Moreover, this ideological work is reinforced by the more repressive powers of law. The result is a mixture of *mystification* (to deliberately perplex or hoax) about law such that the real purpose of law is distorted and legitimated; and *repression*, such that relatively powerless citizens are subject to the threat or application of legal sanctions.

Pashukanis and Marxist Legal Thinking

The Soviet jurist E.B. Pashukanis (1891–1937) remains a key figure in the formulation of Marxist legal thinking. His formidable academic accomplishments—Pashukanis authored approximately 200 works dealing with legal history and legal theory (Beirne and Sharlet 1980, Preface)—are contrasted with his denunciation and eventual execution as "an enemy of the people" (Beirne and Sharlet 1980, 70). Pashukanis believed that, while a measure of social regulation was needed in the *transitional period* between socialism and communism, socialist law was fated to wither away (Beirne and Quinney 1982, 21).

The purge of Pashukanis and others in 1937 signalled a reconsolidation of Soviet jurisprudence as a formal, professional institution. Vyshinsky, the Soviet legal scholar who essentially replaced Pashukanis as a leading force in Soviet jurisprudence, published work that criticized Pashukanis's approach and argued for consolidation of a system of law that reflected the will of the people. Law was thus recast as an authentic representation of the people's will and as a necessary force in the ongoing struggle to establish Soviet socialism. Vyshinsky argued that there was a great need to eliminate previously-dominant classes and to protect the emerging Soviet state from "capitalist encirclement" (Beirne and Sharlet 1980, 33). Far from abolishing the state and its legal structures, Vyshinsky contended that the eventual abolition of the state could not be undertaken post-haste. Instead, law would in the interim have a stabilizing quality, ensuring the orderly development of socialism while protecting against the possible undermining of the Soviet state by outside capitalist forces (Beirne and Sharlet 1980, 33).

Pashukanis was associated with the *commodity exchange* school of law in the 1920s. In this approach, law is not simply a reflection of the interests of a dominant class or classes; instead, law emerges from the development of generalized commodity exchange (Beirne and Sharlet 1980, 20–21). Pashukanis argued that the *legal form* emerged from the economic sphere, specifically from the exchange of *commodities* under capitalism. The production of goods for "direct use" was eclipsed by the manufacture of commodities, which are produced for their "use value" (Milovanovic 1988, 70–71). At its extreme, the commodity-based system and the introduction of currency (money) contribute to a masking of the exploitation of social labour and a concealment of real needs.

Pashukanis claimed that there was a parallel between the commodity form and the legal form. In the legal form, there appears to be equality between individuals. Each person bears rights, and his or her actions are taken to be freely willed. Nevertheless, the *juridic subject* (Milovanovic 1988, 72) is an idealization of individual freedom: in essence, individuals are still constrained by substantive differences in power, and part of this constraint is secured through legal processes. This approach is significant in that, rather than treating law as a neutral, progressive, and natural development in civilization, it sees law under capitalism as rooted in materialist conditions and oriented to the protection of property relations and class power.

Pashukanis provided a valuable framework for understanding law, including his argument that the *appearance* of law was belied by continuing inequalities maintained by the legal apparatus. Just as the commodity form was associated with unequal efforts and rewards (between the bourgeoisie and the proletariat), so also the legal form served to perpetuate inequality. Beirne and Sharlet (1982, 308) note that the logic of the commodity form, and the logic of the legal form "are universal equivalents which in appearance equalize the manifestly unequal: respectively, different commodities and the labour which produced them, and different political citizens and the subjects of rights and obligations."

Criticisms of Marxist and Neo-Marxist Theory

POOR INTEGRATION OF THEORY AND EMPIRICAL RESEARCH

Critics have commented on the gap between *theorizing* about the state on the one hand and *concrete, empirical analysis* of the nature of state control. Knuttila (1987, 119) concludes that the *instrumentalist* perspective developed by Miliband suffers from an underdeveloped theoretical framework, while Poulantzas's *structuralist* approach lacks empirical analysis. Clearly, then, neo-Marxist theory requires an integration of empiricism and theory before it can fully explore the nature of the state and its legal apparatus.

Radical criminology has also been criticized for the weak empirical basis of many of its assertions. Hagan (1985, 224), for example, comments on the imprecise wording used by some Marxist criminologists, including the murky and poorly operationalized concept of the ruling (or governing) class, or their use of the term "interests served under capitalism." Such opaque terminology hinders careful measurement and verification of the claims of Marxist and other radical criminologists.

Durkheim argued that the primacy given by Marx to economic factors had not been verified scientifically, by either Marx or his followers. Durkheim believed that economic factors were important, but that in terms of social development, economic factors were properly regarded as "secondary and derivative" (Lukes 1977, 232).

BIASED ANALYSIS OF LAW AND POLITICS

Some critics express concern over Marxism's myopic analysis of law and politics in capitalist societies. They argue that neo-Marxist approaches are built on a thoroughgoing critique of capitalism without an appreciation of the progressive or positive aspects of capitalist societies. For example, Collins (1987, 14) makes the point that the Marxist ideological critique of liberal-pluralism and the rule of law is not entirely convincing. Such critiques are directed against existing power arrangements, without formulating a more positive theory of law and power (see Collins 1987, 14). We could add that some critical outlooks ignore beneficial aspects of the rule of law, including provisions that safeguard individual freedoms while inhibiting the actions of the most powerful sectors in society. In addition, Marxist theories that hinge on simplified versions of class conflict are open to the criticism that they are falsely simplistic: they reduce the complexity of social and economic conflict (Collins 1987, 45–47).

IRRELEVANCE OF MARXIST THEORY

Marxist theory has also been dismissed as no longer pertinent to modern political and economic issues, since Marx was writing about an earlier form of capitalism. The Marxist tenets of the decline of the state and escalating class conflict lead some theorists to argue that the Marxist approach is antiquated and irrelevant. Some believe that Marxist doctrinaire thinking, like all forms of dogma, is no longer relevant in a changing world. Consider the following exchange between Bill Moyers (1989, 501) (host of the PBS program "A World of Ideas") and the late Professor Northrop Frye:

Frye: Doctrinaire Marxism will not work anywhere in the world—not because it's Marxism, but because it's doctrinaire. I don't think anything doctrinaire will work anywhere.

Moyers: And by "doctrinaire," you mean—?

Frye: I mean a simplified deductive pattern that carries out policies from major premises about ideology—

Moyers: —instead of from the experience of the real world.

Frye: Yes.

A related criticism is that Marxist theories of law have become stale and catechismal, not subject to empirical verification. This criticism has not gone without challenge. Collins (1987, 5), for example, charges that contemporary Marxism is far from dogmatic, and that contemporary Marxist research involves the refinement and replacement of various facets of classical Marxist theories. There has been a dramatic revival of interest in Marx and neo-Marxism in Western scholarship, including attempts to apply Marxist approaches to such major developments as the welfare state (see Gough 1979).

UNCLEAR FRAMEWORK OF LAW
The analysis of the nature of law in neo-Marxist writing is at times not very coherent. Marx did *not* emphasize the study of law in his writing, and Marxists have not yet resolved whether or not law is to be retained under communism. There exist substantial splits on the topic of law among neo-Marxists, centring on such questions as (1) should the legal apparatus as we know it be abolished? (2) should reform be undertaken, since it may simply consolidate the hegemonic powers of the state by giving legitimacy to the law? and (3) should particular elements of law, for example, human rights safeguards, be retained?

POLITICAL REPRESSION
Critics also point to the danger that neo-Marxist practices may be implemented in a manner that destroys popular political expression. Writing in 1918, the German socialist leader Rosa Luxemburg foresaw that, as political life became repressed, "life in the soviets must become more and more crippled. Without general elections, without unrestricted freedom of the press and assembly, without a free struggle of opinion, life dies out in every public institution ..." (cited in Carnoy 1984, 63).

Critics also have reservations about the actual implementation of political power. For example, although Emile Durkheim respected socialism for its potential in reorganizing the economic system and securing a higher morality, he was leery of the potential for violence and class-divisiveness he saw in late nineteenth century struggles for socialism (see Lukes 1977, 246–47). Woodcock (1990, 6) cautions against the repressive aspects of leftist administrations.

Political repression may take other forms. Some argue that the development of Marxist-influenced policies has tended toward nationalism, while repressing possibilities for international solidarity. Karenga (1981, 238–39) illustrates this tendency with the transition from German socialism to German nationalism and the growth of "Russification" in the USSR. Karenga (1981, 239–40) also raises two related points: first, that Marxism suffers from "Eurocentrism"—the tendency to exalt European countries and struggles as "the hope of mankind"; and second, that Marxism tends to reduce struggles for justice and equality to class. Marxism that places the economic base as the primary focus of study and struggle thus must be aware of racism and other factors. Karenga (1981, 240) puts this bluntly: "The Marxist expectation of working class unity across racial and ethnic lines is complicated by the racial ideology, privileges, status and access which the white working class possess and treasure."

Interestingly, the repressive aspects of Soviet life have become something of a media staple in North American culture. From the 1939 film *Ninotchka*, to the more recent film *Moscow on the Hudson*, material deprivation and political repression are presented as a central motif in Soviet life. This equation of "Marxism = political repression and totalitarianism" has been challenged by Marxists. Beirne and Quinney (1982, 2) contend that there is a renewed interest among Marxists in law and social regulation. Moreover, this modern interest is not static, but more open and rigorous. Overturning simplistic stereotypes of Marxism includes moving beyond instrumentalism. Instrumentalism—about which Marx and Engels wrote (as noted earlier), "The executive of the modern state is but a committee for managing the common affairs of the whole bourgeoisie"—is now widely seen as overstated. More sophisticated theories and approaches have since been mounted within the Marxist tradition. While acknowledging the value of instrumentalism in uncovering the extraordinary influence of powerful economic interests in capitalist societies, Beirne and Quinney (1982, 16–17) note that not all legislation is so influenced by dominant classes.

The point here is that many contemporary Marxists claim to have shifted away from the more doctrinaire, stultifying aspects of political rule or scholarly theorizing. This renewed interest in Marxism thus stems largely from an interpretation of Marx and his more humanistic, emancipatory objective, and less from political regimes ostensibly modelled on his original or revised principles. Svitak (cited in Benn 1980, 38) is quite clear about the humanistic objectives prized by Marx and by contemporary Marxists who object to some of the repression in socialist bloc countries. Svitak, arguing against the stereotype of Marx as the father of fascism, claims that Marx "strove for a wider humanism than that of the bourgeois democracies that he knew, and for wider civil rights, not for the setting up of the dictatorship of one class and one political party" (cited in Benn 1980, 38).

OPPOSITIONAL AND NEGATIVE APPROACH

Fine (1984, 1–3) expresses concern over the polarization of some legal critiques; specifically, that some doctrinaire Marxists fail to appreciate the contribution of liberal principles and achievements. He laments a "sectarian refusal" among some Marxists to forge alliances with liberals. He notes that Marxism may appear to be little more than "a negation of liberalism" (Fine 1984, 1), in which liberal ideals of equality before the law, judicial neutrality, and the like may be dismissed as fraudulent, and propertied relations cast as essentially exploitative under capitalism. Fine clearly recognizes the importance of critiquing the *class* nature of capitalist law, but adds that a monolithic critique of liberalism is unsatisfactory and mistaken.

To summarize, Marx and his followers have insisted on setting any analysis of law in the wider context of economic and political relations. This is true for law under capitalism as well as for socialist legality. The *historical* dimension is crucial to neo-Marxist perspectives on law, especially the view that laws protect such capitalist features as private property, investment, and profit-maximization, while *mystifying* the substantive inequalities through an idealization of law as essentially just and impartial. Worsley (1984, 23–33) provides a thoughtful critique and appreciation of the complexity of Marxist theoretical approaches. Worsley credits Marx with revealing in holistic fashion the moving forces of history, thus challenging the more bourgeois, event-filled approaches to human history. Marx also positioned the ordinary people—the great mass of labourers—as a decisive force in this unfolding history. Worsley suggests, however, that the extension of Marx's thought has been troubled by some more doctrinaire approaches, which involve untenable, "Jesuitical casuistries" [deceptive or false arguments] about capitalist and noncapitalist societies (Worsley 1984, 32). He believes that for Marxism to develop fully, it must grapple with the "relative autonomy" of the social systems it seeks to understand and appreciate the pitfalls of imposing a deterministic framework on these complex societies (Worsley 1984, 26).

SUMMARY

Emile Durkheim, the most famous French sociologist of the late nineteenth and early twentieth centuries, was a proponent of the importance of "the social," that is, the importance of social rules and societal needs in explaining social development. Durkheim's approach thus emphasized *collective* forces as influential on individual conduct and beliefs: "Collective life is not born from individual life, but it is, on the contrary, the second which is born of the first" (cited in Milovanovic 1988, 24). Durkheim formulated the concept of the "social fact," which is external to the will of individuals and which *constrains* individual action. Societies survive through the development of the *collective conscience*, which represents the sentiments and identities of the social group. Earlier forms of society were held together by *mechanical solidarity* in which individuality was minimized, and legal forms were primarily *repressive* and punitive, akin to penal law.

With the advent of industrialized societies, and the more complex division of labour, social solidarity evolved into *organic solidarity*. This new form of solidarity reflected the greater dependence of individuals on others, as folk customs and bonds became loosened. The collective conscience in these industrialized, specialized societies was weakened, but did not vanish altogether. Indeed, according to Durkheim, organic solidarity represented an even stronger force than mechanical solidarity. It reinforced complementary obligations in these complex societies. *Law* became important as a means of ensuring social solidarity. Ostensibly, law took on a more *restitutive character* in industrialized societies.[13]

Durkheim opposed the system of inheritance of wealth and privilege, as this contradicted the ethos of individualism in modern societies. Inheritance constituted a form of inequality in societies that were of a more meritocratic spirit (Milovanovic 1988, 34). Overall, legal forces were a part of wider structural constraints that permitted societies to function. Legal rules and customs were seen, ideally, to operate in ways that preserved the overall order of these complex societies.

The metaphor of society-as-organism is evident in much of Durkheim's writing. He wrote of the necessity of establishing regulatory mechanisms to co-ordinate social functioning: "It is necessary that the way in which organs should co-operate ... at least in the most frequent circumstances, be predetermined" (cited in Lukes 1977, 155). For these newer societies to survive, however, the bonds of organic solidarity needed to be strong; hence the need for a state regulatory body. This *structural-functionalist* approach remains influential in contemporary sociological analysis and political ideology. Durkheim's approach highlights the importance of social equilibrium and social order. Nevertheless, as outlined by Caputo et al. (1989), more critical, conflict-oriented interpretations of law have become prominent in recent decades.

Max Weber investigated many themes that Durkheim had addressed. Like Durkheim, Weber placed great importance on the influence of law on social life and argued for comparative (cross-cultural) studies of legal and social phenomena. For Weber, the study of legal systems was something that was to be undertaken in a comprehensive empirical and theoretical manner. Weber's substantial contributions have influenced the development of sociological theory generally and the theoretical framework of the sociology of law in particular. Weber's scholarship encompassed sociology, jurisprudence, philosophy, and economics. The development of capitalism, and its relation to Protestantism and law, was one of his primary concerns. He is widely acknowledged as the first writer to seek to establish a comprehensive sociology of law.

Weber contested Marx's premise that the legal order and the social order were largely determined by economic factors. Law was influential in shaping economic development; moreover, a number of factors interacted in a matrix, to produce a particular legal and political order. Käsler (1988, ix) credits Weber with developing intellectual approaches with great scope and flexibility, unlike Durkheim who "set out a systematic position early in his writings and thereafter persistently maintained and elaborated it."

Weber categorized three "ideal types" of *domination*: (1) *traditional domination*, in which obedience is based on custom or habit; (2) *charismatic domination*, an unstable form of domination based on the personal qualities of a particular leader; and (3) *legal domination*, in which there is a widespread belief that laws are legitimate and properly administered in an efficient, impersonal manner by a legal bureaucracy.

Marx offered a thoroughgoing critique of capitalism and its overall tendency to develop systems of law that were, in the final analysis, more favourable to bourgeois interests than to those of the proletariat. Unlike Durkheim or Weber, Marx envisioned that the growing infrastructure of capitalist-worker relations and the looming powers of the modern state contained irreconcilable contradictions. These contradictions would, he thought, usher in a transition from capitalist domination, to socialism, and finally to communism.

It is in the writings of Marx that such topical concepts as hegemony, mystification, and bourgeois legality were developed, even if they were not directly set in the systematic study of legal systems. Marx envisioned an end to formal legality as we know it, as the antagonistic relationships between worker and owner led to a transformation of society. Law was not only associated with direct expressions of coercion and repression; it also served a key ideological function in (mis)representing legal relations as equal for all and as a source of progress and social betterment. Modern movements such as feminist and civil rights groups often incorporate some aspects of Marxist thought, especially the notion that economic stratification and the undue consolidation of wealth among the few are used to exclude or exploit more marginal groups.

STUDY QUESTIONS

1. Emile Durkheim and Max Weber addressed legal processes as a means of establishing a general theoretical framework of social development. Review the key points of Durkheim's and Weber's approaches to the evolution of law, social solidarity, and social conflict. Provide at least *three* criticisms each of Durkheim's and Weber's approaches to law. What do you see as the key strengths or applications of the two authors' perspectives on law, social solidarity, and conflict?

2. Review the key elements of neo-Marxist approaches to law. Where does law originate from? Whose purposes does law serve? Outline the repressive, facilitative, and ideological functions of law under capitalism.

3. Contrast instrumental Marxism with structural Marxism, including their theoretical approaches to the autonomy (or lack of autonomy) of the state.

4. What specific reservations or criticisms do you have regarding a Marxist-based sociology of law? To what extent is this approach useful in understanding the nature of legal control?

NOTES

1. Durkheim was deeply involved in the French efforts to resist the Germans during World War I. Lukes (1977, 548) observes that almost one-third of Durkheim's students were killed in the First World War. Durkheim sought to counter German war propaganda and completed an analysis of events leading to the declaration of war in 1914 (Lukes 1977, 548–50).

2. The connection between Durkheim the objective scientist of society and Durkheim the man can be seen in Durkheim's childhood experiences in the Jewish community of Alsace-Lorraine. Durkheim admired the cohesiveness of such groups as religious minorities whose communities afforded them "a feeling of relief that is immeasurably bracing and sustains one against the difficulties of life" (Lukes 1977, 40).

3. The concept of the "social fact" was presented as a force that was external to the consciences of individuals and had a general constraining effect throughout a group. This emphasis on social factors acting upon people and constituting "beliefs, tendencies, practices of the group taken collectively" (Lukes 1977, 14) helped to establish a structuralist framework of social regulation of individuals and the groups they formed.

4. Giddens (1971, 80) notes that the conditions for organic solidarity require an occupational system based on merit not privilege. The forced division of labour would consist of the "unilateral imposition" of rules by one class against the interests of another. Giddens (1971, 80) adds that, for Durkheim, "these conflicts can be obviated only if the division of labour is co-ordinated with the distribution of talents and capacities, and if the higher occupational positions are not monopolised by a privileged class."

5. Weber based much of his argument on passages from Marx and Engels's *Communist Manifesto*. Weber maintained that the bourgeois class had to provide a minimum standard of living for workers to maintain bourgeois domination. The theory of emmiseration ("increasing misery") of workers as capitalism developed "has nowadays been explicitly and universally abandoned in this form as incorrect by all sections of the Social Democratic movement ..." (Runciman 1980, 257).

6. The ideal type was used to outline ideal forms of law or other social phenomena. Weber was aware that in reality few societies would fit this ideal conceptualization (see Hunt 1980, 101).

7. Weber wrote that "pure charisma recognises no 'legitimacy' other than that conferred by personal power, which must be constantly re-confirmed" (Runciman 1980, 229).

8. "Relations of production" is used to refer to the ways in which human labour and existing economic and technological resources are organized, producing, in the Marxist tradition, "forces of production" that profoundly influence politics and law, and indeed all aspects of human existence (see MacLean 1986, 9).

9. Biographical sketch of Karl Marx is paraphrased from E. Kamenka, ed. (1988) *The Portable Karl Marx*. Harmondsworth: Penguin.

10. Other neo-Marxist approaches include *capital logic* (in which economic forces become more prominent in determining social formations and law) and *class conflict*, epitomized by the work of the late Italian scholar Antonio Gramsci. For Gramsci, the balance of class conflicts meant that the state had to "win the consent" of the governed, using not only repressive measures but also ideological appeals to gain legitimacy; for example, the use of repressive force (police, militia) and ideological persuasion, in which the state mediates labour-capital relations (see Ratner and McMullan 1989).

11. "Surplus value" refers to the value of work beyond that which the worker is paid for (known as *exchange*). A key point of Marxism is that workers are oppressed under capitalist relations: they must sell their labour power for wages, and these wages do not reflect the actual worth of the labour performed.

12. The criminal justice apparatus in the modern state can be viewed from a relative-autonomy perspective. Different levels of the criminal justice system can be distinguished, with conflicts emerging at the macro level of economy and justice, through intermediate levels, and down to the micro level of interstaff and interagency conflicts (see Ratner, McMullan, and Burtch 1987).

13. As noted earlier, Durkheim's premise that law had become more restitutive in character has not been borne out by anthropological studies of law and custom. Earlier societies were not necessarily as punitive (repressive) as Durkheim assumed (Clarke 1976) and modern industrialized societies have developed an extensive system of jails, prisons, and other punitive institutions that contradict the restitutive spirit envisioned by Durkheim (Culhane 1985; Rutherford 1986).

REFERENCES

Beirne, P., and R. Quinney, eds. (1982) *Marxism and Law*. New York: John Wiley & Sons.

Beirne, P., and R. Sharlet (1980) *Pashukanis: Selected Writings on Marxism and Law*. London: Academic Press.

———. (1982) "Pashukanis and Socialist Legality." In *Marxism and Law*, edited by P. Beirne and R. Quinney, 307–27. New York: John Wiley & Sons.

Benn, T. (1980) *Arguments for Socialism*. Harmondsworth: Penguin.

Binnie, S. (1988) "Some Reflections on the 'New' Legal History in Relation to Weber's Sociology of Law." In *Canadian Perspectives on Law and Society: Issues in Legal History*, edited by W. Pue and B. Wright, 29–42. Ottawa: Carleton University Press.

Cain, M., and A. Hunt, eds. (1979) *Marx and Engels on Law*. London: Academic Press.

Caputo, T., M. Kennedy, C. Reasons, and A. Brannigan, eds. (1989) *Law and Society: A Critical Perspective*. Toronto: Harcourt Brace Jovanovich.

Carnoy, M. (1984) *The State and Political Theory*. New Jersey: Princeton University Press.

Chambliss, W. (1986) "On Lawmaking." In *The Social Basis of Law*, edited by S. Brickey and E. Comack, 27–51. Toronto: Garamond Press.

Clarke, M. (1976) "Durkheim's Sociology of Law." *British Journal of Law and Society* 3 (2): 239–55.

Collins, H. (1987) *Marxism and Law*. Oxford: Oxford University Press.

Cotterrell, R. (1984) *The Sociology of Law: An Introduction*. London: Butterworths.

Culhane, C. (1985) *Still Barred From Prison: Social Injustice in Canada*. Montreal: Black Rose Books.

Durkheim, E. (1966) *The Division of Labour in Society*, translated by G. Simpson. Toronto: Collier-Macmillan.

Fine, B. (1984) *Democracy and the Rule of Law: Liberal Ideals and Marxist Critiques*. London: Pluto Press.

Giddens, A. (1971) *Capitalism and Modern Social Theory: An Analysis of the Writings of Marx, Durkheim, and Weber*. Cambridge: Cambridge University Press.

Gough, I. (1979) *The Political Economy of the Welfare State*. London: Macmillan.

Hagan, J. (1985) *Modern Criminology: Crime, Criminal Behavior, and Its Control*. New York: McGraw-Hill.

Horton, J. (1966) "Order and Conflict Theories of Society as Competing Ideologies." *American Journal of Sociology* 71: 701–13.

Hunt, A. (1980) *The Sociological Movement in Law*. London: Macmillan.

Kamenka, E., ed. (1988) *The Portable Karl Marx*. Harmondsworth: Penguin.

Karenga, M.R. (1981) "The Problematic Aspects of Pluralism: Ideological and Political Dimensions." In *Pluralism, Racism and Public Policy: The Search for Equality*, edited by E. Clausen and J. Bermingham, 223–46. Boston: G.K. Hall.

Käsler, D. (1988) *Max Weber: An Introduction to His Life and Work*. London: Polity Press.

Knuttila, M. (1987) *State Theories: From Liberalism to the Challenge of Feminism*. Toronto: Garamond Press.

Kronman, A. (1983) *Max Weber*. London: E. Arnold.

Lachmann, L. (1970) *The Legacy of Max Weber*. London: Heinemann.

Lowman, J., and R. Menzies (1986) "Out of the Fiscal Shadow: Carceral Trends in Canada and the United States." *Crime and Social Justice* 26: 95–115.

Lukes, S. (1977) *Emile Durkheim: His Life and Work: A Historical Study*. Harmondsworth: Penguin.

MacLean, B. (1986) "Some Limitations of Traditional Inquiry." In *The Political Economy of Crime: Readings for a Critical Criminology*, edited by B. MacLean, 1–20. Toronto: Prentice-Hall.

Marx, K., and F. Engels (1979) *The Communist Manifesto*. Harmondsworth: Penguin.

Milovanovic, D. (1988) *A Primer in the Sociology of Law*. New York: Harrow and Heston.

Moyers, B. (1989) "Northrop Frye: Canadian Literary Critic." In *A World of Ideas*, edited by B. Flowers, 494–505. New York: Doubleday.

Parkin, F. (1982) *Max Weber*. London: Tavistock.

Pearce, F. (1989) *The Radical Durkheim*. London: Unwin Hyman.

Ratner, R., and J. McMullan (1989) "State Intervention and the Control of Labour in British Columbia: A Capital-Logic Approach." In *Law and Society: A Critical Perspective*, edited by T. Caputo, M. Kennedy, C. Reasons, and A. Brannigan, 232–49. Toronto: Harcourt Brace Jovanovich.

Ratner, R., J. McMullan, and B. Burtch (1987) "The Relative Autonomy of the State and Criminal Justice." In *State Control: Criminal Justice Politics in Canada*, edited by R. Ratner and J. McMullan, 85–125. Vancouver: University of British Columbia Press.

Runciman, W., ed. (1980) *Weber: Selections in Translation*, translated by E. Matthews. Cambridge: Cambridge University Press.

Rutherford, A. (1986) *Prisons and the Process of Justice*. New York: Oxford University Press.

Taylor, I., P. Walton, and J. Young (1973) *The New Criminology: For a Social Theory of Deviance*. London: Routledge and Kegan Paul.

Tucker, E., ed. (1972) *The Marx-Engels Reader*. New York: W.W. Norton.

Weber, M. (1968) *Economy and Society: An Outline of Interpretive Sociology*, edited by G. Ross and C. Wittich (originally published in 1921). New York: Bedminster Press.

Wood, A. (1980) "The Marxian Critique of Justice." In *Marx, Justice, and History*, edited by M. Cohen, T. Nagel, and T. Scanlon, 3–41. Princeton: Princeton University Press.

Woodcock, G. (1990) "Gary Geddes: Political Poet." *The Canadian Forum* 69 (792): 5–9.

Worsley, P. (1984) *The Three Worlds: Culture and World Development*. London: Weidenfeld and Nicolson.

3

Historical Foundations of Law

INTRODUCTION

Our understanding of contemporary legal processes—lawmaking, law enforcement, and social change—would be very limited if we did not explore the *origins* of law. This chapter presents an overview of how law emerges as an institution and whose interests it served. We will review several works on Canadian labour history as well as certain historical bases for criminal legislation affecting women (laws concerning prostitution, rape, and sexual assault). This chapter also provides historical backdrops to Native land claims and other issues considering aboriginal peoples. To begin with, we will consider the origins of criminal law in England. As noted above, we will also outline the historical treatment of prostitutes in Canada as an example of the conflicting values over legal regulation and crime control.

HAY: "PROPERTY, AUTHORITY, AND THE CRIMINAL LAW"

Douglas Hay has written an extensive treatment of the origins of English criminal law and its reliance on a complex repertoire of terror, majesty, and mercy in advancing the interests of a propertied class and a government bent on social order. Hay (1975, 17) begins with a reference to the popular appeal of the death sentence, a severe sanction that was, in Hay's words, "cherished" by eighteenth century rulers in England. Criminal law was thus based on *terror*, in the form of punishments meted out to the "labouring poor." Hay emphasizes that the exercise of law was closely associated with the protection of private property. He cites John Locke's assertion that "government has no other end but the preservation of property" (Hay 1975, 18). This economic foundation of criminal law contrasted sharply with the dominant ideology that linked crime with *moral degeneracy* (Hay 1975, 20). The symbolic apparatus of terror and the proliferation of offences that might be sanctioned by death did not result in a great increase in actual executions of criminals (Hay 1975, 22). There were difficulties in implementing this "bloody code." These difficulties included the refusal of juries to convict their peers, and the reluctance of some people to prosecute others, knowing the convicts might face the death penalty.

Hay states that during this period, a number of reforms were made to the English criminal law, partly along the classical lines recommended by the eighteenth century scholar Cesare Beccaria. "Real progress," however, did not occur until the 1820s and 1830s (Hay 1975, 24). Against the obdurate working-class offenders, the diminishing power of terror had to be refashioned into "a much more effective instrument of terror" (Hay 1975, 25). Hay thus interprets law as a dynamic force in which the repressive elements of the legal order are complemented by more sophisticated control measures.[1] In this conception of law, we see the play of symbolism and ideology complementing the state-approved executions. Hay outlines three aspects of English legal ideology: majesty, justice, and mercy.

Majesty refers to the development of criminal law as a "formidable spectacle" (Hay 1975, 27) in the quarter sessions (every three months) and the assizes (twice a year). The costumes and demeanour of the judges and the pomp of the ceremonies created a theatrical aspect in which "the powers of light and darkness" (Hay 1975, 27) were drawn out and ritualized for the greatest impact on the throng. The need for social order, presented as desirable, natural, and progressive, was accompanied by the need for vengeance against the wretched offenders, who were not uncommonly portrayed as a kind of contagion (Hay 1975, 28–29). In this theatre, the judge played the roles of priest, deity, and, sometimes, the mere mortal (see the Chelmsford example from 1754 in Hay 1975, 29). Law became a kind of "secular sermon"—mysterious and imbued with the gravity of divine as well as earthly punishments and justice. The occasional theatres of the quarter sessions and the assizes were assisted by exemplary punishments, as meted out by the special commissions (Hay 1975, 31). These "rituals of justice" were presented as healing processes, which restored moral balance in eighteenth century English society.

Justice, the second aspect of English legal ideology, is established through the veneration of the rule of law. The adherence to "strict procedural rules" and the formalities of assessing cases were facets of a legal structure that claimed to be rooted in the principle of *equality before the law* (Hay 1975, 32–34); the gallows became, symbolically, a great leveller. Hay argues that the law was applied unevenly: some people were convicted on flimsy evidence, while others escaped punishment through legal loopholes. Nevertheless, the doctrine of legal equality and a *universal morality* obscured the fact that the protection of property was the very bedrock of the criminal law: "The trick was to extend the communal sanction to a criminal law that was nine-tenths concerned with upholding a radical division of property" (Hay 1975, 35).

Hay notes that the third aspect—*prerogative of mercy*—was present throughout the administrative structure of eighteenth century England (Hay 1975, 40). Indeed, the discretionary elements of (1) the pardon and

(2) the lenient disposition attracted criticism and praise. Hay outlines a legal system that is checked by fear and compassion and in which the hope of mercy—and the granting of merciful dispositions—served in "justifying the legal order" (Hay 1975, 43).

Pleadings of the day placed great emphasis on the *respectability* of the accused, and his or her witnesses and supporters, not simply on their *social class*. Nonetheless, Hay (1975, 45) notes that pardons were often used to favour the more privileged sections of English society, and, in turn, patronage and favours were returned (Hay 1975, 45–48). As Hay notes, the criminal law again fronted its selective, or biased, operations on the principle of its fairness and neutrality:

> *[The law] allowed the rulers of England to make the courts a selective instrument of class justice, yet simultaneously to proclaim the law's incorruptible impartiality, and absolute determinacy. It allowed the class that passed one of the bloodiest penal codes in Europe to congratulate itself on its humanity (Hay 1975, 48–49).*

At the conclusion of his essay, Hay notes that the apparent *benevolence* of the ruling class, as expressed through law, was not simply altruistic: "It contained within it the ever-present threat of malice" (Hay 1975, 62). The *repressive* powers of the state, then, were aided and leavened by the appeal to its merciful and egalitarian promises, forces that served in general to consolidate the powers of the ruling class.

Hay's interpretation of the nature and implications of criminal law in eighteenth century England has generated criticism. Langbien (1983, 96) contends that Hay's conclusion of a "ruling-class conspiracy" against the working class is "fundamentally mistaken." Langbien (1983, 99) indicates that Hay was preoccupied with larger-scale disturbances such as "food riots" and work-related protests, actions that fit the class-conflict explanation in eighteenth century England. Langbien counters, however, that if criminal behaviour as a whole is examined, one will find far more intra-class offences. Most of the offences studied by Langbien—that is, offences prosecuted at four sessions of the Old Bailey Court, between 1754 and 1756—involved crimes against the person (homicide, assault), theft, burglary, forgery, and the like. He concludes that there is little sense of "romantic crimes"—those committed by the oppressed against the powerful; many crime victims were themselves poor[2] (Langbien 1983, 100).

Langbien (1983) also criticizes Hay's assumption that the death penalty was used to a greater extent in eighteenth century England. Langbien (1983, 96) reports that the death penalty was being used less often for convicted felons. He notes that prosecution of criminals was not largely the prerogative of wealthier persons. In fact, prosecutorial discretion was limited in many ways, including the automatic investigation of suspicious deaths by the coroner's system. In addition, "potential prosecutors" sometimes decided not to prosecute but rather to forgive the offender or simply forgo prosecution for reasons of time and expense. Langbien (1983, 103) therefore challenges the premise that wealthier victims could substantively "manipulate" prosecutorial power in their private interests. Langbien (1983, 104) also mentions the practice in which juries devalued the estimated worth of stolen goods or down-played the seriousness of offences. Building on these and other practices, Langbien (1983, 105) takes strong exception to theories that use available documents to construct an argument for a ruling-class, elitist interpretation of English criminal law in this period:

> I concede, although the actual evidence for it is thin, that elite victims must have been treated with greater courtesy.... What I resist is the idea that such practices justify treating the prosecutorial system as having been constructed for the purpose of furthering the class interests of the elite .... The whole of the criminal justice system, especially the prosecutorial system, was primarily designed to protect the people, overwhelmingly non-elite, who suffered from crime.

BEATTIE: *CRIME AND THE COURTS IN ENGLAND, 1660–1800*

Beattie (1986) provides a magnificent account of changes in the application of criminal law in his award-winning book, *Crime and the Courts in England, 1660–1800*. The book is too exhaustive in scope to review in detail. We can, however, summarize Beattie's account to trace some key transformations in the nature of judicial administration and the corresponding institutions concerned with crime and its punishment.

Beattie (1986, 619) traces a shift from the more severe, and quite limited, range of punishments in 1660 (branding, public flogging, or hanging convicted offenders) to the creation of "secondary punishments," including imprisonment or transportation (sending the convicts to penal colonies, such as Australia). Beattie (1986, 619) acknowledges the spirit of humanism that accompanied this transformation of punishments; however, he concludes that their creation "derived as much from a concern for effectiveness in penal matters as for fairness and humanity."

Beattie does not adopt an explicitly Marxist approach in his study of crime and the courts. Nevertheless, he builds his study in conjunction with a number of social-historical studies of English law and punishments. Beattie's assessment of these earlier studies, together with his study of court records in Surrey and Sussex, underscores the importance of class factors in establishing and reforming particular laws. Beattie (1986, 621–22) concludes that criminal law in eighteenth century England served to preserve "the established social and economic and political arrangements of the society" and also to implement certain changes sought by more powerful groups. The influence of the "propertied elite" was maintained by the broadened range of discretionary charges and punishments embedded into criminal law as it evolved (Beattie 1986, 621–22).

Beattie does not restrict his analysis to an instrumentalist reading of elite interests and state powers. Acknowledging the symbolic and material powers served by the edifice of criminal law, Beattie (1986, 622) argues that the ideological power of law had to attract a considerable degree of public approval:

> If the criminal law had served only the interests of the propertied classes it would hardly have attracted the widespread approval that was clearly bestowed upon it.... However constrained in practice access to the courts was for the working population, the law appears to have been widely accepted in society as a means of settling disputes and ameliorating public grievances.

Beattie (1986, 624) dramatizes the difficulty in challenging the use of capital punishment, particularly throughout the seventeenth century; there was little organized ferment against the administration of criminal law. Beattie (1986, 623) found that there were few signs of opposition to such principles as hanging during the century or more following the Restoration. The need for new measures—well beyond the brutal spectacles epitomized by public hangings and mutilations—is traced to the burgeoning developments in the mercantile and commercial spheres of the English economy. New concerns were voiced, calling for the establishment of a disciplinary network of reformatories and workhouses. Again, Beattie (1986, 624–25) interprets this mobilization of concern not as mere philanthropy, but as an imperative for the good of the economy and for those who benefited inordinately from it. Beattie (1986, 624–25) writes that the growth in social concern and the call for new institutions "were all related concerns to the propertied classes of London." He notes that new forms of coercion were necessary to establish sufficient discipline and levels of health for the labouring classes.[3]

CRIMINAL LAW, PROSTITUTION, AND MORAL REFORM

McLaren (1988) examines the origins of early twentieth century laws governing prostitution in Canada, especially streetwalking and keeping a bawdy-house. Focusing on the period between 1900 and 1920, McLaren notes the development of organized reform movements, which espoused a *social gospel* rooted in Protestant evangelism. Seeking the eradication of vice and immorality, such groups as the Women's Christian Temperance Union and the Young Women's Christian Association sought to improve the "moral health and harmony" of Canada, using rescue work, public education, and legal reform (McLaren 1988, 329–30). These groups viewed prostitution in moral terms, with very little attention to the economic forces that might impel women to prostitution. Prostitutes and those thought to be in danger of becoming prostitutes were liable to a strict regimen of labour, frugality, and "moral education" (McLaren 1988, 330). Prostitutes brought before nineteenth century magistrates were often sentenced to jail—and in cases thought to be incorrigible, for quite lengthy terms (McLaren 1988, 334).

While law is credited with a dynamic character, adopting new procedures and principles to deal with changing social conditions, early twentieth century law concerning prostitution was quite contradictory. For example, prostitutes were routinely prosecuted, while their customers were initially immune from prosecution. The double standard re-emerged when prostitutes later faced possible charges of being inmates in a bawdyhouse (which was a more serious, indictable offence), while clients "found in" bawdyhouses were liable only to a summary conviction charge (McLaren 1988, 330–31).

Another contradiction was evident in the variety of magistrates' attitudes and decisions concerning prostitution. McLaren (1988, 336–47) identifies three types of magisterial responses to prostitution: toleration, traditionalism, and activism. *Tolerance* was perhaps most evident in frontier areas of Canada. In Fort William, Ontario, Magistrate William Palling suggested in 1880 that prostitutes provided necessary, or understandable, sexual services to transient men; in addition, prostitutes may have served to help more reputable women avoid being accosted by these "rough men" (McLaren 1988, 337).

Magistrates who took a more *traditional* outlook did not espouse complete tolerance of prostitution. Nor were they heavily swayed by the efforts of more zealous reformers to eradicate prostitution. Prostitution was generally seen as inevitable and as a reflection of working-class practices and values that could not be easily transformed. Management of prostitution, especially its more extreme forms of exploitation, was thus sought.

The third kind of response to prostitution took the form of *activism* on the part of women magistrates who sought to attain political, social, and economic rights for women. These magistrates were also sensitive to biases in law enforcement that allowed men who preyed on, or otherwise exploited, girls and women to escape prosecution. When such men were prosecuted, it was not unusual for the case to be dismissed altogether or the man to be given a lenient disposition (McLaren 1988, 344–45). These reform-oriented magistrates, among them Judge Emily Murphy of Edmonton, were also critical of the state's financial interest in prostitution, which was most transparent in the fining of prostitutes and the lack of services to assist in rehabilitating them.

McLaren (1988, 347) concludes that despite the differences concerning the seriousness of prostitution as a social problem and the extent to which the law ought to (or could) remedy the problem, there was a widely-shared belief among the magistrates that prostitution would prevail, partly due to the strong sexual drives of men and what was seen by some as "the inherent looseness of working-class women." Criminal law was used to contain some aspects of prostitution, often without enquiring into the social and economic forces influencing prostitutes. McLaren notes that instead of providing a deep influence on magisterial practices, the social reform movements were often resisted, illustrated by the judicial practice of giving more lenient sentences for prostitutes over time.

Lowman (1989, 32–37) sees a legacy of entrenched contradictions in Canadian efforts to regulate or prohibit prostitution. At various times, police have simply tolerated forms of brothel prostitution, while at other times—in Vancouver from 1903 to 1917, for example—police have shut down brothel operations. Lowman cites the example of the 1976 closure of the Penthouse Cabaret in Vancouver, which resulted in the displacement of prostitution onto the street (Lowman 1989, 32). One of the ironies that emerges from this attempt to eliminate prostitution is that it forces prostitutes out of the closed quarters of brothels into the more public (and more dangerous) form of street solicitation. Lowman (1989, 39) observes that street prostitutes are especially vulnerable to violence. He refers to the deaths of over 20 prostitutes in the Vancouver area over a three-year period in the late 1980s, and the killings of nearly 50 prostitutes in the vicinity of Seattle. The latter killings have been linked with the so-called "Green River Killer" (Lowman 1989, 39).

The visibility of street prostitution has generated calls to abolish prostitution, or at least remove it from residential neighbourhoods. Lowman (1986, 207–08) notes that opposition to street prostitution by neighbourhood groups is not confined to concerns over noise and public safety; it also involves a concern over the "blight" (Lowman 1986, 207) associated with prostitution, and concerns over further deterioration of the neighbourhood. The point remains that attempts to legislate prostitution out of existence have been unsuccessful in Canada. Moreover, the legacy has been that such laws discriminate against women who work as prostitutes, and these laws tend to deflect attention away from the *structural* factors (such as sexual socialization and unemployment) that underlie prostitution (Lowman 1987, 110–11; Lowman 1991, 130).

CANADIAN RAPE LAW: WOMEN AS PROPERTY, WOMEN AS PERSONS

The crime of rape has traditionally been ignored or downplayed as a part of legal history (Backhouse 1983, 200). Despite a growing number of studies it has still not attracted considerable attention as a part of research on criminal law in Canada or the United Kingdom (Clark and Lewis 1977; Smart 1976, 93).

Backhouse (1983) reviewed the development of rape legislation and rape trials in nineteenth century Canada. She noted that as rape law evolved in Canada, it gradually departed from the influential legislative model adopted from England. In 1869, the Canadian Parliament passed the Canadian Counterpart Act, which retained the death penalty for rape even after England had abolished it. The Canadian legislation was considered more severe than English law and practice of the day, especially the provision for capital punishment for those found guilty of statutory rape of a girl under 10 years old. Backhouse (1983, 207–8) adds that this relatively harsh legislation had a less stringent requirement of proof for rape cases; specifically, even slight degrees of vaginal penetration would suffice for conviction. Over time, the Canadian Parliament modified some of the harsher elements of the law, replacing the death penalty with life imprisonment (Backhouse 1983, 208). Backhouse's research is valuable not only in pointing out the different ways in which countries frame such criminal laws but also the ways in which women came to be regarded under legal ideologies of the time. Backhouse interprets changes in nineteenth century rape legislation as a reflection of society's changing views of women, as property and as persons. Women were increasingly acknowledged to possess their own integrity. This was the beginning of a break from the ideology of women as property. Backhouse described the latter view:

Historically, the view was that men held property rights in women and that the value of this property was diminished if the woman had sexual relations with someone other than her husband. Ownership implied exclusivity, and sole control over the woman's potential for childbearing (Backhouse 1983, 208).

Over time, it became important for defence counsel in a rape trial to establish that the woman had "resisted" the assault. Women who could not meet this requirement were often seen as contributing to the rape itself. Backhouse (1983, 219) draws a portrait of the kind of woman who might properly resist such attacks. The "ideal" victim would be respectable and domesticated, choosing to "remain safely in the home, surrounded by family responsibilities," not exposing herself to the threat of sexual attack; when confronted she would resist, succumbing only because of the rapist's sheer "physical force."

Clark and Lewis (1977) use a historical framework to assess their research on rape in Metropolitan Toronto in 1970. The authors present a feminist interpretation of how women became viewed as property—of their fathers or husbands—within a general legal framework that was based on the dual notions of (1) the importance of private ownership of property and (2) the natural superiority of men, including their rightful mastery of women (Clark and Lewis 1977, 112). Rape law reflected this historical valuation of women as property. Not all women were treated equally under the law. For some women, deviation from the expected female role left them without effective legal recourse. These "open-territory victims" of rape were seen as devalued in their sexual and reproductive worth and were described variously as promiscuous, welfare-dependent, divorced, and so forth (Clark and Lewis 1977, 123–24). Box (1983, 157–59) remarks on the substantial influence of media accounts of rape—characterizing women as deserving victims, for example—and also comments on the criminal justice system's contributions to distinguishing between "legitimate" and "illegitimate" victims of rape. The rationalizations of the rapist are thus echoed and supported by the mass media and the courts.

Clark and Lewis's (1977) research serves to underscore a critical interpretation of sexual politics, including the pervasiveness of coerced, rather than freely chosen, sexuality. Clark and Lewis's study, together with other commentaries on rape and criminal law, signals a movement away from the perception of rape as an isolated criminal act or a psychological aberration and toward the idea that rape is situated in a social context.[4] This movement pressured reform, and led to the enactment of sexual assault legislation in Canada.

Canadian legislation dealing with the sexual offences of rape, attempted rape, and indecent assault was replaced in 1983 by legislation dealing with various kinds of sexual assault. The movement to sexual assault legislation has attracted some criticism from researchers concerned about the limits of such legal reforms. Gunn and Minch (1986) interviewed victims of sexual assault in Manitoba and followed the process of legal investigations of alleged sexual assaults. The authors found that only a tenth of the original charges led to conviction; the vast majority (approximately 70 percent) of the charges were "filtered out" of the legal system. Gunn and Minch (1986, 133) concluded that women bringing forward allegations of sexual assault face "social and structural" opposition. The legal system, like the social system in general, manifests considerable skepticism and explaining-away of sexual assaults. Even when a conviction was registered, average sentences were only 3.2 years for an offence that has a maximum penalty of life imprisonment. The authors added that despite the removal of a spousal immunity approach, spouses convicted of sexual assault tended to receive even more lenient sentences—for example, six months' imprisonment and one year's probation in a 1983 case and three months' imprisonment for a husband convicted in 1987 (Gunn and Minch 1986, 98, 118–19).

More recent research from the United Kingdom gives us cause for concern over the impact—or lack of impact—of efforts to erase leniency for spouses. It was only in 1992 that the House of Lords abolished the marital exemption in rape. Kate Warner (2000) reported that this late-in-the-day initiative has not resolved many problems associated with sexual assault in common-law or married situations. Specifically, there are concerns over persistent ideologies that promote myths of marital rape; for example, that such actions are less traumatic, less a breach of trust than assaults by strangers. Warner challenges several such myths, arguing that such violations may be even more traumatic than stranger-rape, and that the judiciary has sometimes been slow to regard "relationship rape" as a serious crime.

This research illustrates the gulf between legal reforms and actual protections for women and underscores the myriad reasons why many victims are discouraged from proceeding with sexual assault charges. Various myths about sexual assault are reinforced by the legal system and the media—for example, that some assaults are provoked, or victim-precipitated, others can be attributed to the victim's conduct or appearance (blaming the victim), or the lack of palpable injuries on the victim as a defence argument that no harm was done (Gunn and Minch 1986, 17–18). The authors pointed out that there is considerable inertia in moving the legal system and changing public attitudes so as to facilitate successful prosecutions and appropriate sentencing for persons convicted of sexual assault.

Others have also questioned the extent to which the new sexual assault legislation was a victory for Canadian women. Hinch (1988) found that police in Halifax, Nova Scotia might be reluctant to recommend charges for "open territory" victims—women who might be exposed to "potential character assassination" in court if the defence was allowed to explore the victim's previous sexual history (Hinch 1988, 291). Hinch views the law as contradictory in this respect, as it leaves some room for admission of reputational evidence about the complainant. Hinch (1988, 284–85) also found that in some incidents, "sexual assault" was defined in such a way as to hinder potential prosecutions. Such narrow interpretations and the retention of the "honest but mistaken belief" defence (Hinch 1988, 292) underscore some tangible limitations to a legal reform that was widely hailed as a victory for women.

LABOUR LEGISLATION IN CANADA: CRITICAL-HISTORICAL STUDIES

Conflicts over legislation are also evident in the history of labour law. Caputo and his associates (1989) provide an overview of labour-related laws, together with critical studies of labour law at various points in this century. They begin with two accounts of contemporary Luddism[5] to highlight the topic of worker alienation.

Many critical scholars agree that law has played a significant role in the structural conflicts between worker and management. Since World War II, North American labour relations have been described as "business unionism," in which the more revolutionary elements of the labour movement have been discarded, and a more co-operative style of negotiating established. Caputo et al. (1989, 208) indicate that this is a complex process. The law takes on a *repressive* character when it restricts such activities as union formation, picketing, and so on. Most scholars are well aware of the coercive aspects of provincial and federal labour law from earlier in this century (Morton 1980); however, they also draw our attention to ways in which such laws and regulatory agencies seek to soften violence and dissent among the work force. At the same time, labour law provides a level of protection and benefits for many workers. This balancing of interests is not interpreted as a justification of the neutrality associated with liberal-pluralist ideals of law and the state. Rather, critical theorists see this as a dialectical model of law that emphasizes the role of law in resolving specific contradictions in specific situations, leaving the overall economic structure intact (Chambliss 1986).

Caputo et al. (1989, 210) trace the use of law in labour conflict to Industrial England and the efforts by merchants to establish themselves in the production process, as feudalism was being eclipsed and eventually replaced by capitalism. The terrible conditions of eighteenth and nineteenth century industrial capitalism in England are outlined, along with the harsh, disciplinary nature of work in the factories (Caputo et al. 1989, 211). This Dickensian motif of brutality was alleviated over time, as protections for workers became embedded in law—limitations on hours of work and on the use of child labour as well as some safety provisions—despite resistance from such groups as the National Founders Association (Caputo et al. 1989, 211).

Court decisions in the United States and Canada in the early twentieth century were largely favourable to capitalist interests in restricting labour organization and promoting the ideology of free trade and capital accumulation. Thus, it is argued that capitalism and its corresponding labour laws reflected struggles over work and a process of legal development that, in the long run, facilitated capital accumulation and was largely contrary to a socialist approach to control over the work process.

Huxley (1989) provides a detailed account of the nature of collective bargaining, focusing on Canadian labour relations and legal decisions. Huxley's essay is a reprint of an article published a decade earlier. Nevertheless, Huxley's theoretical approach is useful in the general context of the nature of law in mediating social conflicts. He notes that the pattern of strikes in Canada is distinctive, implying that we should be careful about generalizing from one nation to another, or from a specific period of time to another. This caveat is significant if we are to avoid broadbrush generalizations that ignore significant differences in state and law between countries or within smaller jurisdictions (e.g., provinces, states, and the like). The main impact of Canadian labour legislation, according to Huxley, has been (1) to significantly restrict the implementation of the "strike weapon" and (2) to legitimate the ideology of the involvement of the state in resolving or controlling labour conflicts (Huxley 1989, 218).

One problem confronting workers and owners alike has been the disruptive effect of work stoppages due to strikes. Huxley argues against a "strictly economistic" interpretation of these prolonged strikes. Thus, other (noneconomic) factors need to be understood, including the power of ideas and of political organization in the contest between workers and owners (Huxley 1989, 219–20). This labour contest has resulted in the successful institutionalization of industrial conflict, that is, in securing the state's three functions of favouring management's capital accumulation, coercing labour's compliance (such as through back-to-work legislation), and legitimating government involvement in labour issues (Huxley 1989, 220). Notwithstanding legal protections for workers, Canadian labour legislation appears to have promoted lengthy strikes by banning strikes during the life of a collective agreement and by deferring specific negotiations or demands until after the expiration of an existing agreement. Structurally, then, law and management tactics are presented as encouraging strikes in a manner that facilitates capitalist accumulation.

A study by Ratner and McMullan (1989) complements Huxley's (1989) article. Ratner and McMullan focus on the evolution of labour conflicts and legislation in British Columbia, a province with a history of high levels of capital-labour conflict. The authors take a dynamic approach to labour conflict, arguing that the turn-of-the-century policies of state coercion and repression have largely become replaced by a more benign policy of *stabilization* of capital-labour conflicts. Once again, this objective of stabilization does not imply that it is in everyone's interest to acquiesce to labour law procedures.

For Ratner and McMullan (1989), capital-logic theory is rooted in a Marxist approach to class conflict and capital accumulation. The capital-logic approach is distinct from some neo-Marxist approaches that stress *economic factors* (also known as "economism") or *ideological factors* as pivotal in state-labour relations. The logic of capital is "predominant" in capital-logic theory. Ratner, McMullan, and Burtch (1987, 99) note that in capital-logic theory, the "state and law function to secure the conditions for capital accumulation according to the developing 'logic' of capitalist economic relations," and that the balance of class forces is partly influential for state policies. While the ideological power of law is important in distorting or mystifying the exploitative nature of the work process (Ratner, McMullan, and Burtch 1987, 234), the specific forms of *class struggles* and the *appropriation of surplus value* are decisive in creating economic relations and the corresponding form of the state, including its legal apparatus.

Ratner and McMullan's (1989, 237–45) discussion of industrial strikes and state intervention uses specific examples of B.C. labour conflicts as a "test" for the capital-logic theory. The Nanaimo coal strike (1912–1914) is depicted as the most bitter and prolonged strike in B.C. labour history. The authors see this strike as typical of B.C. labour relations prior to 1930, pointing to the extremely dependent nature of the B.C. economy on external markets, the need to establish safeguards for union organization and workers' safety, and the limited repertoire of the state, which could either refuse to become involved in the labour-capital conflict, or use the *coercive* powers of the court, police, and militia against the strikers. The authors conclude that this situation led to division and disorganization among B.C. workers.

Another example—the Blubber Bay lumberworkers' strikes of 1937 and 1938—reflects the protracted and bitter conflicts within the forestry sector.

The exacerbation of "already poor health and safety conditions" (Ratner and McMullan 1989, 240) led to growing antagonism among workers and managers alike. The affiliation of Blubber Bay workers with the International Woodworkers of America (IWA) was also a point of contention during the strikes. In 1937, the province passed the Industrial Conciliation and Arbitration (ICA) Act, which recognized the right of labour to organize and promoted the use of conciliation as a means of resolving labour conflicts. As Ratner and McMullan (1989, 240) note, the state was now acting in a coercive and adjudicative role.

The third example—the B.C. lumberworkers' strikes of 1946 and 1947—is set in the context of the Industrial Conciliation and Arbitration Act of 1947 (Ratner and McMullan 1989, 243–45). While gaining protections for labour against outlawing union shops and checkoff clauses (i.e., membership in the union became compulsory, not optional), the ICA Act meant that unions could be sued, since unions were now accorded legal status. Ratner and McMullan (1989, 244) argue that this Act helped to consolidate the regulatory powers of the B.C. government, and blunted the radical character associated with communist activity within the union movement. Indeed, Morton (1980, 210) notes that by 1950, the Communist influence once prominent within Canadian labour politics had given way, leaving a less radical union stance.

As Ratner and McMullen point out, the legislation could be interpreted as an advance for labour or as a new, more sophisticated means of containing labour. The authors place great emphasis on the latter interpretation (containment). Ratner and McMullan (1989, 247) conclude, however, that there was an increasing *centralization* of state, labour, and capital in the late 1940s. The locus of resolution of capital-labour conflict shifted from the workplace to the courts where the "class bias" of the state was obscured, and the legitimacy of state intervention was entrenched in provincial labour law. Class bias has been identified in other legislative initiatives, including a structural-Marxist interpretation of the development of anti-combines legislation in Canada. Smandych (1985) discounts liberal-pluralist interpretations of this legislation as well as the rather crude instrumentalist approaches. He points to differences *within* the capitalist class over the need for regulation of unfair practices, and the significance of "a threatening confrontation" that is likely between capitalists and workers.

Labour law in the United States has also been attacked for the discrepancy between the ideal of neutral arbitration between employers and workers, and concrete decisions that support a "corporate counterattack against labor" (Swidorski 1995, 174). The author outlines several examples of how U.S. Supreme Court actions have blunted union powers and channeled conflicts (1995, 173–74). He also concludes that many labour-capitalist conflicts are now funnelled into closed settings, rather than a "visible public agenda" (1995, 163). This critical approach is applied not only to work-related issues, but also to race relations and civil liberties. Again, it is concluded that court decisions have often undermined affirmative action initiatives and the importance of race discrimination in the United States (1995, 176–77). One methodological limitation of Swidorski's approach is the reliance on particular cases—which may be selective—and the lack of quantitative analyses of a larger number of cases over time.

Keep in mind that there have been challenges to these critical outlooks on historical legal measures. For example, critics charge that Marxist-based explanations of labour relations fail to account for relatively high levels of satisfaction reported by citizens in contemporary Western societies. It is best to keep a critical eye on the assumption that labour relations invariably constitute an "unrelenting guerilla war" (Caputo et al. 1989, 207) in the workplace. Clearly, there are elements of subversion and resistance in worker-employer relations but there are alternative approaches as well that stress harmony in the work force in such a way that employees become willing participants in the workplace, even accepting layoffs and firings without extensive protests.

LAW, ECONOMY, AND RACIAL ISSUES

The dynamic quality of law pertaining to the economy is also evident in societies subjected to colonization. Prior to European contact, many societies had not implemented the formal economic systems associated with capitalism. Moreover, relying more on custom than on Western-style use of due process and rule of law, these societies were faced with overwhelming pressures to suit their dispute-resolution processes to the laws of colonial regimes. This section provides a consideration of recent work on economic and legal transformations in some areas of Africa, and foreshadows more contemporary discussion of legal conflicts and racial discrimination brought forward in Chapter Six.

Kennedy (1989) raises several important questions about the nature of law in the context of colonial regimes. Native labour needed to be harnessed in order to exploit the vast natural resources of sub-Saharan Africa. This process of enlisting, or even conscripting, indigenous labour was facilitated by diverse systems of colonial administration (see Kennedy 1989, 30). As with other scholars exploring historical developments on a wide scale, Kennedy's (1989) analysis appreciates the diversity of state structures, rather than oversimplifying the question of particular means of establishing state control and legal orders. Kennedy (1989, 30) adds that one major step in the colonizing process was the creation of *reserves*. These reserves, designated for indigenous Africans, required the movement of Africans away from lands now needed by the colonizers for economic reasons.

Kennedy's essay pays particular attention to the creation of laws that forced Africans to be wage labourers and thus altered their livelihood from subsistence to the more surplus- and profit-oriented requirements of capitalism. Kennedy thus seeks to apply historical and economic factors in analyzing the introduction of *formal, legal systems* to societies that had been primarily based on custom. Social changes are also significant in modifying forms of law and colonial administration. Kennedy (1989, 30) shows that the need for these laws emerged with the depopulation of many African territories. The practice of slavery in the Americas and Europe required the forced emigration of Africans, resulting in a labour shortage in Africa. The laws of the day thus reinforced the rights of property owners and reflected the economic needs of the colonial era: conquest, increased production of commodities, and cheap labour.

The international dimension also emerges in Kennedy's (1989, 31) discussion of rivalry between nation-states. Colonial regimes were required to exploit natural resources in colonized lands. This requirement became even more important in the face of three decades of economic depression in Europe in the late nineteenth century. The costs of war among competing nations were temporarily averted through a form of "détente" (Kennedy 1989, 31–32), with African territories partitioned by agreement of the colonizing nations themselves—Portugal, Belgium, Germany, and France.

Kennedy's approach is valuable, inasmuch as he develops an international framework for analyzing the origins of a variety of laws that reshaped social and economic life throughout the sub-Sahara. His broad approach remains sensitive to *variations* within particular regimes, ranging from the finer details of colonial administration to the larger developments of the repeal of slavery and the granting of nationhood to territories once deemed colonies of various European nation-states.

Kennedy's essay also contributes to Marxist or neo-Marxist theories of economic development. For Kennedy, the political economy of specific territories is a crucial factor in shaping legal systems. These legal systems are, in turn, useful in protecting powerful economic interests. Nevertheless, the safety of capitalist colonial interests is not guaranteed by these legal forms, although Kennedy suggests that, on the whole, these colonial laws have left an indelible mark, establishing capitalist systems throughout Africa.

There are weaknesses in Kennedy's analysis that should be considered. First, Kennedy does not provide substantial detail on the *process of colonization*—the combinations of inducements and force that were brought to bear on Africans. Second, there is little discussion of *human agency* as a force in the colonial and postcolonial periods. What forms of resistance were generated against imperialism and partitioning, for example? Where did uprisings occur, and how did imperialists react? In short, Kennedy fails to take into account the human factor—the actions and beliefs of the Africans who were subjected to colonization. It would also be useful to consider such forces as the anti-slavery movement, including the work of William Wilberforce and his supporters in England.

We might also consider the implications of systems other than colonial capitalist systems with respect to land use and ownership in Africa. Sue Fleming, writing of northern Mozambique, criticizes various forms of centralized control, including socialist and capitalist approaches. She argues that decentralized approaches may be more advantageous for "peasant farmers" who are often overlooked (Fleming 1996, 69). She also highlights the power of globalization, especially the ability of international capital organizations to purchase land "despite the legal framework protecting peasants" (ibid).

The strength of Kennedy's essay, nevertheless, is his realization that the economic impetus underlying the dramatic social changes in Africa under colonization is linked with legal structures. His essay is also useful for purposes of comparison with similar developments in Western societies. One example of the imposition of legal and economic regimes on aboriginal peoples is the settlement of what we now know as Canada.

Havemann (1989) also brings forward the international dimension in law-making and economic forces. Havemann's outline of Canada's treatment of Native peoples underscores the irony of the Canadian government's official opposition of South African apartheid and its own history of ignoring Native land claims at home.

Havemann (1989, 55) allows for the *contradictory* nature of law in Canada, whereby (1) legal enactments promoted a form of "pacification" of Native peoples, but (2) law also served as "an arena for struggles to define and assert rights for indigenous peoples in the Americas since the sixteenth century." The law that was forced on indigenous peoples served as a kind of legitimation for the developing cultural and economic forms of the European settlers. Havemann asserts that discrimination against indigenous peoples is frequently invisible, and that policing patterns are frequently oriented toward maintaining "social hygiene" or blaming the victims for their poverty (Havemann 1989, 62). This process of placing blame on economically and politically less powerful groups deflects attention away from underlying historical and economic realities. The maintaining of material interests and legal ideologies, and the suppression of indigenous peoples' interests are thus combined.

There is clearly a strong public and scholarly tradition that links discrimination against indigenous peoples to a history of conquest. Legal processes ranging from land claims, to citizenship issues, to the overrepresentation of Natives in criminal sentencing, legitimated this discrimination (Havemann 1989, 68–72). The issue of race discrimination in law is developed in Chapter Six, which considers international studies of criminal justice, civil rights, and the treatment of aboriginal peoples.

SUMMARY

The works discussed in this chapter share a common interest: placing contemporary social conflicts concerning criminal law and other forms of legislation (e.g., labour law) in the context of historically rooted conflicts over the nature of law and society. These works also reinforce the importance of *legit-*

imation of political and legal authority, buttressed by more *repressive* threats or actions that coerce specific populations. These studies thus touch on a fundamental issue of the politics of law: the use of the criminal sanction against those who, in general, are least able to defend themselves. As Beattie (1986) and others have emphasized, criminal law, historically, has not been deployed primarily to protect people's lives and health. The most commonly used laws were those designed to protect property. As set out in this chapter, current scholarship on the history of the criminal law in England still raises the question of whether English criminal law simply reflected popular concerns over property and safety, or whether it was a hegemonic device designed to serve the interests of a propertied, privileged class.

Lowman (1989) and McLaren (1988) discuss the application of criminal law to sexual offences. Lowman (1989) notes that prostitution has been evident in North America for many years, and that ongoing attempts to curb prostitution have ironically led to "displacement" of prostitutes and a failure to establish a coherent framework for protecting prostitutes from violence and exploitation. Lowman (1989, 45) proposes regulation of prostitution—and the sex trade in general—through administrative law, not the criminal law. Critics of modern legal reform point out that there has been no dramatic improvement in either protecting women from the act of rape itself or in establishing methods of punishment or treatment for rapists, beyond the legal reforms associated with the prosecutorial process.

A number of studies have addressed the repressive elements of labour legislation, especially that designed to address unionization and work stoppages. As noted earlier in this chapter, most scholars agree that the historical evolution of labour law could not have been restricted to use of repressive sanctions (e.g., police arrests, deployment of the militia, heavy fines for violation of labour injunctions, and so forth). Rather, the repressive function of law has been offset—but not eliminated—by formal and informal processes of labour negotiation and mediation through the state.

An appreciation of the historical application of laws would be incomplete without reference to ways in which criminal laws, and other laws regulating conduct, were developed along racial and class lines. As outlined earlier, this includes profound transformations in how work was governed, and how property (including entire tracts of land) was defined. Students should be aware that for centuries, such institutions as slavery were crucial in limiting the legal status of millions of people. At the same time, there emerged a growing sense among these oppressed people, and within western societies generally, that such racist practices ought not to be sustained. The anti-slavery movement mounted in many countries, including England and America, was a direct effort to abolish slavery and the laws which supported it (see Genovese 1976; Jordan 1968, Chapter 9). Much of the remainder of this book will address attempts to reverse legislation and legal practices that discriminate on the basis of race, gender, and other factors.

STUDY QUESTIONS

1. How does Hay's account of English criminal law point to elements of mystification and class interest in the exercise of law, and not to the more consensual perspective developed by Durkheim?

2. Critically evaluate Kennedy's (1989) discussion of the relationship between colonization and capitalist interests. To what extent was law useful in promoting an ideology of civilization while masking the necessity of exploiting labour and other resources? Indicate clearly to what extent you agree or disagree with Kennedy's argument.

3. Contrast Hay's interpretation of eighteenth century English criminal law with that of John Langbien. What elements of elitism and popular protection are highlighted, or overlooked, by each author?

4. Many scholars have drawn our attention to the *repressive* qualities of labour law. Discuss whether laws are in fact directed in a repressive way against workers or other groups in work-related disputes. Critically assess the liberal notion that law can act in a neutral manner and serve the public interest.

5. What is the value of the "instance study" approach that Ratner and McMullan take in explaining labour disputes and legal interventions? Critically assess the merits of Marxist-derived theories of the state in regulating labour-management conflicts.

NOTES

1. See Michel Foucault's *Discipline and Punish: The Birth of the Prison* (1977) for an articulation of how the ethos of discipline developed in France. Foucault's work is a critical and innovative treatise on the dynamics of power.

2. Langbien (1983, 101) is hardly sympathetic to these criminals, whose trials were held at the Old Bailey. He suggests that most were employed and had not committed crimes out of necessity, but from temptation. He adds that it is a distortion of fact to "turn these little crooks into class warriors."

3. Beattie (1986, 624) observes a transformation in the value accorded to labourers in the eighteenth century. Labourers were increasingly recognized for their contributions to the changing industrial and financial ventures in England that made up the "mercantilist state" in this era.

4. Many writers have contested the premise that rapists are essentially pathological. Clark and Lewis (1977, 136) cite research to support their conclusion that rapists are in many respects "average" men. Smart (1976, 105) maintains that, in the context of sexual socialization,

rapists are seen as normal: female sexuality is repressed and made passive, whereas the aggressive character of male sexuality is amplified.

5. Luddism was a nineteenth century English movement that protested the introduction of machinery into the workplace, which the Luddites saw as a threat to workers' employment. The term "Luddite" is loosely applied to those protesters who sabotaged some aspect of their workplace. For an account of the Luddite movement, see Thompson (1968). Thompson (1968, 549) observes that, while the Luddites are conventionally depicted as motivated by a "blind opposition to machinery," in fact, they were protesting the introduction of the factory system, the reduction of wages, and other facets of nineteenth century capitalism.

REFERENCES

Backhouse, C. (1983) "Nineteenth-Century Canadian Rape Law, 1800–92." In *Essays in the History of Canadian Law: Volume II*, edited by D. Flaherty, 200–74. Toronto: The Osgoode Society.

Beattie, J. (1986) *Crime and the Courts in England, 1660–1800*. Princeton: Princeton University Press.

Box, S. (1983) *Power, Crime, and Mystification*. London: Tavistock.

Caputo, T., M. Kennedy, C. Reasons, and A. Brannigan, eds. (1989) *Law and Society: A Critical Perspective*. Toronto: Harcourt Brace Jovanovich.

Chambliss, W. (1986) "On Lawmaking." In *The Social Basis of Law: Readings in the Sociology of Law*, edited by S. Brickey and E. Comack, 27–51. Toronto: Garamond Press.

Clark, L., and D. Lewis (1977) *Rape: The Price of Coercive Sexuality*. Toronto: The Women's Press.

Fleming, S. (1996) "Trading in ambiguity: Law, rights, and realities in the distribution of land in northern Mozambique." In *Inside and Outside the Law: Anthropological studies of authority and ambiguity*, edited by O. Harris, 56–71. London: Routledge.

Foucault, M. (1977) *Discipline and Punish: The Birth of the Prison*. New York: Pantheon Books.

Genovese, E. (1976) *Roll, Jordan, Roll: The World the Slaves Made*. New York: Vintage Books.

Gunn, R., and C. Minch (1986) *Sexual Assault: The Dilemma of Disclosure, the Question of Conviction*. Winnipeg: University of Manitoba Press.

Havemann, P. (1989) "Law, State, and Canada's Indigenous People: Pacification by Coercion and Consent." In *Law and Society: A Critical Perspective*, edited by T. Caputo, M. Kennedy, C. Reasons, and A. Brannigan, 54–72. Toronto: Harcourt Brace Jovanovich.

Hay, D. (1975) "Property, Authority and the Criminal Law." In *Albion's Fatal Tree: Crime and Society in Eighteenth Century England*, edited by D. Hay, P. Linebaugh, J. Rule, E.P. Thompson, and C. Winslow, 17–63. New York: Pantheon Books.

Hinch, R. (1988) "Inconsistencies and Contradictions in Canada's Sexual Assault Law." *Canadian Public Policy* 14 (3): 282–94.

Huxley, C. (1989) "The State, Collective Bargaining, and the Shape of Strikes in Canada." In *Law and Society: A*

Critical Perspective, edited by T. Caputo, M. Kennedy, C. Reasons, and A. Brannigan, 218–31. Toronto: Harcourt Brace Jovanovich.

Jordan, W. (1968) White Over Black: American Attitudes Toward the Negro, 1550–1812. Chapell Hill: North Carolina University Press.

Kennedy, M. (1989) "Law and Capitalist Development: The Colonization of Sub-Saharan Africa." In Law and Society: A Critical Perspective, edited by T. Caputo, M. Kennedy, C. Reasons, and A. Brannigan, 30–35. Toronto: Harcourt Brace Jovanovich.

Langbien, J. (1983) "Albion's Fatal Flaws." Past and Present (98): 96–120.

Lowman, J. (1986) "You Can Do It, But Don't Do It Here: Some Comments on Proposals for the Reform of Canadian Prostitution Law." In Regulating Sex: An Anthology of Commentaries on the Findings and Recommendations of the Badgley and Fraser Reports, edited by J. Lowman, N. Jackson, T. Palys, and S. Gavigan, 193–213. Burnaby, British Columbia: School of Criminology, Simon Fraser University.

——. (1987) "Taking Young Prostitutes Seriously." Canadian Review of Sociology and Anthropology, 24(1): 99–116.

——. (1989) "Prostitution Law in Canada." Comparative Law Review 23(3): 13–48.

——. (1991) "Prostitution in Canada." In Canadian Criminology: Perspectives on Crime and Criminality, edited by M. Jackson and C. Griffiths, 113–34. Toronto: Harcourt Brace Jovanovich.

McLaren, J. (1988) "The Canadian Magistracy and the Anti-White Slavery Campaign, 1900–1920." In Law & Society: Issues in Legal History, edited by W. Pue and B. Wright, 329–53. Ottawa: Carleton University Press.

Morton, D., with T. Copp (1980) Working People: An Illustrated History of Canadian Labour. Ottawa: Deneau and Greenberg.

Ratner, R., and J. McMullan (1989) "State Intervention and the Control of Labour in British Columbia: A Capital-Logic Approach." In Law and Society: A Critical Perspective, edited by T. Caputo, M. Kennedy, C. Reasons, and A. Brannigan, 232–49. Toronto: Harcourt Brace Jovanovich.

Ratner, R., J. McMullan, and B. Burtch (1987) "The Relative Autonomy of the State and Criminal Justice." In State Control: Criminal Justice Politics in Canada, edited by R. Ratner and J. McMullan, 85–125. Vancouver: University of British Columbia Press.

Smandych, R. (1985) "Marxism and the Creation of Law: Re-Examining the Origins of Canadian Anti-Combines Legislation 1890–1910." In The New Criminologies: State, Crime, and Control, edited by T. Fleming, 87–99. Toronto: Oxford University Press.

Smart, C. (1976) Women, Crime and Criminology. London: Routledge and Kegan Paul.

Swidorski, C. (1995) "Constituting the Modern State: The Supreme Court, Labor Law, and the Contradictions of Legitimation." In Radical Philosophy of Law: Contemporary Challenges to Mainstream Legal Theory and Practice, edited by D. Caudill and S. Gold, 162–78. New Jersey: Humanities Press.

Thompson, E.P. (1968) The Making of the English Working Class. Harmondsworth: Penguin.

Warner, K. (2000) "Sentencing in cases of marital rape: toward changing the male imagination." Legal Studies 20(4): 592–611.

4
Feminist Theory and Law

Feminism, as I know it, is resistance to invisibility and silencing. It is the recognition that resistance to gendered power relations is both integral to and distinct from all other resistances to global injustice. Feminism is a willingness to reckon with gender disparities as a universal but "unnatural" power reality, a structural process affecting both male and female, which can be deconstructed through consciousness-raising and social change. Feminist resistance is articulated through women's movements and through individual actions, including refusals and separations.

(Karlene Faith 1994, 37)

INTRODUCTION

Karlene Faith's definition of feminism captures the spirit of resistance and redefinition long associated with the women's movement. The contemporary women's movement has influenced legal policy and thinking, as well as political, cultural, and social institutions. There are now substantial efforts to make women's issues and interests more visible within societies that have traditionally limited and discounted these interests. The continuing interest in sociological approaches to law has been accompanied by a dramatic growth in women's studies, including feminist research and theory.

Canada has received praise and criticism for its approaches to women and multiculturalism. Chant and McIlwaine (1998, 181) applaud the number of women involved in the paid workforce and other income-related activities. Nevertheless, they express concern over the continuing gap between women's and men's wages, with women earning just under two-thirds of men's earnings, on average. They credit the "rich mosaic" of Canada and "economic opportunities" associated with Canada (1998, 177). This chapter develops themes we have considered previously, including a skeptical approach to the legal order and the ways in which women are limited by the ideological and repressive powers of law. Contradictions in law are especially important in understanding how conflicts surrounding gender are reproduced in legal settings, and how law can further women's interests. Boyd and Sheehy (1989) offer insights into the limits of liberal conceptualizations of law and the merits of feminist rethinking.

FEMINISM AND CANADIAN LAW REFORM

Boyd and Sheehy provide an extensive review of theoretical work concerning feminism and law in Canada. They note that the feminist movement in law is not strictly a twentieth century phenomenon. Women's
groups have been lobbying for legislative and judicial reform since the late
nineteenth century. The feminist perspective, like the Marxist perspective,
challenges the dominant *liberal* perspective of law as just and impartial. It
is significant, however, that the bulk of scholarship and literature on
women and the law in Canada can be traced to a liberal outlook, which
accepts basic social institutions and assumes that the law can be made into
a "neutral body of rules," such that women can be treated fairly as legal
subjects (Boyd and Sheehy 1989, 255).

Feminist scholarship thus tends to draw a bold line at jurisprudential
approaches that ignore gender as a factor in society at large or in the legal
sphere. Feminist scholarship "takes into account a woman's perspective or
interests" (Boyd and Sheehy 1989, 255); thus, any discussion of citizens'
rights or powers must take seriously the role of *gender relations* in the exercise of law. These discussions must also consider the differences—biological, social, economic, and political—that often define and influence
women's statuses and perspectives. The abstract notion of an individual
treated as an equal in social life, before the courts and other legal mechanisms, is seen by feminists as false and misleading. Such abstract ideologies
serve to exaggerate the actual gains secured for women and use the artificial measure of formal rights and enactments to assess social reforms.

Although feminism grew out of liberal philosophy, some feminists are
critical of the "gender-neutral," liberal emphasis on individual rights. They
place greater emphasis on the *limited* achievements of legal reforms and the
need to analyze women's roles within society (Boyd and Sheehy 1989,
254). Critics of liberal feminism thus argue that law has long served as an
instrument of patriarchy, defining women's place in all social spheres. It is
hardly surprising that the task of bending existing laws and institutions
away from this patriarchal legacy will require more than amendments and
reforms to law.

The 1970 Royal Commission on the Status of Women in Canada documented patterns of *discrimination* against women and recommended liberal
solutions to women's inequality. These liberal solutions included eliminating legislation that differentiated on the basis of gender. This meant
removing, for example, conventions that barred women from certain occupations or pension arrangements that benefited male but not female
workers (Boyd and Sheehy 1989, 256). Liberal feminist approaches centred
on the gap between *formal equality* as an ideal and *substantive inequality* as
practice. Boyd and Sheehy (1989, 256) note that liberal feminist approaches
highlighted discrimination in the socialization of female law students and
in women's career patterns within the legal profession generally.
Limitations on women's access to abortion was also emphasized, together

with a critique of the lack of action on women's equality claims under the Canadian Bill of Rights and federal and provincial human rights codes (Boyd and Sheehy 1989, 257). This situation speaks once more of the gulf between law on the books and the "living law"—law as it is actually applied.

Susan Wendell (1987) offers a "qualified defense" of liberal-feminist principles. Stating that her primary commitment is to socialism (discussed below), she asserts "... liberal feminism is committed to promoting women's recognition of their own value as individuals and public and private recognition of that value by others" (1987, 82). Wendell also contests the premise that obtaining formal legal equality may be the end-point of liberal feminist strategies, arguing that it may be a passageway out of oppression. "Those who fear that obtaining legal equality will fool women into believing that we are the social and economic equals of men are under-estimating women and ... not paying enough attention to the historical evidence. Surely history shows that oppressed groups do *not* tend to be satisfied with legal equality, and that obtaining it helps to uncover the other sources of oppression" (Wendell 1987, 89).

Following the passage of the Charter of Rights and Freedoms in 1982, feminist approaches to law were extended to *result-equality feminism*. That is, the focus shifted away from considering whether or not laws were equally applied, to questioning the actual impact of legal processes in a society where men and women are not equal. Boyd and Sheehy (1989, 257) claim that result-equality feminism provided a "major transformation" in liberal feminist theory. There was greater attention to ensuring that women had input in the drafting of legislation and litigation of issues pertaining to women's equality. Boyd and Sheehy (1989, 257) credit result-equality feminism with creating an awareness of the gender bias that underlies law and social relations. As such, result-equality feminism "demands an extensive rethinking of the underlying assumptions and content of legal rules, on the theory that equal application of a male-oriented legal system cannot drastically alter women's disadvantaged position."

Not all research has confirmed a lack of progress in the legislation against sex discrimination. Malarkey and Hagan (1989) note that in Ontario the Female Employees Fair Remuneration Act of 1951 appears to have reduced disparities between men and women in certain occupations. The Ontario law was also known as the Equal Pay Act, and stated that "no employer and no person acting on his behalf shall discriminate between his male and female employees by paying a female employee at a rate of pay less than paid to a male employee employed by him for the same work done in the same establishment" (Malarkey and Hagan 1989, 301). The authors note that, historically, some occupations have blatantly discriminated against women. In 1858, male teachers in Toronto earned approximately twice as much as female teachers, although women teachers greatly outnumbered men: in 1858 there were 6297 female teachers in Toronto, compared with 2200 male teachers. Malarkey and Hagan (1989, 296) add that great disparities in teachers' incomes remained "well into the twentieth century." Such gender-based disparities were challenged. Since the 1950s, trade unions, women teachers' associations, and government officials, among others, sought to have the egalitarian spirit of the Equal Pay Act established concretely. Malarkey and Hagan (1989) used a time-series regression analysis of male-female incomes up until 1981. They found that the legislation appeared to have a modest effect in narrowing the wage differential, in some occupations, while in others, the disparity became greater. The authors conclude that equal pay legislation, for its inconsistency, provides some basis for encouragement, and that more effective legislation is warranted.

It has been said that Marxist and socialist analyses are "often abstract at the expense of context" (Boyd and Sheehy 1989, 259) and masculinist in that they ignore women's perspectives. There are, of course, exceptions. Boyd and Sheehy (1989) cite the work of Shelley Gavigan, a socialist feminist, who acknowledges women's resistance to law and the importance of continuing struggles for women's autonomy. Gavigan appreciates that law has served as a means of securing state dominance, as well as the dominance of the professions. Law is not one-dimensional, however. Gavigan credits law with the ability to react to pressures from women to regulate their own conception and pregnancy (see Gavigan 1986), for example. Other examples include the refusal of the courts to uphold arguments favouring a "male veto" over therapeutic abortion decisions and the establishment of mandatory arrest policies for police called to attend at domestic assaults.

Feminist approaches to law can only be understood in relation to women's position in society. This is a very controversial area. Some people assert that women's position has been dramatically improved with respect to equality; others state that this supposed improvement has been greatly exaggerated, and that, indeed, regressive measures are eroding women's status. Stanko (1990, 97) documents "the daily indignities of sexual intimidation" experienced by women in England. For Stanko, a *gestalt* of fear of assault, experience of sexual harassment, and other forms of victimization leads to strategies of avoidance—taking precautions in public areas as well as in more "familiar" surroundings, such as the workplace and the home. Implicit in these accounts of women's experiences of threat and intimidation is a sense that law is not designed to offer adequate protection to women.

Some critics note a clash between gains of the latest wave of feminism and backlash against feminist principles. A range of policies, including greater access to daycare, pay equity, and increased hiring of women in positions in which they are underrepresented, have all been subject to backlash (McCormack 1991). Even the most shocking forms of violence against women, including the murder of 14 female engineering students at l'École Polytechnique at l'Université de Montréal in 1989, generate explanations of personal madness and individual culpability, rather than a larger structure of woman-hating and male control (Baril 1990; Lakeman 1990, Malette and Chalouh 1991, Rathjen and Montpetit 1999).

Demands for the integrity of women's bodies have yet to alter some practices, however. The practice of female sexual circumcision, which includes cutting of the clitoris as well as stitching to close most of the vaginal opening, is one example. In some African and Middle Eastern societies these operations are used to reduce women's sexual desire and decrease the chance that women will be sexually active before marriage. Female circumcision has been interpreted as a custom that inhibits sexual pleasure for women and, as such, represents a form of control and domination over women. It has been estimated that in 1982, 84 million females were circumcised in African countries (Seager and Olson 1986, 3–4). The realpolitik is that non-governmental organizations and grassroots ("community") organizations are more likely to achieve social change than governments acting in isolation. In the case of female genital mutilation, it is important that women seeking to reserve such practices are allied with other people, including government leaders, religious authorities, lawyers, and health care professionals. Successful efforts hinge on " ... the participation of broad sectors of society in an ongoing dialogue and consolidated efforts" (Rahman and Toubia 2000, 73–75). Robert Ameh reached a similar conclusion in his analysis of initiatives to abolish trokosi, put simply, a form of female slavery in some parts of Ghana (Ameh 2000).

Ameh reviews the embattled practice of "trokosi," variously presented as a form of child slavery/bondage or, more positively, as a distinctive, valuable traditional practice in some areas of Ghana (Ameh 2001). He traces the transformation of trokosi from a traditional practice in Ghana to a "national social problem" at the end of the twentieth century (p. 35). Ameh traces three waves of anti-trokosi efforts. The first began in 1977 with a revelation by a Ghanaian national, Mark Wisdom, and the relatively small organization, Fetish Slaves Liberation Movement (FESLIM). This original wave of protest and research was followed by the second wave—extensive media coverage—and a third wave, centred on governmental ministries, and "international and local non-governmental organizations" (p. 45). The net effect of these successive efforts has been the partial abolition of a long-established practice.

Thousands of females subject to trokosi were "liberated" from shrines, and there have been efforts to abolish and criminalize the practice (pp. 35–36). Ameh argues that even as the end of trokosi is to be welcomed, the process of eradicating it should respect local customs and values. He reviews the ongoing debate between *universalism* in international human rights—where there is a clear common ground of understanding across different cultures and nations—and *relativism*, which allows for differences in outlook between cultures. More to the point, relativists express concern over a Western, imperialistic-like invasion of autonomy exercised by non-Western nations (p. 38). African societies have often been cast as primitive, as lacking civilization, something that could be provided by more advanced societies. Ziyad (1989, 380) refutes this condescending philosophy. In fact, African societies traditionally "… had a sense of justice and were remarkably democratic in that all members of the group participated in the decision-making process…. Integral to the African understanding of human rights was the concept of group or community; the group was seen as more important than the individual." Ameh's thesis is that the success of the anti-trokosi forces rests in large part on "cultural sensitivity" rather than wholesale adoption of Western outlooks and calls for international human rights (see p. 40). We see a clash between established "magico-religious mechanisms of social control" in Ghana (p. 41), and an increasingly secular society in which individual rights, including those of women, might eclipse traditional outlooks on social control and the status of girls and women. This takes the form of concern about sexual exploitation of trokosiwo, lack of choice whether to stay in the shrine or to leave, and poverty experienced by some trokosiwo who lack financial support from shrines or their families (p. 42). A key point is that cultural practices are not easily legislated away; rather, without considerable public support, they may simply go underground, well out of the reach of most enforcement efforts (Ameh 2001). Robert Ameh contends that pressure groups, individuals, and mass media all played a part in exposing trokosi-related practices and working for its abolition. Political officials and researchers were active in this social movement, presenting recommendations for dramatic reform of practices, including substituting animals for human beings as a form of reparation (p. 44).

It is important to appreciate, however, that much of the literature on women's status and efforts to achieve equality has concentrated on less dramatic and more pervasive forms of social control of women than violent assaults. One example of gender socialization and social control is the power of school curricula to stream female students into studies and into occupations that are considered appropriate for their sex. Some writers see the formal ideology of equality in schools—in which each student is free to pursue his or her interests and to develop his or her potential after formal schooling—as an egalitarian fiction. Beyond the more overt "streaming" of male and female students into courses and programs, there has also been evidence of less perceptible forms of discrimination. These "micro-inequities" (Sandler and Hall, cited in Renzetti and Curran 1989, 97) include gender-laden references (e.g., assuming all physicians are men and all nurses are women), and quite subtle behaviours, such as a teacher's tendency not to call on female students for responses or to interrupt females' responses more frequently than males' (Renzetti and Curran 1989, 97). The influence of social class and gender relations in schooling systems is significant, according to Marxists and feminists. The school is interpreted as a control institution that perpetuates capitalist and patriarchal relations rather than as a truly public resource, tailored to personal needs and aptitudes (Russell 1987, 229).

Feminists have also drawn attention to gender issues in post-secondary education. Judith Okley remarks on the gender gap in academic research and publications: "Even in the 1990s, the majority of undergraduates, whose task it is to read the academic publications, are largely female, yet women researchers relative to men are still grossly underrepresented, and the proportion of women in university positions in British social anthropology remains miniscule" (1996, 204). The main character in Carol Shield's novel, *Unless*, attacks what Shields calls the "colonization" of women. Reta Summers assails those who ignore women's contributions and recreate a "testicular hit list of literary big cats", ensuring that some women face an "apprenticeship in self-denigration" (Shields 2002, 164–65).

Another example of discrimination is the pattern of disparity between men and women in personal income and assets. In Canada, the tremendous increase in women working outside of the home in recent decades has not necessarily produced parity in earnings or social power with their male counterparts. A study published by the Canadian Advisory Council on the Status of Women—*Women and Labour Market Poverty* (Gunderson and Muszynski 1990, 66–67)—found that while women constituted only 29.9 percent of the working poor in 1971, they formed nearly half (46.4 percent) of the working poor in 1986. The authors refer to such processes as the "feminization of poverty" (Gunderson and Muszynski 1990, 66–67). Renzetti and Curran (1989, 195–96) claim that sexist ideologies about women and work still structure hiring practices. In North America, women's role was traditionally restricted to domestic matters; when women worked outside the home, it was often seen as "secondary" to men's employment. Renzetti and Curran add that, although it is commonplace for people to view this traditional ideology as obsolete and irrelevant to modern life, a number of U.S. studies point to the persistence of sexist beliefs about women's work, specifically, that women are more likely to leave their jobs to raise children, or that women's physical limitations make them unsuitable for certain jobs (Renzetti and Curran 1989, 196). They report that sex segregation in the workplace remains "extensive" and that narrow interpretations of court decisions have often served to reduce the impact of affirmative action doctrine; in some cases, such as flight attendant work, traditionally female jobs have been opened up to men, again on the grounds of sex equality (Renzetti and Curran 1989, 200).

Nellie Wong (1991) traces many examples of women's involvement in liberation movements in Korea, Poland, Russia, the United States, and other countries. Wong features several women who have reversed injustices: (1) Rosa Parks, who challenged the colour line by refusing to sit in the back of a Montgomery, Alabama bus in 1959; Clara Fraser, a Jewish woman who struck against Seattle City Light in 1974, and helped to reverse sex discrimination policies at this public utility; and Merle Woo, a lecturer at the University of California who was fired in 1972, ostensibly because of a four-year limit on lecturers' employment. Woo won her case against the university, claiming she was discriminated against with respect to her "race, sex, sexuality, and political ideology" (see Wong 1991, 293). Wong believes that *socialist feminism* is the best political approach to women's oppression and other forms of oppression. "Socialist feminism is a radical, disciplined, and all-encompassing solution to the problems of race, sex, sexuality, and class struggle. Socialist feminism lives in the battles of all people of color, in the lesbian and gay movement, and in the class struggle" (Wong 1991, 290). Identifying herself as a Chinese American, she links her generation's experiences of racism to a wide grouping of others: "... blacks who have been enslaved, and who are still fighting for their civil rights; of Japanese Americans who were incarcerated during World War II; and of other groups of workers who were brought in to build America" (ibid). Socialist feminists are thus concerned with many levels of oppression experienced by women, visible minorities, workers, and others excluded from full participation in a capitalist economic system. Significantly, this feminist approach rests on the possibility of revolution and substantial social change. It also recognizes the role of men and women in challenging oppression.

Economic disparities are but one part of the feminist critique. Many researchers have also highlighted differential treatment in law and social services. For example, Susan C. Boyd's recent work on *Mothers and Illicit Drugs* (1999) dispenses with the all-inclusive concept of "addict," introducing powerful ideological constructs of femininity and motherhood. Boyd demonstrates, for example, how an ideology of motherhood is often co-opted by control institutions such as law and medicine. Boyd also traces different images of motherhood, ranging from extremely positive depictions of motherhood as virtuous to what she sees as a less romantic, more realistic image: "long hours of unacknowledged and unpaid work and total responsibility for the care of dependants and household." (Boyd 1999, 9). Boyd emphasizes that just as the term "addict" must be deconstructed, so also must we break down a generic term of women. Specifically, issues of social class, race, and ethnicity must be considered as part of feminist analysis. Boyd found that many First Nations women reported "overt and covert racism" in their encounters with social services personnel, and many reported abuses in foster care and other institutions (1999, 116–17). Again, activists challenge policies such as imprisoning expectant mothers who test positive for illicit drugs (see Ms. Editors 2001, 10).

Garrett (1987, 97–103) indicates that employment patterns for women altered with industrialization in England. In pre-Industrial England, all family members worked, without the artificial distinction between "domestic" work and waged work, or other forms of labour. With industrialization, labour was generally divided along gender lines, with women excluded from heavy work, skilled trades, the professions, sciences, and the civil service (Garrett 1987, 98). Approximately two-fifths of women workers are concentrated in a handful of occupations, a persistent pattern documented in several European countries and North America (Garrett 1987, 102).

Boyd and Sheehy (1989, 257–58) warn us of the consequences of abstracting legal principles such that the social context of gender and law is not considered. Specifically, the ongoing push for gender-neutrality in law includes the formal provision for men to claim maintenance (spousal and/or child support) from women in the event of separation. What was previously referred to as "maternity leave" was extended to men, in the more inclusive term "paternity leave." In a sense, these developments could herald new options in childrearing, with men now enabled to spend more effort and time with childrearing. There is little evidence that most men are even approximating parity with women in terms of such responsibilities as child care and other forms of domestic work. Many critics have also noted that the tendency for women to assume caretaking functions— for dependent children, elderly parents, and so on—has been compounded by lack of support services, such as daycare facilities. There have been numerous studies documenting women's contributions in such spheres as household labour (see Luxton 1980). Feminist work thus highlights unrecognized—and often unpaid—work.

Studies of women's status before the law bear on the nature of legal domination for women and possible strategies for changing legal structures. A common point of these studies is the limited progress women have made within Western societies, including rather small gains in the legal sphere and in social policy.

EISENSTEIN: *THE RADICAL FUTURE OF LIBERAL FEMINISM*

Eisenstein's approach to the politics of feminism in her somewhat self-explanatory title—*The Radical Future of Liberal Feminism* (1981)—is a landmark work. Eisenstein provides a detailed review of historical writings on state and law, using this backdrop to argue for the necessity of feminist politics that move beyond the gradual approach of liberalism. Eisenstein (1981, 114) defines *liberal individualism* as "the view of the individual pictured as atomized and disconnected from the social relations that actually affect his or her choices and options." As such, liberal individualism is extremely limiting, ignoring political and historical contexts, while celebrating opportunities for individual expression and rights. Eisenstein counters that *structural forces* impede individual expression. These structural forces could include cultural definitions of appropriate roles for women, economic forces that limit women's work, and legal forces that define or constrain women's freedoms. The promise of equality via liberalism cannot be fully met, given these limiting forces. Students interested in Eisenstein's approach may wish to read some of her other writings concerning capitalism, patriarchy, and laws affecting reproductive choice (see Eisenstein 1979, 1988).

Eisenstein provides several insights into the collaboration between the acclaimed English philosopher John Stuart Mill, and Harriet Taylor, his collaborator and spouse. She contends that Mill and Taylor offered a vision of liberation that, ultimately, is available primarily to middle-class men and "an elite of middle-class women" (Eisenstein 1981, 115). This remains a contentious point, for Mill, as a utilitarian, supported public education. It is arguable that his vision of liberty was not as narrowly focused on a small elite as Eisenstein implies.

Mill and Taylor place great emphasis on gifted, educated individuals as leaders in society. For Mill and Taylor, the danger of democracy and socialism is that the masses may become unduly influential in shaping politics despite what is seen as their lack of knowledge (see Eisenstein 1981, 118–19). A system of *plural voting* is favoured over the democratic formula of "one man, one vote." An opposing view was taken by Engels, who believed that the working class was aware of the contradiction between the national interest and the specific interests of the bourgeoisie (Eisenstein 1981, 120). This is a very useful counterpoint, as it brings forward a less optimistic view of the educated classes and a more positive outlook on the capacities of manual workers.

Eisenstein addresses the concepts of *ideology* and *gender* in her discussion of how Victorian married women were defined by their domestic status. Eisenstein (1981, 131) contests the stereotype of Victorian married women as idle, noting that few middle-class households could afford the domestic helpers needed to manage the household and raise children. This relegation to the household was offset, to some extent, by efforts to enfranchise women, a project that became the "major political concern" of Mill and Taylor (Eisenstein 1981, 132). Further to this, Mill and Taylor linked the emancipation of women, including greater freedom within marriage, with economic independence (Eisenstein 1981, 133).

For Mill and Taylor, the supposed weakness of women's constitutions was not in-born, and many arguments to the contrary were ill-founded. Eisenstein (1981, 134) cites excerpts from Mill's writings in which he outlines how "women's nature" is an *artificial construct*, reflecting the "societal needs" affecting women, not their innate abilities or their potential powers. Eisenstein adds that Mill and Taylor nevertheless accepted the patriarchal division of appropriate male and female spheres (Eisenstein 1981, 134–35), for example, the assumption that women are best suited to childrearing, and men for work that requires more "muscular exertion." Eisenstein (1981, 136) underscores the contradictions between Mill and Taylor's emphasis on individualism and independence of women, on the one hand, and their acceptance of women's proper responsibilities within the household. This linking of women's nature to the domestic sphere undermines the emancipatory message of Mill and Taylor; the exclusion from public life impeded the development of the "exceptional woman":

There is no way that any single "exceptional" woman can become com-
pletely free of the patriarchal structural relations of society. She remains
defined in relationship to this structure even when, as an "exception," she
tries to defy it. This is the consequence of the structural reality of power
rather than a reflection of liberal individualist options (Eisenstein 1981,
138; emphasis added).

One concern with Eisenstein's approach is the ease with which she criticizes the limitations of such concepts as "citizen rights" (Eisenstein 1981,
115). Eisenstein is correct in arguing against a "simplistic reading"
(Eisenstein 1981, 116) of liberal individualism that divorces the topic of
individual rights from the concepts of patriarchy and the structural discrimination against women as a group. What is troubling about
Eisenstein's approach is that she seems to diminish these struggles for
greater liberties, especially in the context of greater respect for women's
rights. Specifically, the writings of Taylor and Mill on utilizing one's faculties, on securing the vote, and the dangers of government censure remain
central to political theory and daily practice. Eisenstein also fails to sub-
stantiate certain generalizations. For example, she contends (1979, 117)
that the middle class is more likely to accept customary practices and ideas
uncritically. Eisenstein provides no basis for this portraiture of Babbitry
(Babbit is the character in and the title of Sinclair Lewis's novel), but she
nevertheless provides an articulate critique of liberal ideology and the
effects of capitalism and patriarchy for working-class men, and working-
class and middle-class women (Eisenstein 1981, 138).

SMART: *FEMINISM AND THE POWER OF LAW*

Carol Smart's *Feminism and the Power of Law* (1989) provides a careful theoretical discussion of feminist jurisprudence. As a feminist, Smart examines
several examples of how the law has been misapplied in such areas as rape
(or sexual assault, as it is now defined in Canadian criminal law), child
sexual abuse, pornography, and the wider issue of how women's bodies
may be subject to the power of law. Smart's research focuses primarily on
the United Kingdom but is clearly applicable to feminist jurisprudence in
Canada and elsewhere.

Smart's work rests on the belief that women need to promote "a new
way of seeing" in such a way as to reconceptualize existing models of literature, law, and social activities (Smart 1989, 1). This process of seeing anew
is difficult, especially in the relatively short time span of modern feminism.
Nonetheless, Smart (1989, 2) notes that voices that have previously been
suppressed are now surfacing, illustrated by the growing contributions to
literature and art by women of colour. This point is also made clearly by
Chrystos, a Native woman and poet who has written a collection of poems
entitled *Not Vanishing* (1988) and a more recent book of poetry, *Dream On*

(1991). Her work offers a stark and vivid portrait of American history, including genocide and everyday patterns of discrimination against and assimilation of minorities. Building on her experience of Asian, Native, black, Latin, and white people, Chrystos asserts that, despite the material and spiritual deprivations of her people, "we are not Vanishing Americans."

Smart (1989) supports the development of a new consciousness of gender and race that will effect a change in dominant discourses and definitions. This objective is, however, subject to the power of law. The growing feminist knowledge base, and the feminist critique of law and social control, are often "disqualified" by law. Thus, while some legal reforms may be advantageous to women, feminists should be cautious in resorting to legal solutions. The co-opting power of law is a factor that feminists and others must address. Debates over equality and the utility of law are necessary, but

> *they have the overwhelming disadvantage of ceding to law the very power that law may then deploy against women's claims. It is a dilemma that all radical political movements face, namely the problem of challenging a form of power without accepting its terms of reference and hence losing the battle before it has begun (Smart 1989, 5).*

Smart sees law and masculine culture as essentially congruent. Smart (1989, 3) adds that the liberal emphasis on rights has ironically become more of a weapon against women than a force that acts in favour of feminism. Smart (1989, 67) notes that some strong battles on the part of the women's movement have not resulted in substantial legal reforms but, rather, in measures that provide only slight improvements in the position of women.

For Smart, the task of developing a *feminist jurisprudence* requires a shift away from conventional, liberal law reform—in which women are "added" into existing legal considerations—and toward a fundamental rethinking of legal values and justice principles. The promise of feminist jurisprudence—as a general theory of law, accompanied by practical measures to transform women's status—has not been fully met, according to Smart; feminist jurisprudence has become divided and fragmentary. Moreover, there is disagreement over the value of legal struggles (Smart 1989, 66). Smart (1989, 72) cautions against "grand theorizing." Taking the conventional definition of jurisprudence—in which law is presented as an entity, unified and guided by "basic principles of justice, rights, and equality" (Smart 1989, 69)—she insists that a feminist-based approach can "deconstruct" abstract, overgeneralized theories of law, and thus outline everyday applications of the power of law. Further, Smart (1989, 70–72) is critical of a tendency to present feminist jurisprudence as a superior, scientific theory. In other words, she warns against the tendency to view this approach as "the truth," which, in turn, is validated by its methodologies and epistemology. This approach can become a variant of legal positivism or of the "privileged discourse" that others have used—the very tendency that some feminists decry in legal theory. Smart (1989) appears to argue against such catechismal, dogmatic approaches, allowing instead for a more flexible kind of feminist jurisprudence that respects the value of intellectual comparisons and modifications.

SEXUAL OFFENCES AND LEGAL DISCOURSE

Smart addresses the ways in which women's sexuality is defined and distorted. Using the examples of rape (in Canada, legally redefined as "sexual assault") and child sexual abuse, Smart offers a powerful critique of cultural representations of women's sexuality. Beyond this, she views the criminal trial for accused rapists not as a corrective for hateful actions against women, but as a forum that reinforces a cultural depiction of women's sexuality as problematic and pathological. Her work thus stands as a direct challenge to the complacent view that women have benefited from what has been dubbed "the sexual revolution," or that reforms in criminal law have been a major contribution toward sexual equality. Rape, as a legal definition, is a narrow construct (Smart 1989, 26). This narrow, legalistic definition serves to disqualify other possible discourses that are seen as irrelevant or inferior. Rape law thus acts to disqualify women and their sexuality. Smart (1989, 26–27) notes that in Western societies, the rape trial constitutes a celebration of women's lack of power. The trial also magnifies the ways in which female heterosexuality is constructed as fundamentally different from male heterosexuality.

In Western cultures, sexuality is conventionally presented as "phallocentric," that is, focused on male pleasure. In contrast, other forms of sexuality that challenge this phallocentrism are discounted as "incomprehensible and pathological" (Smart 1989, 28). Smart acknowledges that female pleasure in sexuality is of course possible; however, the weight of a male-oriented construction of sexuality does not coincide with the realization of women's sexual potential. It follows that, as female sexuality is seen as mysterious, capricious, and unrealized, the solution to sexual problems is paternalistic in character: "If all women are seen as having the thing that men most need, if they are also seen as grudging with it, or as so out of touch with their 'real' sexual feelings that they deny it to themselves and to men, then the problem for men is how to gain control of women's sexuality in spite of women themselves" (Smart 1989, 30).

Thus, women become separated, or alienated, from their own sexuality. In a sense, this idea of patriarchal control of women's sexuality can be greatly oversimplified, as sexuality is reduced to a "one-dimensional prudery" that undermines women's potential for sexual satisfaction (Smart 1989, 30).

Smart uses the rape trial to illustrate the ways in which women's experience of sexuality is distorted and disqualified. If women themselves are unable to know their own sexuality, some defence attorneys and other officials could use this premise to argue that women might enjoy "sex" even in its more violent manifestations. Smart thus raises the fundamental question of how sexual misconceptions permeate the workings of law and society. Reviewing some rapists' excuses for their attacks—women led them on, rape was a man's right, and so forth—Smart (1989, 31) states that this rape discourse is not restricted to the rapists, that is, to the minority of men who have been convicted of rape or sexual assault. Instead, this forceful denial of female sexuality permeates male discourse, taking the forms of resentment, frustration, and anger, which are translated into the "material and psychic oppression" of women (Smart 1989, 32).

One of Smart's central points is that law presents an authoritative claim on truth. As such, it is a very powerful mechanism in allowing—or disallowing—conflicting claims about such events as rapes. On the surface, the very existence of rape law would seem to consolidate women's rights to be free of unwanted sex. As Smart (1989, 34) notes, however, there is an obverse side to this view. When the accused in a rape trial is found innocent, this represents "a finding of sexual complicity on the part of the victim. The woman must have lied...." Acquittal thus can be translated into a confirmation of phallocentric values. The very conduct of the trial undermines the high-flown ideal that women warrant protection from men's advances. Smart (1989, 35–36) provides several examples from judicial utterances in rape trials that underscore how women's testimony can be disregarded or trivialized. Women are liable to be "untruthful and invent stories"; "Women who say no do not always mean no"; "Women who hitch-hike are 'asking for it.'" These quotes are excerpts from judges' statements from 1976 to the early 1980s (Smart 1989, 35). Smart adds that even though some men are convicted of rape and imprisoned, only a very small minority of men who sexually abuse women are tried, let alone convicted. This reality confirms research that documents why some rape charges are deemed founded or unfounded. This includes attacks on the character of women alleging sexual assault and masculinist ideologies seeping through courtroom and disciplinary tribunals (Clark and Lewis 1977; Ehrlich 2001). Once again, there is a substantial gap between legal rhetoric of protection and equality before the law, and the reality of rape as a crime almost invariably directed against women, with a very low rate of conviction for accused rapists.

Smart's critique of rape law raises several fundamental questions. It restores a vital link between culture and legal institutions. To the extent that cultures are essentially misogynistic, law will reflect much of this discreditation of women's accounts and actions. Smart's work can also be linked with other work that dramatizes the ways in which women's sexuality is commodified, for example, the way advertising emphasizes youth, beauty, and allure while bypassing women who do not fit this ideal image of beauty. While Smart's arguments mesh with a feminist critique of women's victimization, there are counterarguments to her views, especially the point that others in fact control women in sexual expression and enjoyment. Sheila Kitzinger's *Women's Experience of Sex* (1987), breaks ground in appreciating the diversity of female sexuality. Exploring the sexual and reproductive powers of women, Kitzinger (1987) provides a thoughtful account of heterosexuality, lesbian sexuality, celibacy, birth control, childbirth, and aging and menopause, bringing forth a woman-centred appreciation of intimacy and expressiveness. Kitzinger, like Smart, is fully aware of the power of the dominant culture in oversimplifying and discounting women, in creating objects out of individual subjects. Nevertheless, Kitzinger's work suggests that the influence of the patriarchal culture is far from complete, that resistance to, and understanding of, sexual politics is underway in many societies. Even so, other writers take a global outlook on rape, citing examples of mass rapes in Indonesia, Rwanda, Haiti and other countries in the late twentieth century and many historical instances of civilian women being targetted for rape and other atrocities (Frederick 2001).

The issue of child sexual abuse is another example of the politics of law. A 1975 police investigation into child abuse at the Mount Cashel orphanage in Newfoundland was suppressed until 1989, when news of beatings and sexual abuse of children was finally brought to light (Harris 1990). Ironically, it is virtually impossible to prosecute those who sexually abuse children, yet it is almost inevitable that children, as part of these proceedings, are damaged (Smart 1989, 51). Describing the response of criminal law in controlling sexual abuse, Smart refers to a mixture of "consternation and complacency" on the part of government officials and social reformers. Legislation in the Victorian era, while providing mechanisms for prosecuting those who violated children, including those who sold girls into prostitution, could also be punitive toward the victims. Greater numbers of girls became subject to monitoring and moral intervention, including incarcerating girls in reformatories or industrial schools. This practice was justified as a protection for girls in "moral danger" (Smart 1989, 51).

The combination of alarm and complacency was also evident in legislation against incest. Some jurists did not believe that such acts were possible; others referred to incest as "mischief," adding that the number of cases must be very small (Smart 1989, 53). In recent times, while legislation and resources—child protection agencies, for example—remain in place, Smart (1989, 55) notes that the criminal law has been "massively under-utilized" to fight child abuse. Protection agencies rely far more on care orders—removing children from their homes—than on applying the criminal law to remove the victimizers, who are almost invariably fathers. Clearly, the limited response of law in addressing child abuse is seen as another example of the superficial treatment of a social problem whose roots lie in male sexual socialization, not in offender pathology alone. Moreover, despite challenges to the therapeutic approach—treatment of abusive fathers and an ideology of family reintegration —traditional family therapy is still used in Britain for many cases of child sexual abuse. The assessment of allegations of abuse through clinical experts and legal discourse combine to silence children's accounts. This tendency to ignore or challenge some statements by children may have been heightened by the much-publicized "Cleveland Crisis" in the late 1980s. The Cleveland Crisis refers to extensive press coverage of the practices of a female pediatrician and, to a lesser extent, a male doctor who assessed child sexual abuse by the physical diagnosis of anal dilation. To use them to recommend removal of the child from his or her home, or to press charges against parents, has been seen as more of a "moral panic" (Smart 1989, 62) than sound medical practice. Smart adds that the attack on both pediatricians and on the social service personnel who placed the children in care appears to have reinforced the ideology of nonintervention in the nuclear family and the notion that child sexual abuse is a rarity. The backlash against the Cleveland doctors seems to have taken a conservative twist, highlighting parents' rights and obscuring real difficulties in detecting and prosecuting child sexual abuse. Such conflicts may serve not to address cases of abuse, but to marginalize the issue and restore a sense of complacency.

The issue of pornography has also been linked with legal repression and legal protections. Again, there are strong divisions of opinion over sexually-explicit imagery. On the one hand, Tania Kindersley contrasts the tendency to see pornography as exciting and chic, with what she regards as the essentially degrading character of hardcore pornography. In reality, such sex trade workers are sometimes injured and required to undergo considerable discomfort as part of their work. She presents this not as a feminist outlook, but a "humanist argument." She also makes a direct comparison with the uselessness of the War on Drugs; that is, there is no point in trying to eradicate pornography (Kindersley 2001). Others take a civil libertarian approach that celebrates free expression and free speech, and offers a more sensual approach, exemplified in de Grazia's book, whose title is taken from James Joyce's *Ulysses*, a book banned under obscenity law (*Girls Lean Back Everywhere*, 1992).

Nicola Lacey (1998) presents pornography as arguably the most divisive topic among feminists. She credits Andrea Dworkin and Catherine MacKinnon with their "inspired" strategy of arguing that pornography is a form of sex discrimination that "exploits and harms women" (Lacey 1998, 71 and 89). Lacey assumes that contemporary pornography "... does contribute to sex discrimination, not just in the sense of sexual violence but also in the sense of contributing to the low esteem in which women are held by men and, all too often, hold ourselves" (Lacey 1998, 91). It is curious, however, that this rationale for attacking pornography is rarely extended to less explicit "women's magazines" that generate unrealistic images of women. Lacey lists several barriers for people considering legal remedies related to pornography. These include substantial costs of litigation, other resources needed to fight such battles, and the possibility that such strategies may be "disempowering" rather than empowering for women (1998, 92–93). Lacey summarizes the historical context of ownership and rape: "... its essence was damage to the proprietary value of virginity or chastity to an 'owing' male rather than recognition of a woman's interest in her own sexual freedom" (1998, 106).

Issues surrounding explicit sexual representations—in literature, films, theatre, dance, etc.—have long attracted praise and censure, including legal actions to protect expression or to limit it. This remains a dynamic, topical area, with clearly-drawn arguments for and against censorship, as well as many "gray" areas where people are uncertain about the applicability of law (see Wray 2001). Karen Busby (1999) begins with a seemingly innocuous event, the 1987 seizure of materials in a Winnipeg video operation. The proprietor, Donald Butler, now has a place in Canadian legal history. The initial charge under "obscenity provisions" in the Canadian Criminal Code [p. 42] led to a Supreme Court review. This review included arguments surrounding sexually explicit materials and equality considerations. LEAF (Women's Legal Education and Action Fund) was allowed to intervene in this case, focusing on the need to revamp the law, highlighting "equality implications for women and children" (p. 43). Critics of this approach to pornography contend that there is no clear *causal* relationship between what we might call pornography and violence against women. Second, the axiom that "violent and degrading materials" serve to denigrate females and thus undermine "the individual's sense of self-worth and acceptance" [see p. 47] also lacks a convincing empirical basis. If the pornography industry, however defined, has expanded dramatically through videos and DVDs, print materials, and the Internet, would we not see a corresponding increase in discrimination against women? Third, this presentation of pornography as wholly pernicious to women does not allow for some sexually-explicit materials helping to empower women or other populations such as gays, lesbians, bisexuals, and transgendered people. Some viewers might be delighted that the dialogue is salty, the scenes explicit. There are sexually-explicit productions of gay or lesbian themes that are not necessarily exploitative. S/M (sado-masochistic) representations seen as repugnant by some may be erotic and exciting fantasies for others (see Kiss and Tell Collective, 1994). Artists of all stripes have expressed considerable concern over the unnecessarily restrictive ideology that is associated with the post-*Butler* years.

Fourth, I would like to see a more complex analysis of gender relations. The sweeping statement—"there is a gross distortion of power in our society in favour of heterosexual white men [p. 44]"—begs at least two fundamental questions. First, what is meant by "power"? Is it property ownership, economic security, decision-making within families, political representation, or other measures? Second, to use the catchall term "heterosexual white men" trades on a rather static view of sexual identity, race/ethnicity, and gender, in my opinion. We might ponder whether other factors such as age, health, disability, literacy, employment, family status, and social class might have equally profound effects for people lumped into this HWM category. For some, Busby's approach is compelling, drawing attention to the near-hegemonic power of men who identify as "straight, white males"; for others, it is merely a starting-point, and may even be misleading and divisive.

The communitarians' focus on reciprocity and solidarity is often linked with critical legal studies and feminism, but it may take a conservative twist, centred on exclusivity, family, and even the subordination of women within certain communities (see Lacey 1998, 135–39). Lacey (1998) underscores a key point in law and society studies. She claims that it is mistaken "... to see direct legal regulation as the touchstone for state involvement. In all sorts of indirect ways—economic, administrative, and political—state institutions have a crucial and often deliberate iimpact on the conduct of family life" (Lacey 1998, 74).

WOMEN, POVERTY, AND VIOLENCE

The study of oppressed peoples has been a staple in literature, social criticism, and the social sciences. George Orwell's *The Road to Wigan Pier* (1937) is a classic study of poverty in the north of England during the depression of the 1930s. *The Road to Wigan Pier* described the life of English coal miners to make an incisive critique of the elitist view that disparaged manual labour. In 1982, an English journalist embarked on a six-month journey to several cities in northern England. Beatrix Campbell retraced the journey taken by Orwell in the 1930s. Campbell's *Wigan Pier Revisited* (1984) is a critical reassessment of Orwell's book, in which the roles of men and women are now viewed from a feminist perspective. Campbell (1984) does not lionize men's work of the men, and in fact masculinity and men together "constitute a systematic bloc of resistance to the women of their own community and class" (Campbell 1984, 5–6).

Campbell refers to women in temporary shelters—meant to offer a "safe house" for women and children who have been abused—as "survivors" (Campbell 1984, 7). Even in the physical safety and camaraderie of the shelter, Campbell (1984, 93) remarks that "all of the women in the refuge are poorer than men," with less income, time, clothing and the like. Campbell (1984, 95) contends that various forms of violence against women (sexual assault, sexual harassment, domestic assault) are not the result of economic deprivation, but, rather, of a dynamic process rooted in "men's power and women's subordination." One can also point to the inadequacy of the legal response, an issue that comes up in the work of Elizabeth Comack (1988) regarding battered women in Canada.

Comack (1988) reviews two legal decisions—Lavallée and Leach—to illustrate the contradictory nature of legal responses, including the usefulness of the battered-wife syndrome argument. Angélique Lavallée was acquitted on a charge of second-degree murder in the fatal shooting of her common-law husband. It was established that her husband had beaten Lavallée on many occasions. She had also been hospitalized several times for treatment of these injuries. A key point in the defence argument was that such a history of abuse may produce battered-wife syndrome, which may be considered in absolving or mitigating punishment (Comack 1988, 9). Lavallée's acquittal was appealed by the Crown, which questioned the relevance of the battered-wife syndrome argument in this case. In the case of Verna Mae Leach, there was also a history of abuse from her common-law husband. Unlike Lavallée, however, she was sentenced to two years' imprisonment for the nonfatal stabbing of her partner. The defence argument was based on self-defence, not on the battered-wife syndrome argument.

Comack (1988) uses these two cases to formulate her argument that the continuing phenomenon of wife assault is linked to *structural conditions* that limit women's choices. Comack does not imply that all women are powerless or that legal decisions are entirely unhelpful to all women who have been abused. Nevertheless, the influence of male bias, and the entrenched misunderstanding of these structural limitations on women, remains central to Comack's critique of the ideology and practice of criminal law. For Comack, the battered-wife syndrome argument is far from a complete legal victory. She foresees interpretations of it that could be used against women, for example, to question a mother's competency to care for her children. Comack (1988, 11) is also critical of the extremely narrow focus associated with the defence; it could, ironically, expand the powers of the psychiatric profession to diagnose and treat women, but without focusing on patterns of inequality between men and women.

Even in jurisdictions that have formally approved resources in support of mandatory arrest policies for alleged domestic assault, police discretion and other factors may interfere with full implementation of such services. Sherman and Cohn (1989, 140–41) found that some officers on the Minneapolis police force reported considerable variations in willingness to use their mandated powers of arrest in such cases. Some officers always arrested suspects on probable cause; others never did. Barrow's report on domestic violence, *Not Worth the Paper...?* (1990) details a shortfall in protection for abused women in England. Many women are intimidated by formal proceedings organized by strangers, there may be language and cultural barriers, and many women may be financially dependent on abusers (1990, 79-80, 129). Similar barriers have been confirmed by studies of sexual harassment (Langelan 1993).

MACKINNON: *FEMINISM UNMODIFIED*

Catherine MacKinnon (1987, 1) offers a strong appraisal of the movement for women's legal rights. She suggests that the women's movement is approaching a "crossroads" and alludes to a "string of defeats and declines" for women, including lack of effective sex-equality provisions for pay, opposition to women's right to safe abortions, a movement toward men gaining or sharing custody of children after separation, and other developments that leave the ideal of women's equality before law far from realized in the United States. Two positive exceptions that MacKinnon refers to are policies concerning sexual harassment and some initiatives with respect to marital rape and domestic assault.

MacKinnon (1987, 2–3) cautions against women's complicity in a politics of male supremacy. An unmodified feminism would thus be leery of co-optation and the dispensation of small concessions. MacKinnon (1987, 4) notes that, in large measure, what is referred to as feminism in law reflects "… the attempt to get for men what little has been reserved for women or to get for some women some of the plunder that some men have previously divided (unequally) among themselves."

MacKinnon's work directly confronts the fusing of sexuality, control, and collaboration between men and women. She notes that feminists believe women's accounts of sexual use and abuse by men. As such, feminism resists attempts to dismiss or trivialize a range of sexual practices that, in fact, constitute sexual violation. Such an approach goes well beyond technical or legalistic definitions of violence to an appreciation of the net effect of women's feelings of subordination to men and the various practices that can intimidate them and lead to feelings of terror. Women face an arrangement based on terror: "Just to get through another day, women must spend an incredible amount of time, life, and energy cowed, fearful and colonized, trying to figure out how not to be next on the list" (MacKinnon 1987, 7). One criticism of MacKinnon's approach is that it tends to settle on coercive expressions of sexuality without balancing this with an appreciation of more positive expressions of heterosexuality. In fairness, however, MacKinnon (1987) is dealing with momentous legal questions, and in keeping with the title of her work—*Feminism Unmodified*—MacKinnon (1987, 5) resists any dilution of the seriousness of these issues, drawing our attention to deep-seated expressions of misogyny in society and even in "liberal legalism."

MacKinnon (1987) emphasizes the importance of exploring power and acting against coercion in other sections of her book. For example, she notes that the concept of sexual harassment as a "law of injuries" is a relatively new invention. It is traced to feminism's insistence that women's experience of coercive sexuality be taken seriously. For MacKinnon, laws against sexual harassment represent a practical strategy for stopping the exploitation of women. It is "a demand that state authority stand behind women's refusal of sexual access in certain situations that previously were a masculine prerogative" (MacKinnon 1987, 104). MacKinnon (1987, 105) concludes that, relative to other legislation concerning sex discrimination, the law against sexual harassment works "surprisingly well" for women. Nevertheless, she notes that most victims still do not file complaints against harassers. Women who are especially abused—"viciously violated"—are often ashamed to report the violation (MacKinnon 1987, 114). Those most victimized may be rendered silent, enduring their victimization for fear of public disclosure and further invasion of privacy. MacKinnon (1987, 116) concludes that legislation against sexual harassment can make a difference if a legal initiative is established from "women's real experience of violation." Legal doctrine and male metaphysics—the tendency by some men to theorize, to abstract issues from their social contexts—clearly predominate, but this does not eliminate the importance of feminist-oriented legal initiatives. As MacKinnon (1987, 116) allows, "law is not everything in this respect, but it is not nothing either."

SUMMARY

The women's movement has uprooted many myths concerning the supposed nature of the sexes and the institutions that promote and benefit from discriminatory practices against women. The sphere of law has attracted considerable attention, in part because much of women's oppression and control is vested in law, and also because many feminists—and others supportive of women's struggles—believe that the law can provide leverage against entrenched patterns of sexism.

It is important to note that much of the work within feminist jurisprudence has emphasized the enduring power of patriarchy. Liberal beliefs to the contrary, some feminists argue that many gains have been illusory, and that conservative backlashes with respect to family structures, hiring practices, access to abortion, and other issues foreshadow new ways of treating women as subordinate, or in Simone de Beauvoir's (1970) words, as "the other."

Feminist issues certainly apply to those of us who work and study in universities and other post-secondary institutions. Social activists have highlighted issues of violence and sexism, and proposed policies to make campuses safer for women. Ledwitz-Rigby (1993) warns of the danger of complaceny through merely cosmetic changes to campuses. "No amount of lighting or shrubbery clearing will protect women from acquaintance sexual assault or sexual harassment, or protect visible minorities, lesbians, and gays from racist or homophobic attacks" (p. 90). As part of a committee exploring women's safety on campus, she notes: "The 'right' of men to dominate the women they date and to expect deferential acquiescent behavior in both sexual and non-sexual interactions has long been a part of North American culture ..." (p. 84). Ledwitz-Rigby acknowledges that many universites have become committed to advancing women's status within the university, but she maintains that "the threat of violence" is largely intact on campuses. She reports that women may often limit their work or study-hours; for example, refusing to work after dark in libraries, and that not all women can afford to limit their study/work hours. As a case-in-point, women in the physical sciences often work long hours in laboratory or field settings. Her point is that women often "self-restrict" their movements, largely due to fear (p. 86).

Other work in this area also explores women's lived experiences. Sue Lees' *Sugar and Spice* (1993) interviewed boys and girls in London, England, with a view to exploring gender relations. She also notes structural changes, such as entrance to university: it was only in 1992 that for the first time, more women than men entered university in the United Kingdom (p. 2). Her work covered language, especially how women's behaviour is so often sexualized, much moreso than men's. She also describes girls' vision of the world as a mix of realism and fatalism. "'We know it is unfair, but what can we do about it?'" (p. 29).

The feminization of poverty, discrimination in workplace settings, exposure to violence in public and private places, and women's lack of political influence are a few examples of the issues addressed by feminist theorists and practitioners. Some of these issues are discussed in more detail in Chapter Nine, where we will examine the politics of family law and human reproduction.

STUDY QUESTIONS

1. Many scholars refer to the gap between *formal equality* and *substantive inequality* in law and society. Using specific examples from this chapter, discuss how this concept can be applied to the issue of legal protections for women.

2. Review Smart's (1989) discussion of the ways in which legal procedures for allegations of rape and child sexual abuse correspond to male-oriented (phallocentric) culture. Critically assess her arguments. In what ways might her approach be qualified? In what ways could her arguments be extended?

3. Catherine MacKinnon (1987) advocates a feminist approach that is "unmodified." Address the issue of how women's experiences, discourses, and solutions are co-opted by legal authorities and other agents.

4. Discuss explanations for patterns of violence against girls and women, and arguments for using legal resources to reduce levels of violence. Consider sexual harrassment, sexual assault, and domestic violence in your discussion.

REFERENCES

Ameh, R. (2001) *Child Bondage in Ghana: A Contextual Policy Analysis of Trokosi.* Unpublished Ph.D. Dissertation, School of Criminology, Simon Fraser University.

——. (1998) "Trokosi (Child Slavery) in Ghana: A Policy Approach." *Ghana Studies,* 35–62.

Baril, J. (1990) "At the Centre of the Backlash." *The Canadian Forum* 68 (786): 14–17.

Barrow, J. (1990) *Not Worth the Paper ...?* Bristol: Women's Aid Federation England Ltd. [WAFE].

Boyd, S., and E. Sheehy (1989) "Overview: Feminism and the Law in Canada." In *Law and Society: A Critical Perspective,* edited by T. Caputo, M. Kennedy, C. Reasons, and A. Brannigan, 255–70. Toronto: Harcourt Brace Jovanovich.

Boyd, S.C. (1999) *Mothers and Illicit Drugs: Transcending the Myths.* Toronto: University of Toronto Press.

Busby, K. (1999) "LEAF and Pornography: Litigation on Equality and Sexual Representations." in *Law in Society: Canadian Perspectives,* edited by N. Larsen and B. Burtch, 42–59. Toronto: Harcourt Brace Canada.

Campbell, B. (1984) *Wigan Pier Revisited.* London: Virago.

Chant, S., and C. McIlwaine (1998) *Three Generations, Two Genders, One World. Women and Men in a Changing Century.* London: Zed Books.

Comack, E. (1988) "Justice for Battered Women? The Courts and the 'Battered Wife Syndrome'." *Canadian Dimension* 22(3): 8–11.

Chrystos (1988) *Not Vanishing.* Vancouver: Press Gang.

Chrystos (1991) *Dream On.* Vancouver: Press Gang.

Clark, L., and D. Lewis (1977) *Rape: The Price of Coercive Sexuality.* Toronto: The Women's Press.

de Beauvoir, S. (1970) *The Second Sex,* translated and edited by H.M. Parshley. New York: Bantam.

De Grazia, E. (1992) *Girls Lean Back Everywhere: The Law of Obscenity and the Assault on Genius.* New York: Random House.

Ehrlich, S. (2001) *Representing Rape: Language and Sexual Consent.* London: Routledge.

Eisenstein, Z. (1979) *Capitalism, Patriarchy, and the Case for Socialist Feminism.* New York: Monthly Review Press.

—— (1981) *The Radical Future of Liberal Feminism.* New York: Longman.

Faith, K. (1994) "Resistance: Lessons from Foucault and Feminism." In *Power/Gender: Social Relations in Theory and Practice,* edited by L. Radtke and H. Stam, 36–66.

Frederick, S. and the AWARE [Association of Women for Action and Research] Committee on Rape (2001). *Rape: Weapon of Terror.* River Edge, N.J.: Global Publishing Co. Inc.

Garrett, S. (1987) *Gender.* London: Tavistock.

Gavigan, S. (1986) "Women, Law and Patriarchial Relations: Perspectives in the Sociology of Law." In *The Social Dimensions of Law,* edited by N. Boyd, 101–24. Toronto: Prentice-Hall.

Gunderson, M., and L. Muszynski, with J. Keck (1990) *Women and Labour Market Poverty.* Ottawa: Canadian Advisory Council on the Status of Women.

Harris, M. (1990) *Unholy Orders: Tragedy at Mount Cashel.* Markham, Ontario: Viking.

Held, D. (1984) "Introduction: Central Perspectives on the Modern State." In *States and Societies,* edited by D. Held, J. Anderson, B. Gieben, S. Hall, L. Harris, P. Lewis, N. Parker, and B. Turok, 1–55. London: Martin Robertson.

Kinderseley, T. (2001) "The Degradation of the Species." *The Spectator* 287 (9044): 12–13.

Kiss & Tell Collective [P. Blackbridge, L. Jones, S. Stewart]. (1994) *Her Tongue on My Theory: Images, essays and fantasies.* Vancouver: Press Gang Publishers.

Kitzinger, S. (1987) *Women's Experience of Sex.* Harmondsworth: Penguin.

Lacey, N. (1998) *Unspeakable Subjects: Feminist Essays in Legal and Social Theory.* Oxford: Hart Publishing.

Ledwitz-Rigby, F. (1993) "An Administrative Approach to Personal Safety on a University Campus: The Role of a President's Advisory Committee on Women's Safety on Campus." *Journal of Human Justice* 4: 85–94.

Lakeman, L. (1990) "Women, Violence and the Montreal Massacre." *This Magazine* 23(7): 20–23.

Langelan, M. (1993) *Back Off! How to Confront and Stop Sexual Harassment and Harassers.* New York: Fireside/Simon and Schuster.

Ledwitz-Rigby, F. (1993) "An Administrative Approach to Personal Safety on a University Campus: The Role of a President's Advisory Committee on Women's Safety on Campus." *Journal of Human Justice* 4: 85–94.

Lees, S. (1993) *Sugar and Spice: Sexuality and Adolescent Girls.* London: Penguin Books.

Lewis, S. (1922) *Babbitt.* New York: Harcourt, Brace & Co.

Luxton, M. (1980) *More Than a Labour of Love: Three Generations of Women's Work in the Home.* Toronto: Women's Educational Press.

Malette, L., and M. Chalouh (eds.) (1991) *The Montréal Massacre.* Charlottetown: Gynergy Press (trans. M. Wildeman).

McCormack, T. (1991) "Politically Correct." *The Canadian Forum* 70 (802): 8–10.

MacKinnon, C. (1987) *Feminism Unmodified: Discourses on Life and Law.* Cambridge: Harvard University Press.

Malarkey, R., and J. Hagan (1989) "The Socio-Legal Impact of Equal Pay Legislation in Ontario, 1946–1979." *Osgoode Hall Law Journal* 27(2): 295–336.

Ms. Editors (2001) "Women to Watch: Wyndi Marie Anderson." *Ms.* 11(6): 10.

Oklely, Judith (1996) "Women Readers: Other utopias and our own bodily knowledge." In *Popularizing Anthropology,* edited by J. MacClancy and C. McDonough, 180–207. London: Routledge.

Orwell, G. (1937) *The Road to Wigan Pier.* Harmondsworth: Penguin.

Rahman, A., and N. Toubia (eds.) *Female Genital Mutilation: A Guide to Laws and Policies Worldwide.* London: Zed Books, in association with Centre of Reproductive Law and Policy (CRLP), and the Research, Action and Information Network for the Bodily Integrity of Women.

Rathjen, H. and C. Montpetit (1999) *December 6: from the Montréal Massacre to Gun Control: the inside story.* Toronto: McClelland and Stewart.

Renzetti, C., and D. Curran (1989) *Women, Men, and Society: The Sociology of Gender.* Boston: Allyn and Bacon.

Russell, S. (1987) "The Hidden Curriculum of School: Reproducing Gender and Class Hierarchies." In *Feminism and Political Economy: Women's Work, Women's Struggles,* edited by H. Maroney and M. Luxton, 229–45. Toronto: Methuen.

Seager, J., and A. Olson (1986) *Women in the World.* London: Pluto Press.

Sherman, J., and E. Cohn (1989) "The Impact of Research on Legal Policy: The Minneapolis Domestic Violence Experiment." *Law and Society Review* 23(1): 117–41.

Shields, C. (2002) *Unless.* Toronto: Random House Canada.

Smart, C. (1989) *Feminism and the Power of Law.* London: Routledge and Kegan Paul.

Stanko, E. (1990) *Everyday Violence: How Women and Men Experience Sexual and Physical Danger.* London: Pandora Books.

Wendell, S. (1987) "A (Qualified) Defense of Liberal Feminism." *Hypatia* 2: 65–93.

Wong, N. (1991) "Socialist Feminism: Our Bridge to Freedom." In *Third World Women and the Politics of Feminism,* edited by C. Mohanty, A. Russo, and L. Torres, 288–96. Bloomington: Indiana University Press.

Wray, K. (2001) *NO SHAME ... Women Creating Sexually Explicit Images of Women.* Unpublished M.A. Thesis, School of Criminology, Simon Fraser University.

5
First Nations and Law

Our object is to continue until there is not a single Indian in Canada that has not been absorbed into the body politic and there is no Indian question, and no Indian Department, that is the whole object of this Bill.

(Duncan Campbell Scott, then Deputy Superintendent of Indian Affairs, 1920, quoted in Cairns 2000, 17)

Now, suddenly, they enjoy unprecedented political power. Their representatives sit with the prime minister and the provincial premiers. Aboriginals are now recognized as one of the founding peoples of Canada. Constitutional talks are incomplete without Native people present. All of this came about because Native people refused to live within the stereotypes White people fashioned for them. They would not disappear; they would not be obedient children and assimilate; they would not go away.

(Dan Francis, The Imaginary Indian *1933, 220)*

INTRODUCTION

Historically, the emphasis has been on containment and assimilation of indigenous peoples, not on extermination (genocide). The Beothuk people of Newfoundland were exterminated in the early nineteenth century in what Dickason (1992, 96) calls an "open hunting season" initiated by Europeans. Dickason points out the considerable animosity between the Beothuk and Europeans, as well as ravages of disease—especially tuberculosis.

In 1991 a claim to aboriginal right by the Gitksan and Wet'suwet'en of British Columbia was unsuccessful in the B.C. Supreme Court. The case took almost four years to hear, at an estimated cost of $25 million. The judge in this case concluded "... the discovery and occupation of lands of this continent by European nations, or occupation and settlement, gave rise to the right of sovereignty" (quoted in Dickason 1992, 354). The approach to aboriginal issues often reveals a wilful blindness, and what anthropologist Dara Culhane (1998, 37) refers to as "creating race in the interests of Empire." Speaking generally of recent Canadian legal decisions concerning Aboriginal title, Bell and Asch predict that there will not be a substantial recognition of autonomy of Aboriginal peoples. Rather conservative judicial decisions help to preserve the status quo; as they put it, such a conservative approach " ... allows one to empathize with the discriminatory treatment of Aboriginal people and at the same time declare helpless bondage to fundamental principles firmly established in the common law" (1997, 45).

DISCRIMINATION AND THE LAW

Despite this often bleak outlook on the situation of indigenous peoples, there are examples in which the state has implemented laws and policy initiatives to move beyond exclusion and neglect of First Nations peoples. Hunter (1981, 160) assesses patterns of social inequality in Canada and concludes that aboriginal peoples in Canada experienced the greatest increase in educational involvement between 1951 and 1971. Hunter (1981, 160) is critical, however, of the federal government's greater involvement in promoting such educational participation and its agenda of acculturation and social integration of aboriginal peoples. He notes also that, despite some gains in educational participation, aboriginal peoples continue to lag well behind average rates of participation.

Access to education—and to what sort of education—is a recurrent theme in First Nations issues. A study of First Nations students at the University of Manitoba identified numerous difficulties in accessing postsecondary programs. Rather than personal or simply familial issues, many respondents presented these as systemic barriers. These included poverty, transition from a rural community to a more impersonal urban setting, poor preparation for academic studies, experiences of "abuse and poverty" (Sloane-Seale, Wallace, and Levin 2001, 26). One student reported that few students in her grade nine class completed high school, and her community suffered greatly from many social problems (2001, 25). Many students who began postsecondary studies reported racist and sexist classroom issues, and lamented the very limited offerings on First Nations issues (2001, 23). The researchers concluded that blocked access to further education for First Nations people and others often limits their chances for employment and income. Even today, in spite of successful programmes run by Native bands in many provinces (see York 1990, Chapter 2), many Native students—and low-income children generally—do not complete school, college, or university studies (Canadian Council on Social Development 1991).

Another controversial issue in the history of discrimination and the law in Canada is the treatment of Native families. In recent years, for example, there has been considerable criticism of legally-sanctioned assimilation policies, including the replacement of tribal language and customs with European languages (primarily English) and the forced relocation of Native children to residential schools. As noted in the previous

chapter, the continuing difficulties surrounding aboriginal land claims testify to the state's reluctance to resolve these longstanding demands.

Even so, seemingly local or national concerns can sometimes be
referred to international tribunals and committees. For example, the intersection of aboriginal rights, environmental concerns, and international law
is evident in the Lubicon Lake Band challenge to oil and gas development
efforts in Alberta. The Band protested environmental damage and their
own threatened survival "as a people." The international Human Rights
Committee became involved in this dispute, and the federal government
eventually agreed to pay the Band $4.5 million in compensation, and to
"... set aside a reserve for the tribe, and to sustain its separate existence
with special community services" (Robertson 2000, 147–48).

Kerry Wilkins provides a comprehensive discussion of arguments surrounding aboriginal self-government as an inherent right. He articulates
the considerable gulf between those who believe that First Nations communities' rights to govern themselves have *not* been extinguished, and
what he describes as "the courts' great caution" in recognizing such rights
(1999, 54–55). Wilkins is not persuaded "Charter discipline" should hold
for such "inherent-right communities" (1999, 57).

Transracial Adoption and Residential Schools

The issue of transracial adoption underscores the fundamental power
imbalance between whites and Natives in Canada. McGillivray (1985, 450)
notes the polarized, conflicting values implicit in debates over transracial
adoption. Interracial adoption procedures are seen by some as desirable—a
reflection of racial integration—while others associate legitimating of such
practices as tantamount to cultural genocide. For the latter, "each child
'lost' by adoption outside the ethnic group represents an incalculable drain
of cultural resources" (McGillivray 1985, 450). McGillivray (1985, 451–52)
reports that, for over a decade, adoption of Native children in
Saskatchewan was primarily approved for nonstatus adoptive parents,
many of whom were white. Between 1972 and 1981, the ratio of nonstatus
adoptive parents to status adoptive parents was 6 to 1 (722 adopted children versus 120 adopted children, during this period). The author notes,
however, that adoption policy has shifted recently toward a stronger appreciation of cultural integrity of Native peoples, with priority given to
minority group rights over rights of prospective adoptive parents outside of
the minority group.

The issue of family integrity goes well beyond adoption, extending to
other services affecting children's welfare: "To date, several British
Columbia First Nations have signed triparate agreements with the provincial and federal governments to give them jurisdiction and some funding
to run their own child and family services. Under these agreements, joint
planning is undertaken for all children in care, and adoptive homes are

sought first within the child's extended family or tribe of origin" (Fournier and Crey 1997, 92). The authors are deeply concerned with the legacy of forced relocation to residential schools. They preface their book, *Stolen From Our Embrace*, with a Sto:Lo story of a phantom-like threat to children, and ways of eluding this creature. The story of Th'ówxeya is used to introduce their detailed account of Canada's residential school policies and resistance to them. The Sto:lo people sometimes used the story, passed on to Dolly Felix's extended family, to caution children from staying out after dark. The "cannibal woman" might get them otherwise. This threat is however balanced by "resistance and self-reliance" as integral parts of the tale, with children eluding the creature (see Fournier and Crey 1997, 7–9).

Former residents of residential schools have chronicled their experiences, including members of the Tsartlip Reserve on Vancouver Island (see Olsen, Sam and Morris 2001). There is growing evidence of shameful abuses of First Nations children taken into residential settings, prompting J.S. Milroy to call this "a national crime" (1999). Margaret Hall compared patterns of institutionalized child abuse in Canada and the United Kingdom. The enormity of such abuse—in residential schools, foster care, orphanages, and the like—is evident in several thousand civil actions against the Canadian federal government, and very substantial awards against the Anglican Church, for example (2000, 283). In the United Kingdom, a report entitled *Lost in Care* was published in 2000, documenting the "wilful blindness" of officials and visitors to direct and indirect physical and emotional sexual abuse in numerous settings (Hall 2000, 282). Legal thinking on this issue has moved beyond blaming individual perpetrators, bringing in institutional accountability. Hall puts it as follows: "Public authority liability is predicated on the assumption that fixing liability to perpetrators *alone* is not sufficient compensation for the victim of institutional child abuse ... the responsibility of public authorities for placing and maintaining the child in an abusive environment over which it exercised ultimate control *should* attract legal liability" (Hall 2000, 297, italics in original). The issue of what to do about such past abuses is of course complex. Redress for past harms may take the place of formal legal proceedings or compensation or "redress" arrangements. Hall mentions that legal proceedings often involve considerable delay, cost, and uncertainty, while properly designed redress initiatives may be desirable in resolving liability issues (2000, 298).

Native Self-Government

Patricia Monture-Agnes has articulated her "impatience" with Canadian governmental and legal institutions as a supposed solution to many problems faced by the First Nations. Drawing from her first loyalty as a Mohawk, she presents a complex outlook on law. She is often critical of "mainstream" legal methods and decisions, yet also draws from Mohawk and mainstream resources in her own sense of justice. Monture-Agnes (1999) is also sensitive to gender, repeatedly pointing out how woman or men may be treated differently in either cultural system. Theoretically, she concludes that the established legal system generates "no significant changes" even though it may result in reforms and betterment in small ways (1999, 79). Not content with ameliorative reforms, she holds to a "transformative" outlook. Using the *Delgamuukw* case, decided by the Supreme Court of Canada in 1997, she points out that such cases create such obstacles as cost, delay, and restrictions of Western-style rules of evidence (1999, 81).

Lenore Keeshig-Tobias (1997) argues that protection of culture includes stopping the theft of Aboriginal stories and appropriation of voice. She compliments Francophone-Canadians on sustaining their own language and culture, and sheds light on marginalization of Aboriginal writers, not only in publishing, but also in the arts and film industry. Rosemary Coombe (1997) also argues against appropriation of voice. She identifies limits of a liberal strategy, preferring a postcolonial outlook that recognizes the continuing impact of Canada's colonial past on indigenous peoples. She also recognizes the colossal power of corporations, together with resistance to such power from individuals and groups (1997, 75 and 80).

Tobias (1994) documents ways in which the Indian Act was meant to "civilize" aboriginal peoples and to eventually bring them into conformity with a nineteenth century Euro-Canadian culture and livelihood, focused primarily on farming. Where Indians rejected this livelihood, instead continuing with traditional hunting and fishing practices, this "was particularly irksome to the government, for it was regarded as a drawback to the Indians' adopting a more 'civilized' economic base ..." (Tobias 1994, 298). Tobias chronicles many initiatives designed to enfranchise Indians and to establish—then attack—a reserve system. Despite these examples of subjugation of Indian peoples, Tobias concludes that today "a more honest effort is being made to involve Indians and Indian views in the determination of a new Indian policy" (1994, 303).

George Erasmus, then National Chief of the Assembly of First Nations, contended that aboriginal rights could not be understood or established through outdated concepts. Erasmus distanced himself from the stereotype of separatism, suggesting "we can work together for a single state with proper power-sharing that would be acceptable to Quebec, the rest of the non-native people that have come here, and to First Nations" (Erasmus 1991, 27). Other commentators have argued that this demand for self-government through negotiation with the non-aboriginal population is deeply rooted and indeed is preferable to litigation (see Culhane 1998, 369). Borrows (1997) discusses the Royal Proclamation of 1763 and a ratified agreement the next year in the context of an affirmation of self-government. Well over two hundred years ago, then, there were efforts to ease conflict between First Nations and

European settlers (1997, 158), and for indigenous peoples, this did *not* include extinction of Aboriginal rights or title.

More recently, in *Citizens Plus*, Alan Cairns (2000, 210–11) articulated the importance of "shared citizenship" and of establishing a third order of government within Canada. The "citizens plus" term incorporates both recognition of difference with respect to Aboriginal peoples, and the benefits of "common citizenship" (2000, 8). Cairns believes that older ideologies of assimilation and mainstream superiority have been eclipsed in many ways by Aboriginal activism and self-expression. Clearly, coercion will not be effective nor will platitudinous efforts without substance. For Cairns, recognition of legitimate claims to Aboriginal self-government may go hand-in-hand with stronger relations and fostering a common cause among aboriginals and non-aboriginals (2000, 212). He puts the issue of assimilation plainly: "The discourse of assimilation enjoyed a long hegemony largely because those who were opposed to it—especially the status Indian population—were silenced by their marginalization and by official policy" (2000, 5). In Cairns' work we detect some postmodern themes, including the importance of reclaiming "voice," of resisting appropriation of Aboriginal voices, and debunking claims to universal truth (2000, 15). We also see the argument that Aboriginal peoples are not simply a "visible minority" but are rather claiming a more established status as a Nation, akin to the founding nations of English-Canadians and French-Canadians (see Cairns 2000, 28). Cairns adds that aboriginal issues are not simply influenced by domestic developments, but increasingly by international developments (2000, 4). He also lists structural factors that may hinder efforts to secure a distinct, empowered status for First Nations people; that is, their relatively small population base within Canada (approximately 3 percent), differences among Aboriginal communities, and the dispersion of First Nations people throughout Canada (Cairns 2000, 27).

Asch regards the 1973 Supreme Court of Canada *Calder* decision as pivotal. It meant that "the Canadian state was required to recognize … that Aboriginal peoples lived in societies prior to the arrival of Europeans and … a likelihood that their institutions, tenures, and rights to government remained in place despite the presumption of Canadian sovereignty" (1997, ix). Asch adds that the perspective on Aboriginal rights shifted from a denial of such rights, to a position where "Aboriginal and treaty rights were recognized and affirmed in the 1982 Canadian Constitution Act" (ibid).

LaRocque (1997) explores several issues in her essay about crime and aboriginal peoples. She begins with the controversial disposition of a Hollow Water, Manitoba community; specifically, where an aboriginal couple—who had repeatedly sexually assaulted their two daughters—had received a disposition of "supervised probation" and a requirement that they continue to heal through "the guidance of the circle members" (1997, 75). LaRocque, who is horrified by this arrangement, questions whether such dispositions are in fact traditional. She comments that there seemed to be no consideration of *severe* penalties that were part of traditional justice. LaRocque suggests that contemporary alternative justice processes for aboriginals seem to import basic concepts from Christianity and from "New Age" perspectives, not from ancient, bedrock practices in aboriginal communities. Since sexual assault victims suffer terribly, oftentimes for their lifetimes, the forgiveness and leniency associated with some alternative dispositions may be inappropriate (1997, 84–85). Emma LaRocque challenges uncritical acceptance of such programs, and wonders if the quest—which she describes as a "hunger"—for a distinctly aboriginal identity is sometimes misplaced. She states: "The strident insistence by the Native leadership on our cultural differences has pushed Aboriginal people to the extreme margins. We have given the message that we are fathomlessly different as to be hardly human. We are supposedly so different as to be exempt from the [Charter], as if our history of oppression has made us somehow immune to ordinary human evils, as if we do not require basic human rights that other Canadian citizens expect" (1997, 90). Another instance of a sharp conflict between cultures is the *Thomas v. Norris* civil case. The plaintiff, David Thomas, alleged "assault, battery, and wrongful or false imprisonment" against the seven defendants, all members of the Coast Salish nation (see Denis 1996, 204).

This spirit of difference and cooperation is brought forward with respect to negotiations between First Nations and Canadian federal and provincial governments. Asch and Zlotkin (1997, 220) favour retention of Aboriginal rights and title rather than its extinction. The authors believe that affirming such rights and title has a pragmatic basis, since it should generate less litigation and foster a stronger sense of cooperation among all concerned parties. Moreover, they argue that extinguishing "is inconsistent with the constitutional recognition and affirmation of existing Aboriginal rights in section 35 of the Constitution Act, 1982 ..." (ibid).

"This [forced assimilation] policy had catastrophic results, and these results are plain to see not just in Canada, but also in Australia, New Zealand, the United States and Brazil—wherever aboriginal peoples were denied the right to rule themselves. This is more than a story of the damage done by racist contempt and imperialist arrogance. It is also a terrible demonstration of why rights matter. For any people, aboriginal or not, the right to be the member of a nation, to be respected as such, is a vital condition for personal respect, honour, and dignity. When such group rights to nationhood are stripped from a people, the individuals within the group often disintegrate" (Michael Ignatieff, 2000, 60). Ignatieff traces conflicting principles in the Aboriginal issue: on the one hand, established principles of exclusive sovereignty and territorial ownership associated with European nationalism, and on the other hand, emerging principles of "shared sovereignty." The latter clearly threatens the ideal of hegemonic powers of government, yet it may be the best means to redress the "long history of hurt and injury" in Aboriginal experiences (2000, 80). Interestingly, Ignatieff favours a mix of aboriginal self-determination and Charter protections provided both are conducted in a spirit of equality between aboriginals and non-aboriginals (2000, 82).

The law and society connection requires that we look beyond court-rooms and other legal institutions to consider ways of achieving justice and recognition. The next section reviews the experience of one prominent First Nations man—Donald Marshall Jr.—with the criminal justice system and the federal Fisheries Department.

The Donald Marshall Case

Donald Marshall, Jr. first came to national attention as a murder suspect, then as a convicted murderer, and eventually as a man who had been wrongly convicted. Following his release from prison, Marshall again attracted national news with his efforts to assert a treaty right for First Nations people. This section begins with his experience with the criminal justice system.

Conviction of people for crimes they did not commit is a subject that is very important in understanding legal processes and principles. Literary works such as *Papillon*—based on the wrongful conviction in 1931 of Henri Charrière in France—and *Les Misérables*—which uses the protagonist, Jean Valjean, to dramatize injustices faced by the poor in nineteenth century, post-Napoleonic France—underscore the reality of wrongful convictions and the difficulties facing people who seek to establish their innocence. In Canada, one can cite a number of cases of wrongful conviction. The execution of Wilbert Coffin in Quebec in 1960, and the conviction of Steven Truscott in Ontario in 1959 generated great controversy over possible miscarriages of justice. The Truscott case is national news again, with Steven Truscott "coming out" of his anonymous life in Guelph, Ontario, and working with the Association for the Wrongly Convicted and other people to gain a ministerial review and clear his name (Sher 2001).

In recent times, other cases in Canada have been investigated to see if the wrong person was convicted. Instead of treating such cases as rarities, some activists and researchers have approached wrongful convictions from a more systemic, sociological vantage point, detailing ways in which vulnerable individuals may be denied due process (Anderson and Anderson, 1997). Of these cases, however, the 1971 conviction of Donald Marshall, Jr. for a murder in Nova Scotia has attracted considerable public and official interest.

The wrongful conviction of Donald Marshall has influenced the ways in which criminal law is understood in Canada. Convicted of the murder of his friend Sandy Seale, Marshall was imprisoned for 11 years before his eventual release and exoneration for the murder. This section provides an overview of events in the Marshall case. These events are linked with sociological factors that may have contributed to his conviction, with the ensuing Royal Commission that investigated the Marshall case and the wider question of racial discrimination in the Nova Scotia criminal justice system.

The conviction of Marshall has not only challenged the legitimacy of the criminal justice system in Canada, especially the administration of justice in Nova Scotia, but has also raised questions surrounding patterns of racism in various sectors of the state: policing, courts, prisons, segregation on and off reserves, and so forth. Harris (1990) addressed the process by which Marshall was convicted and later released from prison. The 1989 *Report of the Royal Commission on the Donald Marshall, Jr. Prosecution* will be reviewed in this chapter, along with criticisms of the reforms and assumptions that seem to characterize the Royal Commission Report (see Mannette 1990). To begin with, however, we will use Harris's (1990) work to review the key events in the Marshall case.

Michael Harris's *Justice Denied: The Law versus Donald Marshall* (1990) is a detailed reconstruction of the events of the Marshall case (for other accounts, see Anderson and Anderson 1997; Burtch 1992, Ch. 5). Harris raises a number of serious questions about official conduct in the case and the actions of ordinary people who were aware that Marshall was innocent of the murder charge. Marshall's release from prison in 1982 and compensation award in 1983 partially vindicated him, but full vindication only occurred after the release of a Royal Commission report (discussed below).

In 1971, Donald Marshall was 17 years old. He was the eldest son of Caroline and Donald Marshall, Sr. Donald had 12 siblings. The Marshall family lived on the Membertou Reserve, an urban reserve that houses 400 Micmac Indians. Donald Marshall, Sr., was the Grand Chief of the Micmac Nation. As Grand Chief, Mr. Marshall represented approximately 5,000 Micmacs, primarily in Nova Scotia. Harris (1990, 17) mentions that the people on the reserve had never shared in the wealth created by the industrial developments in Sydney, Nova Scotia: "Bleak and rundown, Membertou was a world apart, its poverty, alcoholism, and paralyzing social isolation largely ignored by the city in whose midst it existed" (Harris 1990, 17). The decimated status of the Membertou Reserve contrasts sharply with the vibrancy of the Micmac people prior to European contact. York (1990, 55–57) states that several thousand Micmacs thrived on Canada's east coast in the 1500s. He adds: "The Micmacs had their own political structures, boundaries, laws, and a sophisticated culture and language" (York 1990, 55). Through disease, liquor, and the reserve system (which confined the Micmac to barren ground and eliminated their traditional livelihood of fishing and hunting), the Micmac population fell and many Micmac communities disintegrated (York 1990, 57, 64–65).

A similar portrait of community disintegration has been made of other reserves, in which traditional means of employment and culture have been eroded. Shkilnyk (1985), for example, documents the inordinately high rates of alcoholism, family conflicts, suicide, and other forms of violent death, on the Grassy Narrows Reserve in northern Ontario in the 1970s. Shkilnyk (1985) links these problems to wider changes affecting the Grassy Narrows community: specifically, mercury poisoning of surrounding waters, which has eliminated a source of livelihood for the Ojibwa and poisoned their water supply; the replacement of a hunting, trapping, and fishing economy with a social welfare dependency; introduction of alcohol; and the overall neglect of community life on the reserve.

There are at least three levels of analysis that can be applied in understanding the Marshall case. The *macrosocial* level emphasizes broad political and social structures. Harris's (1990, 17) depiction of the "bleak" character of the Membertou Reserve indicates that the Marshall case must be set in the context of the discrimination and poverty experienced in one degree or another by the Micmac people on the reserve. This macrosocial perspective can be linked with the relative helplessness of individuals in the face of broad economic, cultural, and political changes.

At the *subcultural* level, it can be observed that fighting, drinking, and petty crimes were valued by many of the youth on the reserve. Not all commentators, however, agree with Harris's perspective. Mannette (1990, 507) provides a report by one Micmac that Harris portrayed Membertou and Sydney as "Harlem North" and overemphasized gang violence. Mannette (1990) contends that many journalistic accounts of the Marshall case did not adequately portray traditional tribal values such as esteem for elders and co-operation. The subcultural portrait corresponds to classic, criminological works on the nature of gang violence and working-class crime. Thus we can see that resistance to dominant, middle-class norms of discipline, respectability, and restraint was prominent among Marshall's peers, with their emphasis on "macho" ideals and violence.

The *labelling perspective* could be used to explain how Marshall's identity was increasingly constructed as delinquent, dangerous, and in need of incarceration. This construction of his deviant identity could, in turn, lead to a presumption of his untrustworthiness and likely guilt in the murder of Sandy Seale. Marshall was thus relatively defenceless against the police charge and the resulting prosecution, notwithstanding the formal, due process protections of the criminal trial. The labelling perspective is rooted in the dynamics of power and social definitions of deviance. It is important to keep in mind, however, that the labelling perspective has been criticized for its lack of a formal "theory" of deviance, poor operationalization of variables, and its limited value in predicting who is labelled deviant and the nature of social reactions to such labels.

Donald Marshall was born in Sydney, Nova Scotia, in 1953. He had failed school twice by the time he entered sixth grade. Donald remarked that Indians were "treated like dirt" at school. While in grade seven, he was expelled for hitting a teacher. Marshall was involved with the Shipyard Gang and became well known to police for several incidents, including underage drinking, vandalizing tombstones, and assaulting a local bootlegger.

On the evening of May 28, 1971, Marshall set out for a dance in Sydney. Around the same time, Sandy Seale, a black teenager and an acquaintance of Marshall, had unsuccessfully tried to get into the dance. Marshall and Seale teamed up. On the way home, according to Harris (1990, 41), the two agreed to panhandle in the park; if necessary, they could take the money by force. When the boys approached Roy Ebsary and his younger companion, Jimmy MacNeil, they hinted around for money. Without warning, Ebsary stabbed Sandy Seale in the stomach, fatally wounding him. Marshall was also cut by Ebsary, but escaped and sought help. Seale died the next day.

Marshall was at this time the only witness available to police. Sandy had not recovered consciousness and had not been able to identify the attacker. There was also a lack of physical evidence, including the murder weapon. Marshall reviewed a police line-up of seven men, but indicated that the killer was not in the line-up. He described the attacker (Ebsary) as an older man, about 50 years old. He was small, with grey hair, and dressed like a priest; that is, he wore a dark, hooded cloak (Harris 1990, 40 and 63). Marshall stood by his description of the assailant and his companion. He did not admit that either he or Sandy Seale tried to panhandle or "roll" the two men. The Sydney police force had already designated Marshall as a possible suspect (Harris 1990, 63).

Some police investigators doubted Marshall's account. Sgt./Det. John MacIntyre headed the murder investigation. MacIntyre sought to place Marshall at the scene, using the testimony of three teenage witnesses. None were at the murder scene, but all three provided statements that they saw Marshall stabbing Sandy Seale. Harris's point—since reinforced by the Report of the Royal Commission on the Donald Marshall, Jr. Prosecution—is that these witnesses were intimidated into giving false statements. Moreover, information that might have been crucial to Marshall's defence was not released by the police or the prosecutor's office to Marshall's attorneys.

On June 1, 1971, with the murder case still unsolved, a letter from the Black United Front was sent to Sydney police chief Gordon MacLeod (Harris 1990, 67). The police were under great pressure to solve this murder, especially in the wake of an unsolved murder of a Chinese-Canadian man a few years earlier (Harris 1990, 57–58). On June 4, 1971, Marshall was arrested and charged with second-degree murder. At trial, no physical evidence linked Marshall with the crime. The three key witnesses for the defence testified against Marshall. One witness—John Pratico— encountered Donald Marshall, Sr., outside the courtroom during the trial. Pratico confessed that he hadn't seen Marshall kill Sandy Seale (Harris 1990, 157–58). Although one of Marshall's lawyers was immediately advised of this, Pratico was not allowed to recant his statement. Two days after his admission to Marshall's father, apparently afraid of repercussions if he recanted, Pratico testified that he had, indeed, seen Marshall stab the boy. Marshall was sentenced to life in prison. Still a juvenile, he served some time in jail and then was transferred to the Dorchester maximum-security penitentiary in New Brunswick in 1972. In 1974, he was transferred to Springhill, a medium-security penitentiary in Nova Scotia. In 1980, Marshall was returned to Dorchester Penitentiary, where he served the next couple of years prior to his release and eventual acquittal.

MacNeil's brothers, sister, and mother heard Jimmy MacNeil's confession that he had lied about Seale's killer in November 1971 (Harris 1990, 222). Even though the Sydney police had heard of this confession the day after MacNeil confessed to his family (Harris 1990, 223), and despite the clear identification of Roy Ebsary as the murderer, Donald Marshall was not cleared of the murder. One result of the allegation, however, was that the director of criminal prosecutions in Nova Scotia, Robert Anderson, was contacted, and a *reinvestigation* of the Marshall case was launched, this time under the auspices of the RCMP (Harris 1990, 232). The RCMP investigation began on November 16, 1971, and concluded less than a month later. Harris (1990) depicts this reinvestigation as a "rubber stamp," which depended on the dubious results of a polygraph investigation and used "armchair psychology" (Harris 1990, 238) to dismiss MacNeil's allegation as delusional. Harris (1990) chronicles Marshall's years in prison: physical violence among prisoners, the contraband drug market, unsuccessful attempts to have the murder conviction appealed or reviewed. Marshall faced the dilemma of showing remorse and confessing to a crime he did not commit in order to increase his chances for a day parole or full parole. The turning point was a visit by Mitchell Sarson in 1981. Sarson told Marshall that Roy Ebsary admitted that "he killed a black guy and stabbed an Indian in the park in 1971" (Harris 1990, 305). This information about Ebsary's involvement in the murder was passed on to the Union of Nova Scotia Indians who immediately contacted the Sydney Police. In 1982 Marshall was released from prison and in May 1983 he was acquitted of the murder of Sandy Seale.

Marshall's suffering did not end with his pardon and release from prison. Harris (1990, 359) documents the adjustments that Marshall faced on release, including legal costs that cut his settlement in half (CBC News 2002). Harris notes that no convicted criminal had ever had his conviction overturned, with a full pardon, despite provisions for this in the Criminal Code (Harris 1990, 359). This situation underscores a central theme in this text: the gulf between formal legal provisions and the structural barriers to putting these provisions in practice.

Provincial Royal Commission on the Marshall Case

In 1990, the Commission investigating the Marshall case released its Report. The Commission examined the particulars of the case and, more broadly, the question of criminal justice and Natives in Nova Scotia. National media coverage reviewed the recommendations of the Report and discussed whether the recommendations were merely symbolic or designed to change current, discriminatory practices against Native people in the criminal law. The Report was unusually blunt in its critique of the Nova Scotia criminal justice system: "The criminal justice system failed Donald Marshall, Jr. at virtually every turn from his arrest and wrongful conviction for murder in 1971 up to and even beyond his acquittal by the Court of Appeal in 1983" (Nova Scotia 1989, 1). The Report outlined 82 recommendations for improving the justice system in Nova Scotia, including reopening the compensation settlement agreed to by Marshall, and criticizing the prosecutor, the Sydney police chief, the defence lawyers, and the judiciary (trial and appeal). The Report rebutted the "gratuitous defence of the justice system" that was part of the 1983 Nova Scotia Appeal Court's statement that any miscarriage of justice in the Marshall case was more apparent than real.

The 82 recommendations covered many aspects of the Marshall case. The recommendations were subdivided into six general categories: dealing with the wrongfully convicted; visible minorities in the criminal justice system; the specific issue of the Nova Scotia Micmac and the criminal justice system; blacks in the criminal justice system; administration of criminal justice; and police and policing. A summary of these recommendations is listed below.

WRONGFUL CONVICTION

The Commission recommended that an independent review mechanism be established to assist in reinvestigation of wrongful conviction cases; second, that this review body have unrestricted access to documents and material in any particular case, and have coercive power to compel witnesses to provide information. Compensation claims by people who were wrongfully convicted should be considered by an independent judicial inquiry. The judicial inquiry would consider all factors pertinent to the case, and there would be no preset limit on the amount of compensation that might be recovered. Legal fees and disbursements of the wrongfully convicted person would be assumed as part of the inquiry's expenses. These general recommendations were followed by a specific recommendation concerning Donald Marshall, Jr., "that Government recanvass the adequacy of the compensation paid to Marshall in light of what we have found to be factors contributing to his wrongful conviction and continued incarceration" (Nova Scotia 1989, 26).

VISIBLE MINORITIES AND CRIMINAL JUSTICE

The Commission recommended that the Nova Scotia government continue to support the minority admissions program in Dalhousie Law School. This admissions program—for Micmacs and indigenous blacks—was designed to provide greater access for these groups. Other recommendations expressed support for the appointment of members of visible minorities as judges and administrative board members. Crown prosecutors would be exposed to educational programs that would focus on "systemic discrimination toward black and Native peoples in Nova Scotia in the criminal justice system" (Nova Scotia 1989, 26), and to specific measures that prosecutors could employ to reduce the effects of systemic discrimination in Nova Scotia's criminal justice operations. More blacks and Native people would be employed within the correctional services, and institutional programs would emphasize the educational, religious, and cultural needs of Native and black offenders.

A cabinet committee on race relations was also recommended. The cabinet committee would meet on a regular basis with representatives of visible minority groups to discuss criminal justice matters. The Attorney General would explore measures to reduce the impact of systemic discrimination in the current criminal justice system. Members of visible minorities would be encouraged to join the correctional services. Where a "significant number of Natives and Blacks are incarcerated" (Nova Scotia 1989, 27), institutional programs would respect the cultural, educational, and religious needs of these offenders.

NOVA SCOTIA MICMAC AND CRIMINAL JUSTICE

A five-year pilot project was recommended for the Nova Scotia Micmac. A Native criminal court would appoint a Native justice of the peace with jurisdiction to hear summary conviction offences. Diversion, mediation, and community work projects would be included in the mandate of this community-controlled court. The court would be designed to encourage "resolution of disputes without resort to the criminal courts" (Nova Scotia 1989, 28). Aftercare services, community input into sentencing decisions, and courtwork services would be made available as part of the court's resources.

The Report recommended a Native justice institute to provide research on Native customary law, to funnel community needs and concerns to the Native criminal court, and to train court workers and other personnel. It would also work with the professions and law schools and monitor discriminatory treatment of Native people in the criminal justice system. All courts in Nova Scotia would have the services of an on-call Micmac interpreter. Legal aid provisions would be strengthened, and regular sittings of provincial courts would be held on reserves. Recruitment of Native constables would be encouraged within the RCMP and municipal police forces. The spirit of these recommendations thus centred on providing a stronger ratio of Native personnel in the criminal justice system. Overall, there was a call for greater sensitivity to the unequal treatment of Micmacs and other Native people in criminal justice.

BLACKS IN THE CRIMINAL JUSTICE SYSTEM

Before we discuss the specific recommendations of the Marshall Commission with respect to black people, it is important to note that discrimination against blacks in Canada has become a major political issue. In Toronto and Montreal, police forces have been strongly criticized for their treatment of black people. The Black United Front in Nova Scotia has publicized discrimination in work, education, and in various other settings (e.g., restaurants, retail stores) to underscore how racism is, for many blacks, an everyday occurrence.

The Marshall Commission made four recommendations concerning blacks in the criminal justice system, among them the establishment of a race relations division within the provincial Human Rights Commission. One full-time commissioner would be designated a race relations commissioner. This commission should be adequately funded in order to provide (1) independent legal counsel and (2) a public awareness program, with particular emphasis on Native and black concerns. Other recommendations involved improvements to legal aid funding for black clients. The Commission recognized that there was a "dependence of Black clients on legal aid services" (Nova Scotia 1989, 30). This dependence could be understood in the context of patterns of lower incomes for black people and other structural limits that impeded equal access to lawyering. Instead, the Marshall Commission appears to have opted for a reinforcement of legal aid services rather than more dramatic reforms in race relations.

ADMINISTRATION OF CRIMINAL JUSTICE

The Marshall Commission made 15 general recommendations for criminal justice administration. The office of director of public prosecutions should be created. The director would be appointed by the provincial Governor in Council. Employment benefits and salary would be equivalent to those of a county court judge. The director would provide an annual report to the Attorney General concerning public prosecutions in Nova Scotia.

The Marshall Commission listed 16 factors that might indicate if prosecutions are in "the public interest" (Nova Scotia 1989, 33). These involved a blend of considerations of general deterrence, special infirmities and age of the accused person, triviality (or seriousness) of the offence, and so forth. A key point is that the discretion to prosecute remained with the powers of the Attorney General's office. It was recommended that prosecutorial decisions should not rest on such factors as race, religion, political beliefs, and the prosecutor's "personal feelings" concerning either the alleged offender or victim. This approach is challenged by arguments that racial discrimination is not the work of individuals but is, rather, part of the history and everyday experience of visible minorities in Nova Scotia.

Disclosure by the Crown was a key factor in the Marshall case. The Commission recommended that accused persons be entitled to various kinds of information before electing the mode of trial (jury or judge as trier of fact) and before entering a plea. This would include verbal and written statements, exhibits contemplated by the prosecutor, copies of witnesses' statements, criminal records of witnesses who might be called to testify, and so forth. The general spirit of the recommendations is that the accused should have access to such information and "any other material or information known to the Crown and which tends to mitigate or negate the defendant's guilt," or which might reduce the accused's punishment (Nova Scotia 1989, 34). Again, it is significant that government discretion would be provided for; specifically, that applications to limit disclosure by the Crown could be considered. A formal application by the prosecutor, coupled with evidence that disclosure would threaten the safety of a person or "interfere with the administration of justice," might therefore be supported.

POLICE AND POLICING

The Marshall Commission's tendency to reinforce official state institutions is evident in its recommendation that the resources of the provincial police commission be sufficient to its mandate. Co-ordination of different levels of state agencies was recommended with respect to the "municipal-provincial partnership" (city police and RCMP forces) in Nova Scotia (Nova Scotia 1989, 36). Adequacy of resources, liaison between different levels of police operations, and co-ordination of police information were highlighted in these recommendations. Recruitment of visible minorities should be "actively encouraged" by both RCMP and municipal police to create a more multiracial composition at all levels of policing. In this spirit, a specific recommendation stated that members of visible minorities should be part of police management positions (Nova Scotia 1989, 37). The Commission seems to have placed faith in the power of policies and guidelines. For example, in order to eradicate racial slurs and stereotyping in municipal police departments throughout Nova Scotia, it was suggested that official policies be developed akin to those adopted by the RCMP and the Metropolitan Toronto police force (Nova Scotia 1989, 38).

The Marshall Inquiry has been described as a forum in which the tribal values of the Micmac people prevailed "within the context of segregationist social reality" (Mannette 1990, 522). Mannette (1990, 506) emphasizes the irony of an Inquiry whose discourse could be read as an ideological defence of "an essentially reformable system," yet which allows members of the Micmac and other groups outside of the dominant culture some voice in the Inquiry proceedings. While the Inquiry did not result in criminal sanctions against anyone implicated in the wrongful conviction of Donald Marshall, Jr.—it has been described as a trial "in which no one goes to jail" (Mannette 1990, 522)—it does underscore the vitality of tribal culture in the face of racial segregation and attempts by the provincial government to assimilate tribal cultures. The aftermath of the Marshall case has left serious questions about the links between politics and justice in Nova Scotia; not the least of which is the tremendous discretionary power of police, judges, and other government officials in withholding information (Harris 1988).

Donald Marshall and The Fisheries Act

Several years after his release from prison, Donald Marshall, Jr. was again arrested in Nova Scotia in the summer of 1993. He was charged with "selling of eels without a license, fishing without a license, and fishing during the close season with illegal nets" (Interactive Science Group, 2001). Despite his defence of an agreed right to fish and sell the catch—under treaties signed in 1760 and 1761—he was found guilty. This decision was appealed to the Nova Scotia Court of Appeal where he was again found guilty. Eventually, the case was heard by the Supreme Court of Canada which "acquitted him on all charges" (ibid). The Supreme Court of Canada determined that while Marshall's activities could be regulated to a certain extent, he "had a treaty right to secure a 'moderate livelihood' by hunting, fishing, and gathering natural resources" (ibid).

This apparent legal victory was followed by social conflicts and legal arguments, perhaps most notably in the case of Burnt Church in the fall of 1999. The Esgenoopetitj (Burnt Church) people fished for lobsters, challenging federal regulation of the fishery. Lobster traps were destroyed and there were altercations between native and non-native people (ibid). In the wake of this conflict, the Supreme Court of Canada issued a clarification of this 1999 treaty right decision in the Marshall case. Part of this clarification was that "The paramount regulatory objective is conservation and responsibility for it is placed squarely on the minister responsible and not on the aboriginal or non-aboriginal users of the resource. The regulatory authority extends to other compelling and substantial public objectives which may include economic and regional fairness, and recognition of the historical reliance upon, and participation in, the fishery by non-aboriginal groups" (Supreme Court of Canada, outlined in Interactive Science Group, 2001).

The Interactive Science Group adds that this spirit of regulation—and arguably, accommodation between conflicting interests—appeared in negotiations between the federal Department of Fisheries and Oceans (DFO) and 43 native bands in Atlantic Canada. Despite a recommendation by the Atlantic Policy Congress of First Nations Chiefs (APCFNC) to not sign such agreements, the majority of affected bands signed (Interactive Science Group, 2001). In the fall of 2000, the Burnt Church community, which refused to sign an agreement, was again in the headlines, with accounts of trap seizures, boat rammings, and injuries suffered by native people and a DFO official (Interactive Science Group, 2001).

The events surrounding Donald Marshall's experiences with criminal law and fisheries law underline historical and contemporary conflicts over the meaning of being aboriginal (First Nations), legal protections and penalties, and efforts to establish self-government by the First Nations within the context of established governmental rule over citizens. Widely regarded as a "legend" or icon among First Nations people, Marshall is uneasy with this high-profile role but nevertheless active in asserting aboriginal rights and working with aboriginal youth (CBC News 2002). The next section provides an overview of First Nations and Law. It is, of course, not an exhaustive review, but one that illustrates points of conflict and attempts at resolution.

ABORIGINAL PEOPLE AND JUSTICE

The Marshall case could be seen as merely a miscarriage of justice, an example of "rotten apples" in the police and prosecutorial services. In quite another sense, it has been argued that the Marshall case is part of a far wider pattern of social and economic discrimination against people of colour. The 1971 killing of Helen Betty Osborne, a Native teenager in The Pas, Manitoba also sparked concerns over racism and criminal justice. It was not until 1987 that charges were laid, with only one of four suspects in the murder eventually convicted. Priest (1990) links this killing—and the difficulties in transforming common knowledge about the likely murderers into a conviction—to factors that include community disorganization and racial conflicts. The recommendations of the Commission investigating the Marshall case seem to reinforce state powers. The Commission implies that the administration of justice is fundamentally sound within Nova Scotia, and that through a series of improvements to existing services, the ideal of equal justice can be realized. Many commentators on criminal justice are not convinced by this reformist approach. Glasbeek (1989, 133–35) argues that the state is not committed to the ideal of justice for individuals, but rather to intervening in ways that legitimate a competitive market economy and social structure. Considerations of property and authority often outweigh attention to principles of justice.

Many researchers have noted very slow progress in attempts to improve conditions for Native peoples. Shkilnyk (1985) published a critical account of the destructive effects of relocation and pollution on an Ojibwa community at Grassy Narrows, near Kenora, Ontario. Shkilnyk (1985) combined her observations of life at Grassy Narrows with official statistics to document a host of social problems that had troubled the residents of Grassy Narrows. These problems included high rates of violent death, increased admissions for care at psychiatric hospitals and detoxification centres, widespread unemployment (and hence, welfare dependency), increased rates of assault, and high levels of alcoholism and other drug abuse. Shkilnyk (1985) points to several structural factors that contributed to the decline of a previously isolated and stable community structure, especially the relocation of the Grassy Narrows people from the English-Wabigoon river site to a new reserve eight kilometres away. This relocation was instigated by the Department of Indian Affairs office in Kenora. The new reserve was close to a logging road, and government authorities thought that the Ojibwa would have better access to electricity, running water, professional health care, and schooling (Shkilnyk 1985, 53). This forced "exodus" had a dramatic effect on the long-established kinship ties among the Ojibwa and this was compounded by a drastic environmental problem: mercury contamination of the English-Wabigoon river, and subsequent poisoning of some members of the Grassy Narrows band.

Mannette (1990, 511) points out that, despite efforts to physically isolate tribal members and to assimilate these cultures—for example, through inculcation of English as the preferred language, or social practices that discourage the "cultural integrity" of groups such as the Micmac—the vitality of Native culture is evident in the proceedings of the Marshall Inquiry. The co-existence of a renaissance of tribal culture and the continuing patterns of discrimination against Native people points to a lack of certainty as to whether Native cultures will be marginalized, will disappear, or will flourish. There are many Native artists, however, who have overcome the barriers of discrimination. There is a growing body of poetry, literature, and other work by First Nations writers (e.g., Scofield 1996, Robinson 2000, Ryan 2001). Politically, the decisive actions of Native leaders that led to the failure of the Meech Lake Accord speak of the greater militancy and political organization of aboriginal peoples. Elijah Harper, a member of the Manitoba legislature and former chief of the Red Sucker Lake band in Manitoba, stalled the Meech Lake proposal on June 23, 1990, and thereby succeeded in killing it. Native leaders have also made progress in their claims for a Native sovereignty that is distinct from federal and provincial civil jurisdictions. If successful in their claims, aboriginal peoples would constitutionally be able to determine their own future and to manage their own resources and communities.

A number of studies have critically assessed the process of colonization in Canada. Thatcher (1986) notes that Native peoples have tended to be labelled as a problem population in the official statistics of various control agencies: social welfare, courts, policing, prisons, and the practice of adopting-out of Native children to white families. LaPrairie (1987) found that Native women were "heavily overrepresented" in jails and prisons in Canada. In B.C., for example, while Native women made up only 5 percent of the population, they constituted 20 percent of all incarcerated women in the province (LaPrairie 1987, 103). She adds that this incarceration rate reflects not individual pathology as such, but rather substantial disparities embedded into Canadian society (LaPrairie 1987, 110). Thatcher (1986) concludes that the perception of Native peoples as essentially "deviant" serves a useful function for economically and politically dominant groups in modern Canada. Such negative stereotyping of Indians, Inuit, and Métis serves (1) to justify a history of colonization and racism in Canada, and (2) to rationalize the government's failure to deal with longstanding Native land claims.

Tennant (1990) provides a detailed account of the events that have led up to the current struggles to resolve land claim disputes in British

Columbia. He notes that whites tend to occupy key positions in provincial (and federal) government despite the increase in the number of "non-white" peoples in modern British Columbia. The author points out that aboriginal peoples were clearly a majority at the time of the first contact with European settlers. Despite the initial co-existence between Native people and Europeans, a gradual pattern of white cultural dominance came into effect—Native names became anglicized, for example, and law banned such cultural rituals as the potlatch ceremony. Tennant notes that, despite a tradition of recognizing some Native land claims in the 1860s, official policies worked in such a way as to worsen the prospects of negotiated settlement of these claims. When James Douglas was governor of B.C. (1858–1864), the government established a policy that confined Native people only to the restricted area of villages and fields (not the wider lands they used). Also, pre-emption of vacant land was available through law, thus allowing governments to appropriate land without negotiating with the aboriginal people affected by such transfer of land. This process was accelerated under the subsequent regime of Joseph Trutch. While Douglas had at least left a legacy whereby Native title to lands had not been formally extinguished, Trutch, chief commissioner of lands and works from 1864 to 1871, helped to implement policies that reduced the size of virtually every reserve in the colony (Tennant 1990, 42).

Tennant thus documents a legacy of failure of the B.C. government to resolve land claims beginning in the mid-nineteenth century. He notes that, in modern times, many Native groups have taken actions to settle these land claim disputes. Such organizations as the church and the B.C. Federation of Labour, as well as some municipal officials, have offered Native leaders support in resolving land claim disputes and other longstanding injustices. Ironically, Tennant's book had barely reached the booksellers when the B.C. Supreme Court presented a controversial decision against the Gitksan-Wetsuwetén people. On March 8, 1991, B.C. Chief Justice Allan McEachern ruled that the plaintiffs—the Gitksan Wetsuwetén—were entitled to use "occupied or vacant Crown land" in the region for aboriginal sustenance. However, the thrust of the plaintiffs' case, extending well beyond the issue of reserve lands and Crown lands, was set aside. Chief Justice McEachern put this bluntly: "As the Crown has all along had the right to settle and develop the territory and to grant titles and tenures in the territory unburdened by aboriginal interests, the plaintiffs' claim for damages is dismissed" (*Delgamuukw et al. v. the Queen*, 1991). This court case, which cost approximately $25 million over the three years of litigation and hearings, was in some respects a setback for Native people seeking exclusive title to land (Culhane 1998, 26). She adds that treaty negotiations and legal cases occur in a context of globalization, and in British Columbia there is great pressure to constrict negotiations to better suit "third party" stakeholders such as non-First Nations fishers, loggers, and miners (1998, 345–47). Nevertheless, there are ongoing efforts to settle land claims through the courts and through negotiations with provincial and federal governments. Thus, notwithstanding the negative judgment as perceived by the Gitksan-Wetsuwetén people, there are ongoing efforts to establish Native title to land and claims to self-government.

STUDY QUESTIONS

1. To what extent do the recommendations of the Provincial Royal Commission on the Donald Marshall, Jr. Prosecution address structural problems facing aboriginal people in Canada? Do these recommendations tend to treat the Marshall case as an anomaly—as a case of an individual being mistreated within a fundamentally sound criminal justice system?

2. Discuss ways in which land claims and efforts to secure Native self-government have been facilitated or hindered by legal decisions, government policies, and social and economic factors. Choose a key incident or case to make this question manageable.

3. Legal powers have been praised and condemned as a means of redressing injustices. Using examples from Aboriginal-related cases, discuss whether legal initiatives have played a major or minor role in securing justice for Aboriginal peoples, or whether such initiatives might be counterproductive. Use specific cases from this chapter or from outside sources.

REFERENCES

Anderson, B., and D. Anderson (1997) *Wrongful Conviction*. Halifax: Fernwood Books.

Asch, Michael (1997). "Introduction." In M. Asch (ed.*), Aboriginal and Treaty Rights in Canada: Essays on Law, Equality, and Respect for Difference*, ix–xv. Vancouver: University of British Columbia Press.

Asch, M., and N. Zlotkin (1997). "Affirming Aboriginal Title: A New Basis for Comprehensive Claims." In M. Asch (ed.*), Aboriginal and Treaty Rights in Canada: Essays on Law, Equality, and Respect for Difference*, 208–29. Vancouver: University of British Columbia

Borrows, J. (1997) "Wampum at Niagara: The Royal Proclamation, Canadian Legal History, and Self-Government." In *Aboriginal and Treaty Rights in Canada: Essays on Law, Equality, and Respect for Difference*, edited by M. Asch, 155–72.

Cairns, A. (2000) *Citizens Plus: Aboriginal Peoples and the Canadian State*. Vancouver: University of British Columbia Press.

CBC News. (2002) *Reluctant Hero: The Donald Marshall Story*. "Life & Times" documentary, directed and produced by Donna Lean.

Coombe, R. (1997) "The Properties of Culture and the Possession of Identity: Postcolonial Struggle and the Legal Imagination." In *Borrowed Power: Essays in Cultural Appropriation*, edited by B. Ziff and P. Rae, 74–96. New Brunswick, N.J.: Rutgers University Press.

Culhane, D. (1998) *The Pleasure of the Crown: Anthropology, Law and First Nations*. Burnaby: Talonbooks.

Delgamuukw et al. v. the Queen, 3 W.W.R. 97, 79 D.L.R. (4th) 185 (B.C.S.C.) (1991).

Denis, C. (1996) "Rights and Spirit Dancing: Aboriginal Peoples versus the Canadian State." In *Explorations in Difference: Law, Culture, and Politics*, edited by J. Hart and R. Baumen, 199–226. Toronto: University of Toronto Press.

Dickason, O. (1992) *Canada's First Nations: A History of Founding Peoples from Earliest Times*. Toronto: McClelland and Stewart.

Erasmus, G. (1991) "Sharing Power: How Can First Nations Government Work?" In *Aboriginal Self-Determination: Proceedings of a conference held September 30–October 3, 1990*, edited by F. Cassidy. Lantzville/Halifax: [co-published by] Oolichan Books/Institute for Research on Public Policy.

Fournier, S. and E. Crey (1997) *Stolen From Our Embrace: The Abduction of First Nations Children and the Restoration of Aboriginal Communities*. Vancouver: Douglas & McIntyre Ltd.

Francis, D. (1993) *The Imaginary Indian: The Image of the Indian in Canada*. Vancouver: Arsenal Pulp Press.

Glasbeek, H.J. (1989) "Why Corporate Deviance Is Not Treated as a Crime: The Need to Make 'Profits' a Dirty Word." In *Law and Society: A Critical Perspective*, edited by T. Caputo, M. Kennedy, C. Reasons, and A.

Brannigan, 126–45. Toronto: Harcourt Brace Jovanovich.

Hall, M. (2000) "The Liability of Public Authorities for the Abuse of Children in Institutional Care: Common Law Developments in Canada and the United Kingdom." *International Journal of Law, Policy and the Family* 14(3): 281–301.

Harris, M. (1990) *Justice Denied: The Law versus Donald Marshall* (2nd edition). Toronto: Totem/Collins.

Hunter, A. (1981) *Class Tells: On Social Inequality in Canada*. Toronto: Butterworths.

Ignatieff, M. (2000) *The Rights Revolution*. Toronto: House of Anansi Press

Interactive Science Group (2001). "The Marshall Decision and the Maritime Canadian Fishery." http://www.rism.org/isg/dlp/bc/introduction/

Keeshig-Tobias, L. (1997) "Stop Stealing Native Stories." In *Borrowed Power: Essays in Cultural Appropriation*, edited by B. Ziff and P. Rae, 71–73. New Brunswick, N.J.: Rutgers University Press.

LaPrairie, C. (1987) "Native Women and Crime in Canada: A Theoretical Model." In *Too Few to Count: Canadian Women in Conflict with the Law*, edited by E. Adelberg and C. Currie, 103–12. Vancouver: Press Gang.

LaRocque, Emma (1997). "Re-examining Culturally Appropriate Models in Criminal Justice Applications." In, *Aboriginal and Treaty Rights in Canada: Essays on Law, Equality, and Respect for Difference*, edited by M. Asch , 75–96. Vancouver: University of British Columbia

Mannette, J. (1990) "'Not Being a Part of the Way Things Work': Tribal Culture and Systemic Exclusion in

the Donald Marshall Inquiry."
*Canadian Review of Sociology and
Anthropology* 27(4): 505–30.

McGillivray, A. (1985) "Transracial
Adoption and the Status Indian
Child." *Canadian Journal of
Family Law* 4(4): 437–67.

Milroy, J.S. (1999) *A National Crime:
The Canadian Government and the
Residential School System,
1879–1986.* Winnipeg: University
of Manitoba Press.

Monture-Agnes, P. (1999). "Standing
against Canadian Law: Naming
Omissions of Race, Culture, and
Gender." In *Locating Law:
Race/Class/Gender Connections*,
edited by E. Comack, 76–97.
Halifax: Fernwood Books.

Nova Scotia (1989) Provincial Royal
Commission on the Donald
Marshall, Jr., Prosecution. *Digest of
Findings and Recommendations.*
Halifax: The Commission. Released
January 1990. Olsen, S., with A.
Sam and R. Morris (2001) *No Time
To Say Goodbye: Stories of the Kuper
Island Residential School.* Victoria:
Sono Nis Press.

Priest, L. (1990) *Conspiracy of Silence.*
Toronto: McClelland and Stewart.
*Indigenous Peoples' Rights in
Australia, Canada and New Zealand*,
edited by P. Havemann, 108–22.
Toronto: Oxford University Press.

Robertson, G. (2000*) Crimes Against
Humanity: The Struggle for Global
Justice.* London: Penguin Books.

Robinson, E. (2000) *Monkey Beach.*
Toronto: Random House of
Canada.

Ryan, A. (2001) *The Trickster Shift:
Humour and Irony in Contemporary
Native Art.* Vancouver: University
of British Columbia Press.

Scofield, G. (1996) *Native Canadiana:
songs from the urban rez.* Vancouver:
Polestar Books.

Sher, J. (2001) *"Until You Are Dead":
Steven Truscott's Long Ride into
History.* Toronto: Alfred A. Knopf.

Shkilnyk, A. (1985) *A Poison Stronger
Than Love: The Destruction of an
Ojibwa Community.* New Haven:
Yale University Press.

Sloane-Seale, A., L. Wallace, and B.
Levin (2001). "Life Paths and
Educational and Employment
Outcomes of Disadvantaged
Aboriginal Learners." *Canadian
Journal of University Continuing
Education* 27(2): 15–31

Tennant, P. (1990) *Aboriginal Peoples
and Politics: The Indian Land
Question in British Columbia,
1849–1989.* Vancouver: University
of British Columbia Press.

Thatcher, R. (1986) "The Functions of
Minority Group Disrepute: The
Case of Native Peoples in Canada."
In *The Political Economy of Crime*,
edited by B. MacLean, 272–94.
Toronto: Prentice-Hall.

Tobias, J. (1994). "Protection,
Civilization, Assimilation: An
Outline History of Canada's Indian
Policy." In *Historical Perspectives on
Law and Society in Canada*, edited
by T. Loo and L. McLean, 290–305.
Mississauga: Copp Clark Longman.

Wilkins, K. (1999) " ... But We Need
the Eggs: The Royal Commission,
The Charter of Rights and the
Inherent Right of Aboriginal Self-
Government." *University of Toronto
Law Journal* 49: 53–121.

6

Racial Discrimination, Multiculturalism, and Law

My children stand on the shoulders of a world that has demonized, enslaved, and raped countless people exactly like them. Today, in Canada, in 2001, black people still contend with racism at every level of society. And yet, the way my children will define themselves, and be defined by others, remains up for grabs.

(Lawrence Hill, Black Berry, Sweet Juice 2001)

The only thing I'd say is this: you're also going to be attacked if you stay down there. So you may as well move. Everything costs, all the time ... it costs to lose and it costs to win, so you may as well win, and do what you came here to do.

(Maya Angelou, 1998)

INTRODUCTION

Racial discrimination has generated protest and litigation in an attempt to reduce ongoing patterns of exclusion and repression. These efforts stem not only from liberal reformers but also increasingly from those applying critical race theory. Critical race theorists take racism as an established, commonplace feature not an exception to the rule. They are also concerned with alliances among various racial and ethnic groups, the limits of legal reforms, and backlash against visible minorities and other populations (Delgado and Stefancic 2000). In general, critics explore ways in which laws are applied unevenly to various racial groups, and whether law can advance or protect the interests of those subjected to racial discrimination. We will examine efforts to reduce discrimination through law—in Canada, Europe, the United States, and Australia and the South Pacific. Two key concepts should be considered: race and racialization. The often taken-for-granted concept of race has generated great controversy over its meaning. There are many definitions of "race," including "nation or ethnic group" and "a group of people who are *socially* defined in a given society as belonging together because of *physical markers* such as skin pigmentation, hair texture, facial features ... and the like ...." (Cashmore 1994, 267, italics in original). Other scholars, such as K. Anthony Appiah, warn that the very concept of race is flawed since it does not match "biological reality" and it is "morally dangerous" (see Postel 2002, A11). Other commentators argue that Canada has vigorously promoted multiculturalism, and that this has provided a striking diversity in customs, languages, and religious faiths (Vincent 2001). The related concept of racialization has taken root in anti-racist efforts. Cashmore (1994, 275) defines racialization as " ... any process or situation wherein the idea of 'race' is introduced to define and give meaning to some particular population, its characteristics and actions." We should keep in mind that the seemingly straightforward concept of "race" remains contentious, given its various definitions and implications, and its use as both a term of derogation and affirmation.

Race, gender, and class issues are explored throughout Backhouse's *Colour-Coded: A Legal History of Racism in Canada, 1900–1950*. Backhouse documents some actions in Québec and British Columbia where race-based practices were overturned, drawing on the principle of equality under the law. The pernicious norm of prohibiting sale of land to "Jews or persons of objectionable nationality" was overturned in a "landmark" 1945 Ontario case, *Re Drummond Wren* (1999, 259). Interestingly, the touchstone of "the common good" was invoked in this case. Eliminating or reducing racial divisions was seen as desirable, while previously, keeping such divisions was seen as wholesome and natural. This contrast reminds us that law and social institutions are dynamic, sometimes slow to change, and other times transforming in a short period of time. Backhouse outlines how malleable the term "race" could be, with census-takers and judges alike aiming for certain, "no-nonsense" categories and determinations despite the complexity and ambiguity of racial designations (Backhouse 1999a, 1999b).

In *The Mismeasure of Man* (1981), Stephen Gould addresses the ways in which Western science has reinforced negative, paternalistic stereotypes of non-Caucasian races. Gould (1981, 32 and 35) notes that such American heroes as Thomas Jefferson, and Abraham Lincoln expressed racial views that would today be viewed as embarrassing. Scientific doctrines of racial inferiority and undesirability were applied throughout the world. As Gould (1981) suggests, this led to an ideology of blacks and Indians as "separate and inferior." Eighteenth and nineteenth century politicians and scholars used the ideology of racial superiority to justify slavery and denial of civil rights for aboriginals and people of colour (Lott 1998). Underlying these developments, however, is the play of racial ideologies. Even those who favoured greater rights for nonwhite peoples tended to accept some aspects of the racial inferiority doctrine. Thomas Jefferson ventured: "Whatever be their degree of talents, it is no measure of their rights" (Gould 1981, 31). This labelling of human beings as inferior or superior, as advanced or defective, was bolstered by many legal and administrative policies that would today be dismissed as uncivilized and racist. Some proponents of racial superiority advocated distinct forms of education, with blacks streamed into manual work and whites into more academic work (Gould 1981, 47).

Gould (1981, 323) examines scientists' efforts to debunk these theories of racial inferiority and the radical measures designed to deal with those who were considered inferior. Thus, quasi-scientific methods were employed not to understand racial diversity but, rather, to classify racial groups by Eurocentric standards. Viewing certain races as inferior was widely accepted throughout the dominant culture and was a useful way of promoting assimilation of the so-called inferior races, or alternatively, implementing policies that segregated aboriginal peoples from white people (Gould 1981, 31). Gould's work challenges the notion of science as a neutral field and suggests, instead, that science is deeply involved in political interests, even to the extent of generating and perpetuating mythologies disguised as scientific verities. In the racial inferiority doctrine, quasi-scientific theories justified discrimination on the grounds of intellectual, moral, and social difference. Science and popular culture thus promoted doctrines of racial inferiority, but not without challenges to these pseudo-scientific claims. This brief historical backdrop illustrates how certain laws and state policies have been formulated in colonial societies. Today, the very survival of groups whose economic resources have been weakened through racially-inspired policies and laws may hang in the balance.

RACIAL DISCRIMINATION AND THE LAW

Canada

John Porter's *The Vertical Mosaic* presented an image of Canadian society in which diverse racial and ethnic groupings could be seen to cluster in particular social and economic statuses. Porter (1965, 79) notes that in Canada in 1931, one-third of the Canadian workforce was first-generation immigrants. Stratification was evident when Porter considered the category, "professional and financial occupations" (4.8 percent of the workforce). People of Jewish, Scottish, English, and Irish descent were over represented in this category, while French, Dutch, German, Scandinavian, Italian, Eastern European, Asian, and native Indians were underrepresented. The "elite world" consisted of a small number of people, often intimately linked through associations. This network promoted a "corporate ideology" supporting individualism, productivity, private ownership, and investment ideology. Deep-seated race prejudice and opposition to racism are explored in the next section which reviews a challenge to colour-bar policies, followed by a more general discussion of racism and anti-racism in Canada and other countries.

THE VIOLA DESMOND CASE (NOVA SCOTIA, 1946–47)

The Nova Scotia case of Viola Desmond case highlights ways in which a colour-bar was established in some areas and also how it was challenged. This following discussion is taken from Constance Backhouse's *Colour-Coded* (1999), a series of essays on racism and resistance in Canada from 1900–1950. The case involved charges brought against a biracial woman, Viola Desmond, who was considered "coloured." The case began with a twist of fate: In November 1946, Viola Desmond's car had mechanical troubles in New Glasgow, Nova Scotia. Waiting for the car to be repaired, she bought a ticket for a movie at a local cinema. Instructed to sit in the upstairs area, which was reserved for "coloured" people. Desmond refused to leave her downstairs seat. Backhouse's detailed analysis of the 1946 Desmond trial centres on this alleged infraction of the Nova Scotia Theatres, Cinematographs and Amusements Act of 1915 (p. 230). This wide-ranging act provided for penalties for those who did not pay an "amusement tax," but nowhere did it mention race specifically. Backhouse points out that Viola Desmond's alleged infraction was utterly minor: "Since she had insisted on sitting downstairs, she was *one cent short* on tax" (p. 230, italics added). Viola Desmond was forcibly removed from the Roseland Theatre by a police officer, suffered injuries to her knee and hip (p. 229), and she was jailed overnight.

Backhouse outlines Viola Desmond's middle-class background, the biracial marriage of her parents, and her abilities in school and later in business (pages 232–35). She was committed to increasing work opportunities for black women, beyond the conventional practice of domestic work (p. 240). Backhouse points to the importance of social class in such activism: "… most legal challenges to racial segregation in Canada seem to have come from middle-class individuals … A certain level of economic security furnished a base which enabled such individuals to consider taking legal action against discriminatory treatment" (p. 243). This in turn raises the question not only of who creates legislation and administers law, but also who has the resources and inclination to challenge laws.

Some believed that her maltreatment was a clear overreaction, an uncivilized action even within a still-segregated social system in Canada and the United States. Backhouse reports that many members of "the black community in Halifax" were appalled by this incident (p. 246). Encouraged by her physician to appeal her conviction and also by the Nova Scotia Association for the Advancement of Coloured People (NSAACP), Desmond took legal action. There were few black lawyers available to her, with only one such lawyer practicing in Halifax (p. 252). This in itself speaks to racial stratification in the legal profession. Desmond retained "a white trial lawyer," Frederic Bissett. Backhouse traces the mixed response by the judiciary to race-related cases where black defendants won damages and lower court decisions were upheld on appeal (ibid). The judiciary, and arguably, the general public, was divided over the appropriateness of preserving or removing racial barriers in various settings. Backhouse contends that the competing outlooks boiled down to "the doctrine of freedom of commerce and the doctrine of equality within a democratic society" (p. 256).

Backhouse shifts to a detailed discussion of the civil litigation brought by Vila Desmond against the manager of the Roseland Theatre, and the Roseland Theatre Company itself (p. 261). Bissett contended that his client suffered from "assault ... malicious prosecution [and] false arrest and imprisonment" (ibid). The legal action was moved to the Nova Scotia Supreme Court where Judge Archibald refused to review the initial decision against Desmond, noting that the time frame—a mere 10 days after conviction—for an appeal had lapsed. Backhouse highlights how many contemporary legal protections such as notification of a "right to counsel" or her entitlement to "cross-examine the prosecution witnesses" (p. 264) were not brought to Desmond's attention, nor were these "omissions" considered unusual in the legal climate of 1940s Nova Scotia. Bissett's appeal to the Nova Scotia Supreme Court was unsuccessful, the race implications lost in the welter of technical and procedural arguments and commentary. Only Judge William Hall stated clearly that he had doubts about the motives for MacNeill's actions, implying the paltry tax owing on the ticket was not the issue, but more likely, allegiance to segregation of the races (Backhouse 1999, 266). Rather than face a month in jail, Viola Desmond paid the fine of 26 dollars and returned to Halifax. Desmond was astonished by her conviction. Born in Nova Scotia, and well-travelled, she clearly saw her treatment in the theatre and in the courts as excessive, to say the least (Backhouse 1999, 245). Nevertheless, the humiliation, physical injury, and costs of the criminal case against Desmond seemed to count for nothing in the court's view. Some commentators believed that the decision was correct, given the nature of the law; others were dissatisfied with this legalistic, technical outlook, arguing that human dignity and racial equality needed to be safeguarded through law (p. 269). The leadership in the black community clearly believed that racial barriers must be challenged. Backhouse does not elaborate on subsequent legal cases and social events that were part of a shift to open seating (open to all races, both genders, etc.) in theatres, and similar openness in public venues and private businesses. Nonetheless, it is clear that Desmond's apparently futile stand signalled a challenge to racism and heralded an end to some of its forms.

Backhouse has a sharp eye for divisions within professions and the community. She traces such differences of opinion within the legal community, among politicians, and certainly inside the black community— where some expressed dislike for the legal action, and criticized Mrs. Desmond for attempting to "pass" as white, among other things (Backhouse 1999, 268). Moreover, she brings forward legal precedents and social customs that reinforced discriminatory treatment of black Canadians, or undermined discriminatory practices. For example, the practice of segregating black students from whites was well-established from the mid-1800s to the end of the nineteenth century (p. 250). In addition, many black-only schools were poorly-funded, lacking adequate hours of instruction, library resources, and teaching personnel (p. 250). Backhouse also cites the *Hawes* case in Regina in 1911 where the court held that Hawes, a black Canadian, was aware of (what we would now see as intolerable) a practice of charging black customers double the price of food served to white customers. The case was dismissed, even though this practice was clearly discriminatory (p. 254).

RACISM AND THE CHINESE IN CANADA

Formal and informal discrimination against the Chinese in Canada has long been associated with Canadian public policy. Li (1988, 23) notes that in the 1850s and 1860s, Chinese immigrants were generally well-regarded for their industriousness and general value to a frontier society. Nevertheless, as the British Columbia economy experienced decline in the 1860s and 1870s, various steps were taken against the Chinese, including legislation to take away the right to vote and a ban on hiring Chinese workers for government projects (Li 1988, 23). Even though anti-Chinese sentiments seemed "especially strong" in B.C., Li (1988, 27) found that several attempts to discriminate against the Chinese in Canada—for example, by imposing an annual tax on the Chinese and preventing immigration from China altogether—were defeated or disallowed, although a "head tax" eventually came into force.

Anti-Chinese measures were also applied with respect to labour issues. Comack (1986, 72–75) offers a theoretical explanation of organized labour's broadly based opposition to competition from Chinese labourers. Much of the anti-Chinese action in the late nineteenth century stemmed not simply from racism, but also from an effort by organized workers to keep and improve their conditions of work. Labour organizations in Canada opposed greater use of unskilled labour. In this sense, then, Chinese labourers could be seen as pawns, used by industrial capitalists to divide the labour force and undermine efforts by organized labour to realize better working conditions and wages. Comack (1986, 73) concludes that the "... anti-Chinese posturing of organized labour in British Columbia was therefore not a purely racist reflex but part of a general strategy to oppose the immigration of the unskilled."

Constance Backhouse also documented anti-Asian sentiments and legislation, including legal barriers to full participation of Chinese immigrants around the turn of the twentieth century (1999, 3–4). Such legislation covered many aspects of citizenship: "immigration, taxation, the franchise [voting], employment, business, and social welfare" (1999, 4). She argues that "Small businessmen and male trade-unionists" worked together to offset competition from Asian businessmen (p. 4). One tactic was to forbid the hiring of "white women." As Backhouse explains, such a prohibition would mean that Chinese employers, with a male-only workforce, would have to pay higher wages to the men compared with women employees. Backhouse adds that women of colour were in the minority in early twentieth century Canada, and there were considerable job market obstacles for such women (p. 4). Here, we see a material basis to legislation, rooted in economic interests and an Anglo-Saxon majority in early twentieth-century Canada. We also see considerable rhetoric about protection of white women, combined with stereotyping and even demonization of Chinese-Canadian employers. The 1924 *Yee Clun* court decision in Regina held that municipal councillors had racially discriminated against a Chinese-Canadian businessman (Backhouse 1999c).

Over a decade before the *Yee Clun* case, defence arguments in a 1912 case in Moose Jaw, Saskatchewan, included the slippery issue of "race." While some people may have been content with a clear division between, for example, Chinese and white, defence lawyers and some witnesses refused to follow this racialized differentiation. In the 1912 Moose Jaw case, one white employee adamantly refused to speculate on the defendant's race, stating "I treat him as myself" (Backhouse 1999, 5). Nevertheless, the defendants were found guilty. Angered by this verdict, Chinese business owners raised funds and launched unsuccessful appeals at both the provincial level, and later, the Supreme Court of Canada (Backhouse 1999, 6).

Backhouse uses the legal case against Yee Clun to highlight racist assumptions and practices in Canada. The larger picture in this case includes a clamping-down of immigration policies through the 1923 Chinese Exclusion Act, and also severe problems for "Asian employers" in obtaining workers (p. 8). Note that this is not simply a matter of an application by Yee Clun and a court decision: municipal politicians, police representatives, and municipal employees were also part of this conflict. Backhouse adds that convictions of Chinese-Canadians for criminal offences often generated more media publicity than their Anglo-Saxon counterparts (p. 9). The coalition of Anglo-Saxon business owners and trade unionists mentioned earlier was complemented by lobbying from the Regina Local Council of Women (LCW), a largely middle-class organization committed to morality and social progress (Backhouse 1999, 10).

Against this multitude of people supporting the legislation, a few individuals fought for the principle of "equality under the law" (p. 12). G.F. Blair is mentioned as a lawyer who fought openly for nondiscrimination. Even so, the Saskatchewan statue was in effect until 1969. Note that some provinces—Manitoba in 1940, Ontario in 1947—repealed similar legislation decades before its removal in Saskatchewan. This underscores ways in which social practices and legal statutes are not monolithic, and can be implemented or discarded in very diverse ways across regions and jurisdictions. To use "markers of distinction" (Anderson 1991, cited in Backhouse 1999, 6) to designate racial groupings and even race-based practices is very precarious. This is true not only for visible minority groups, but also for those originating from Italy, Poland, Germany, and the Scandinavian countries (see Backhouse 1999, 7).

United States

Racial injustice is often presented as one of the most intractable and telling indictments of American politics. Worsley (1984, 344), in his wide-ranging discussion of world development, refers to the "social battlefields" and poverty within major American societies and the vast imbalance of wealth in "a society where the race goes to the strong and the weak to the wall." In the view of Hall and his associates (1978, 387), it has been the nature of American capitalism to force American blacks into a "distinct, super-exploited class" within the larger working-class population and to limit them to the lowest reaches of poorly paid "marginal work." It is well documented that black Americans are, on average, disadvantaged with respect to education, income, access to health care, and so forth. This tendency to *substantive inequality* has been offset, not by any dramatic social and economic gains, but by the reinvocation of an ideology of equal opportunity in the social structure, ostensibly backed by legal powers to combat discrimination.

Bond (1987) chronicles the civil rights movement in the United States between 1954 and 1965, a movement that was founded to reverse established patterns of racial discrimination. Bond (1987, 11) notes that black Americans were excluded from higher education at university. Other schools—public schools, high schools, and colleges—were divided along racial lines in states with Jim Crow laws. Jim Crow laws referred to "day-to-day segregation" of whites and blacks. The name was taken from the caricature of a black minstrel, circa 1830 (Bond 1987, 10). The Jim Crow laws were in effect from the 1890s to the 1960s in southern states. Jim Crow laws disenfranchised blacks, blocking their participation in electoral systems and guaranteeing that resources for blacks were typically inferior to those provided for whites (Fredrickson 1981, 238–39). These laws applied to virtually all aspects of life in these states: public transportation, theatres, schooling, restaurants, and so forth (Bond 1987, 12–13). In the 1953 legal case *Brown v. Board of Education*, the judges held that the separate-but-equal doctrine of Jim Crow policies was unjust: "Separate educational facilities are inherently unequal" (Bond 1987, 32–34). This landmark case was seen as a major victory for equal rights; however, many were unconvinced that the legal victory in *Brown* would translate into equality of opportunity and resources. The spirit of the *Brown* decision—that the nature of racial segregation in American schools was injurious for black children—was thus but one step in the overall movement against racism in American life.

The struggle for equality also targetted the practice of racial segregation on public transportation, especially in southern states. In 1953, a one-day boycott of the segregated seating system on buses in Baton Rouge, Louisiana ended unsuccessfully. Nevertheless, partial success was recorded there a few months later, with a compromise result in which one back seat was reserved for blacks, and two front seats were reserved for whites (Bond 1987, 60). In Montgomery, Alabama, in the early 1950s, white passengers enjoyed the privilege of reserved seating. This arrangement prevailed, even though 75 percent of the ridership was black. Bond (1987, 62) recalls "as the whites took their seats, black riders had to get off the bus and re-enter through the back door." In 1955, a protest was launched in Montgomery against segregated seating following the ejection and arrest of Claudette Colvin, a black teenager who refused to give up her seat to a white person (Bond 1987, 62–63). By the 1960s, the scale of the civil rights movement was unmistakable: in 1963, approximately 800 demonstrations took place across America, culminating on August 28, when nearly a quarter-million people marched on Washington to demand action on civil rights (Edwards 1981, 95).

The civil rights movement has, as expected, suffered some reversals, and in virtually all areas of life, black Americans continue to be discriminated against. In more recent times, some researchers have reported substantial differences in perceptions of criminal injustice in the United States. Hagan and Albonetti (1982, 352) conclude that the black Americans sampled in their study were much more likely to perceive injustice in criminal law practices than were white Americans. In contrast to some earlier studies, which indicated no significant differences in such perceptions of injustice, there was clearly an increased perception of "race and class conflict" surrounding criminal injustice in the United States.

Freeman (1982) is very critical of the argument that Supreme Court decisions have improved the overall pattern of racial discrimination in America. Reviewing U.S. Supreme Court decisions concerning antidiscrimination law, he concludes that they have not substantially altered the relatively subordinate position of black Americans with respect to education, voting rights, and housing. Freeman (1982, 210) argues that antidiscrimination law ironically serves to legitimize racially based practices, even while it claims to be against such practices:

> As surely as the law has outlawed racial discrimination, it has affirmed that Black Americans can be without jobs, have their children in all-black, poorly funded schools, have no opportunities for decent housing, and have very little political power, without any violation of antidiscrimination law (Freeman 1982, 210).

Freeman (1982) outlines two theoretical perspectives that are crucial to an understanding of discrimination and the limits of antidiscrimination law: the perpetrator perspective and the victim perspective. The *perpetrator perspective* is used to address racial discrimination as an isolated event, unconnected with the wider conditions of life for minorities. It is a remedial perspective, seeking to correct or punish misbehaviour by racist individuals. This perspective is ahistorical, ignoring or minimizing connections between past and present racial policies. The perpetrator perspective implies that, aside from the inappropriate actions of a minority of perpetrators, the social system is fundamentally fair, affording opportunities for those seeking them. The courts are able to act as a watchdog, correcting instances of discrimination.

The *victim perspective*, while acknowledging that individual perpetrators victimize other individuals, suggests that racial discrimination is an ever present force for subordinated groups. Freeman (1982, 211) thus refers to the existence of a perpetual underclass, which are often denied such basic necessities as adequate housing, employment, and income, and even a sense of their own human dignity and self-worth. Racial problems will not be eliminated by isolated court decisions; rather, affirmative action is needed to correct systemic discrimination against minorities. The victim perspective, with its holistic approach to understanding and addressing racial discrimination, is nonetheless far from a dominant perspective. Freeman (1982, 211) notes that antidiscrimination law in the United States is "hopelessly embedded" in the reformist ideology of the perpetrator perspective.

One weakness of Freeman's approach is its lack of attention to the dialectics of human rights struggles and political response. It fails to take into account the greater representation of blacks and Hispanics on some city councils and other political bodies in the United States or the successful efforts to block conservative initiatives. The failure to appoint conservative nominee Robert Bork to the Supreme Court is one example of this latter trend. On July 1, 1987, Bork was nominated by then President Ronald Reagan to replace liberal Justice Lewis Powell, who had resigned from the U.S. Supreme Court. A coalition of interests—among them the American Civil Liberties Union and groups representing women's issues, the handicapped, racial minorities, and environmental groups—mobilized against this nomination. On October 23, 1987, following 12 days of hearings by the senate Judiciary committee, the Bork nomination was defeated 58 to 42 (see Pertschuk 1989). Due to the malleability of the Supreme Court—liberal in the 1960s and 1970s, more conservative in recent years—it may adopt an even more liberal approach in years to come. Freeman's (1982) work can also be questioned since it was written over a decade ago. There is, however, ample support for his premise that formal legal protections, even those affirmed by the U.S. Supreme Court, have not significantly reversed patterns of substantive racial inequality.

Walzer (1983, 221–24) discusses these complexities of social policy. He points out that the character of compulsory laws, exemplified by the busing of children to achieve racial integration in schools, is laudable in some respects. Nevertheless, the American experience proves that underlying problems—for example, the "tyrannical distributions in the spheres of housing and employment" (Walzer 1983, 224)—cannot be overcome by slight improvements in educational opportunities for racial minorities. Walzer notes that in education, there have been considerable barriers to the recruitment of visible minority teachers and administrators. A study of 45 major metropolitan areas by the National Bureau of Economic Research (NBER 1990) confirmed that unemployment among young black American men was higher than among their white counterparts. This differential increased dramatically when overall economic conditions worsened. Specifically, in areas where the unemployment rate was less than 4 percent, the unemployment rate for young whites and young blacks, respectively, was 5.8 percent and 7.2 percent. For areas where unemployment exceeded 7 percent, the respective figures were 9.7 percent and 24.6 percent. The study found that in better labour markets, young black males benefited from higher wages. This meant "a 1 percent fall in the overall unemployment rate raises the average wage of black youth by 4 to 7 percent, and all youth by 3 to 4 percent" (NBER 1990).

Edwards (1981, 97–99) offers a cogent argument that the initial successes of the civil rights movement have not been followed up to a significant extent after the 1964 Civil Rights Act. Supreme Court rulings against affirmative action policies and cutbacks in education are two of the factors working against the underclass of black citizens in the United States. The ideology of self-improvement faltered in the face of these structural limitations. Edwards (1981, 95) concludes that "White America was not willing, in the main, to submit to the proposition that the problems of Blacks were rooted in the nature of the social structure. Equality was perceived as a right due to the individual as a matter of principle; for Blacks to demand an alteration in their group position was considered unacceptable."

The issue of affirmative action remains controversial. For proponents, affirmative action is an overdue means of alleviating systemic inequalities suffered by visible minorities. Researchers in England listed several factors that undermine anti-discrimination legislation. These include minimal compliance with legal requirements, the traditional practice of blaming individuals rather than exploring systemic discrimination, and reversals in affirmative action initiatives (in the U.S.). They do acknowledge that some legal initiatives, in conjunction with progressive administrative policies, can ease discriminatory practices and attitudes (Lustgarten and Edwards 1992). Others are less sanguine about these programmes. Thomas Sowell reviews affirmative action initiatives, also termed "positive discrimination" in the United Kingdom, and "compensatory preferences" in India. Sowell, a leading African-American scholar, expresses strong misgivings over affirmative action polices. These include a general lack of rigorous, longer-term studies of their impact, and evidence that such initiatives often favour more advantaged members of visible minorities, e.g., middle-class children, recipients of business grants while offering little or nothing to the most marginalized members. Sowell adds that not all minorities are forever consigned to a subordinate status. As he puts it, "Despite the assumption that past misfortunes predetermine present outcomes, numerous groups around the world have begun in poverty, overcome discrimination, and ended up more prosperous than many around them. The list would include the overseas Chinese in southeast Asia, Jews in America, Lebanese in West Africa, Indians in Fiji, Volga Germans in Tsarist Russia, Japanese immigrants in Canada" (Sowell 2001).

Discrimination against indigenous people in America has also attracted considerable criticism. Alice Feldman, for example, situates the American Indian social movement in a critical context of colonization, racism, and subjugation of indigenous peoples. She notes that "… despite its inherent power to oppress peoples and silence alternative voices, law also has transformative capacities …" and that we must consider oppositional or counterhegemonic "narratives in legal settings …" (2000, 558). Efforts to transform society—which she refers to as "reconstruction"—generate great resistance. Using the example of the American Indian social movement, she states that the Senate Committee on Indian Affairs, begun in 1988, demonstrated a "pervasive unwillingness to 'learn' from indigenous peoples, as well as a nearly insurmountable and pathological resistance to their efforts as a whole" (2000, 560). Like Slaughter (2000), she concludes that disadvantaged groups face a powerful legal order and social order, where norms and values are often in stark conflict. Rather than support this status quo, Feldman makes the argument for appreciating the ongoing power of colonization/post-colonization, and for developing a "critical, sociolegal pedagogy" (2000, 576).

Attempts to challenge the legal and social status quo often generate resistance. The test of formal legal safeguards is in their implementation and reception in the legal sphere and society at large. For example, Slaughter (2000) explores the impact of the 1978 Indian Child Welfare Act (ICWA) in the United States. Despite provisions to reverse oppressive practices such as adopting-out Native children or putting them in federal boarding schools, Slaughter concludes "Indian concepts of identity conflict with some of the most cherished principles of American liberalism" (2000, 227–28). In practice, American judges and jurists often disregard the importance of tribal law and Native identity, clinging to a normative approach of individualism over collective life, nuclear families over extended families or bands, and refusing to see Indian people as sovereign or quasi-sovereign (2000, 230, 241).

Australia and the South Pacific

The use of the criminal sanction against aboriginal peoples is for some researchers a form of paternalism: the imposition of a European-derived system of justice on a people who already had established longstanding tribal customs of dispute-resolution. Foley (1984, 164) states that there has been a pattern of gross overrepresentation of Aborigines in the Australian system of criminal justice and uses official statistics from 1976 to indicate that, nationwide, the rate of incarceration of Aborigines is approximately

12 times that of the population as a whole. Foley (1984, 168–72) outlines a *gestalt* of difficulties facing many of Australia's Aborigines: poor health, including significant hearing loss, which in turn compounds linguistic differences and communication problems during interrogation and trial; discriminatory attitudes and practices among Australian police officers; and the "chronic" problem of serious alcohol abuse.

Ligertwood (1984, 193) outlines the problem of crime, particularly juvenile crime, among the Pitjantjatjara tribe in southern Australia. He cites the erosion of "community authority," including broken rituals and ties with Pitjantjatjara elders as the reason for this problem. Given this weakening of traditional authority, Ligertwood acknowledges that this group, and other aboriginal groups, may need to rely on an outside authority to settle disputes. This process would not, however, require complete abdication of local powers in settling some, or conceivably all, disputes. Ligertwood (1984, 210–11) proposes a number of justice-related options, in order that aboriginal peoples might devise their own systems of justice in accordance with their own traditions, with European systems or possibly with modifications and combinations of the two.

Aboriginals in Australia are approximately 2 percent of the population (Cashmore 1994, 3). Cashmore (1994, 2) points out that aboriginals in Australia resisted the takeover of their lands, and used various strategies including reciprocity with colonizers, to fight against colonial policies. Paul Lauren takes a balanced approach to the politics of racial discrimination. He gives numerous examples of the power of moral suasion in changing policies, noting such exemplars as Nelson Mandela, Mahatma Ghandi, Martin Luther King Jr., and other, less well-known activists such as the nineteenth century anti-slavery/abolitionists William Wilberforce and Thomas Clarkson (1996, 319). He points out many historical instances of attempts to eradicate or lessen racism, but notes realistically that such efforts often generate substantial opposition by government officials and other stakeholders (1996, 26–28). Slavery is also not only of historical interest, but of interest given globalization and forms of "new slavery" (Bales 1999). Globalization is often used as an epithet, but it can be used in a more positive sense. Sarat and Kearns (1999, 5) identify "new globalism" which permits crossover between different identities and cultures and possibilities for "a cosmopolitan consciousness."

Nettheim (1984, 50) points out that the focus of much of international law has been on individual rights. This rather narrow focus has interfered with the full implementation of indigenous peoples' claims for land settlements, cultural survival, and self-determination. Nettheim (1984, 50) observes, however, that both international standards and related structures have been evolving and becoming more relevant to the question of human rights for indigenous peoples. Nettheim (1984, 57) concludes that the dominant practice of assimilation of aboriginal peoples in Australia was abandoned in the mid-1970s, although efforts to respect aboriginal legal claims and cultural identities remain inconsistent. He notes that there is also considerable variation among state and territorial governments in the treatment of aboriginal rights; nevertheless, some infringements of human-rights standards can be taken before international bodies.

Colonization of Maori lands involved the takeover of millions of acres in the 1860s. The combination of colonial governments and economic interests, efforts to Christianize the Maori, and urbanization led to the sub-jugation of indigenous peoples. Nevertheless, there were expressions of resistance, including the spirit of Kotahitanga ("the unification of tribes") and even the beginnings of "Maori nationalism" (see Ranginvi 1999, 111–14). Jane Kelsey uses the example of Aotearoa/New Zealand to contrast the rise of Maori and Pakeha nationalism and efforts at self-determination with the impact of "market liberalism" and enduring problems of poverty, joblessness, and crime rates among minority populations.

The history of colonization in the South Pacific highlights the ways in which minority economic interests have transformed many societies. Moorehead (1974) refers to this transformation as "the fatal impact." Societies such as Tahiti were influenced dramatically by European contact in the eighteenth and nineteenth centuries, especially by such Western institutions and concepts as law and private property. As the Australian continent was claimed as an extension of European society, the aboriginal peoples were generally seen as a hindrance to the newly established colo-nial regime. Once the tribal laws of the Aborigines were subordinated to English legal structures, their numbers dwindled. One estimate shows that the population of 1500 Aborigines near Sydney in 1788 fell to a few hun-dred by 1830 (Moorehead 1974, 211).

The inhabitants of what came to be known as Bikini Atoll are still affected by the U.S. government's decision to evacuate the island for nuclear testing in the 1940s. In all, 23 bombs were detonated on Bikini Atoll, with the largest bomb, detonated in 1954, 1000 times stronger than the atomic bomb dropped on Hiroshima (Ellis 1986, 813–15). The Bikini families had earlier been moved to another atoll, where they faced starva-tion, and later relocated to the island of Kili. The islanders suffered various health problems, including diabetes, and also lost their traditional liveli-hood of fishing and seafaring. The government promise to relocate the Bikinians on their original atoll was unmet, largely due to the radioactive waste that has contaminated the soil, water, and crops (Ellis 1986, 815–19).

LAW AND GENOCIDE: THE HOLOCAUST

Holocaust—"wholly burnt offering; wholesale sacrifice or destruction esp. by fire"

(Shoah 1985)

Early in the twenty-first century, the study of genocide—the "deliberate extermination of a race, nation"—takes us back to history, and to current examples of mass killings and mass rapes. The liberal image of law-making and dispute-resolution stands to one side in such studies, as mass killings of vulnerable populations occur. Recently, there have been examples of genocide. In Rwanda, in just over three months in 1994, upward of 800,000 members of the Tutsi minority were massacred by members of the Hutu majority (Africa). The atrocities included torture, rape, and even desecration of religious "votive statues" (Gourevitch 1995). Other examples of genocide include Bosznia-Hertogovenia. This section explores examples of genocide, focusing on the World War II Holocaust and the aim of exterminating European Jews. This took the form of mass deception, use of lethal technology, and reflected deep roots of anti-Semitism in western societies. The United Nations defined genocide in the context of eradication of "national, ethnical, racial or religious group[s]", listing the following forms of genocide: murder, serious physical or mental injury, policies to limit births, and "forcibly transferring children of the group to another group" (see Bischoping and Fingerhut 1996, p. 483). Genocide is thus many-faced, associated with murder, but also with social and cultural decimation.

It has been estimated that six million European Jews were killed during the Holocaust, including four million killed in concentration camps (Bauer 1982, 204). This total includes an estimated two-thirds of all European Jews, and approximately one-third of the Jewish population of the world. Raul Hilberg sets the most conservative estimate by Holocaust historians at 5.1 million Jewish deaths (see Marrus 1987, 199–200). Dawidowicz (1986, xxxvii) draws an analogy to the destruction of the Jews in WWII as a sacrificial offering, a terrible event that hardly stands alone, but can be connected with persecution centuries earlier. Hitler's *Mein Kampf* was published in 1925, and a second version published in 1926. One passage of *Mein Kampf* presents his belief that if 12,000 to 15,000 "Hebrew corruptors of the people" had been poisoned with gas, "the sacrifice of millions [of German soldiers] at the front would not have been in vain" (see Dawidowicz 1986, 3–5). These anti-Semitic texts are often oblique and dishonest, prompting Marrus (1987, 33) to refer to "euphemistic language" associated with the final solution.

Dawidowicz (1986, ch. 3) traces anti-Jewish legislation between 1933 and 1945. When Hitler took the oath of office on January 30, 1933 a plan was set in motion to undermine the oath, including constitutional protections and democratic laws (p. 448). Voting behaviours were replaced by "mass meetings" and pluralism and discussion lost in the mix of nationalism, anti-Semitism, and militarism (pp. 49–50). Following the burning of the Reichstag building on February 27, Hitler established a number of emergency decrees. The decrees "suspended all fundamental freedoms of speech, press, assembly, freedom from invasion of privacy (mail, telephone, telegram) and from house search without warrant. They gave the federal government the power to take over the state governments as needed to restore public security, and they imposed the death penalty—in place of life imprisonment—for treason, arson, railroad sabotage ... Another set of decrees dealt with high treason, in a manner so deliberately ill-defined as to cover every possible form of dissidence, including the publication and dissemination of certain forms of printed matter" (Dawidowicz 1986, 50).

As part of a coalition government, Hitler's National Socialist party sought to pass an Enabling Act. This act allowed for emergency legislation, without approval of the Reichstag, for a limited period of time. The Act was passed on March 23, 1933. On July 14, any appearance of pluralist politics vanished with the decree that the NSDAP was the sole political party in Germany: those seeking to remain in, or initiate a rival party could face three years' imprisonment (Dawidowicz 1986, 52). These legislative changes were followed by mass expulsion of Jews from the legal profession, the judiciary, journalism, and the universities (p. 54). Even a protest from Hindenburg on April 4, 1933 was denied by Hitler, citing the damage caused by "the Jewish presence in public life and the professions" (p. 55). The point here is that legislation interacted with informal acts of violence against German Jews. Every civil servant was obliged to provide documentation of racial descent, with a view to eliminating non-Aryans from public life (p. 59). The 1935 Nuremburg Laws were adopted unanimously on September 15, 1935 (by the Reichstag): these laws required that intermarriage between a Jew and non-Jew be brought to the attention of the NSDAP, in order to allow the couple to review their decision (p. 63). The *Mischlinge* category ("mixed blood") was designed so that anyone who was 1/16 Jewish, e.g., one Jewish great-great-grandparent, would be considered of German blood (see Dawidowicz 1986, 68–69).

Dawidowicz (1986, ch. 4) sees the S.S. as the key force behind the Final Solution. (S.S. stands for *Schutzstaffel* [Defence Corps]). Bauer (1982, 169) writes that Jewish ghettos served a slavery function; that is, supplying workers for various aspects of the war effort. Ghettos such as the Warsaw ghetto were overcrowded, particularly as Jewish refugees emigrated to these isolated sectors of European cities. Bauer (1982, 170) notes that many ghetto residents died of starvation or from diseases that were exacerbated by malnourished, overcrowded, unhygienic situations. Underground organizations arose within the ghettos, some with the objective of social welfare or preservation of religious rituals that were outlawed; other organizations aimed for direct resistance against the German troops and collaborators. It is important to consider the scale of genocide. In wartime Greece, for example, Jewish firms and property were misappropriated. Jews were made to work at forced labour under 1942 legislation. Deportation of Jews began in 1943, following ghettoization of some Jews. Up to 45,000 Jews were deported from Salonika. Most of the 60,000 Jews deported from Corfu, Athens, Crete, Rhodes and elsewhere were sent to Auschwitz (see Dawidowicz 1986, 393–94).

Dawidowicz (1986, 396–97) traces three key periods in the Final Solution as implemented in wartime Poland: (1) Expulsion of the Jews from many Polish territories (except Lodz), and their concentration in larger cities. This involved isolation of Jews from Poles, with provision for special identification, forced labour, smaller food rations than non-Jewish Poles, etc.; (2) Ghettoization—such as the Lodz and Warsaw ghettos (1940); (3) Liquidation—including the death camps (Chelmno, Belzec, Treblinka).

Hilberg (1961, 5) draws a parallel between canonical measures (Church law) and various decrees and measures under the Nazis. Such laws as the Protection of German Blood and Honor (1935) are mirrored in prohibitions of intercourse and intermarriage between Jews and Christians, in the Synod of Elvira, 306 B.C. Other examples of canonical law include forbidding Christians to "patronize Jewish doctors" (692 B.C.), forbidding Christians from living in Jewish homes (1050 B.C.), marking of Jewish clothing with badges (1215), and a ban on construction of new synagogues (Council of Oxford, 1222). Consider the order from Heydrich to Goring, 1938, to destroy all synagogues in the Reich (Hilberg 1961, 5).

Hilberg (1961, 567) draws our attention to industrial interests in the annihilation of the Jews. Private factories manufactured Zyklon B (hydrogen cyanide), a product that was viable only for three months after manufacture. Hilberg (1961, 1) connects the final solution with 12 centuries of anti-Jewish policies, starting in the fourth century B.C. Church laws forbade intermarriage (of Jews and Catholics), prohibitions on Jews holding public office, and the Talmud was burned (Hilberg 1961, 2). Jews were rarely converted to Christianity however. The failure of the first anti-Jewish policy (conversion) led to the second policy (expulsion, in England, France, Germany, Spain, Italy, from the 1400s through the 1700s). The third anti-Jewish policy (annihilation) began in 1941, with the formulation of the "final solution" in the context of what Hilberg (1961, 3) calls German involvement in "a total war." Laqueur's book *The Terrible Secret* (1980) traces how news of the death camps and extermination of ghetto residents was known three years prior to the ghastly revelations by western journalists and soldiers at Bergen-Belsen in April 1945. Eyewitnesses who had escaped from Poland and other regions testified to these atrocities as early as 1942. News was leaked to the English-speaking world.

Abella and Troper's *None Is Too Many* (1983) chronicles immigration policy in Canada. The title of the book is taken from a conversation in 1945 between Canadian journalists and a government official. Asked how many Jews might be brought to Canada, he replied: "None is too many" (Abella and Troper 1983, v). The efforts of the Canadian Jewish Congress and Jewish Immigrant Aid Society to dramatize the tragedy often fell on deaf ears in Canada. In the Bermuda conference of 1933, Canadian officials, including Lester Pearson, did not attend. Closer to home, Abella and Troper (1983, vi) draw our attention to barriers facing European Jews seeking to emigrate to Canada: less than 5,000 Jews successfully emigrated to Canada between 1933 and 1945, compared with Argentina (50,000), Brazil (27,000), and the U.S.A. (200,000). Between 1933 and 1945, even as the Jews faced escalating repression and the eventual implementation of the "final solution" (genocide), Canada's record of admitting Jewish refugees was, arguably, "the worst" of all nations that were in a position to accept them (Abella and Troper 1983, v). Canada admitted only 5,000 Jews between 1933 and 1945, under an implacable doctrine that rejected almost all Jewish applicants.

Today, these historical legacies of racial discrimination and anti-Semitism in Canada (see Bolaria and Li 1988) have not been forgotten. We can look to official policies by the federal government favouring multiculturalism in Canada, and to attempts by governments to redress some of the more shocking examples of racism and anti-Semitism. Actions by the Crown and by school boards have been taken against some individuals who have denied that the European Holocaust before and during World War II took place. For example, Jim Keegstra, formerly a high school teacher in Alberta (Appelbaum 1985, 7; Bercuson 1985), was charged with the wilful promotion of hatred, under section 319 of the Canadian Criminal Code. In New Brunswick, school teacher Malcolm Ross was relieved of teaching duties following complaints after he published material alleging that the Holocaust had not occurred, and in Toronto, Ernst Zundel, who had also denied the existence of the Holocaust (Weimann and Winn 1986, 19–20), was convicted on the criminal charge of "spreading false news," under section 181 of the Canadian Criminal Code. Such examples can be seen as a signal by governments that extreme forms of anti-Semitism will not be tolerated. Financial compensation and an official apology to Japanese Canadians interned during the Second World War (1991) can be seen as another example of a more tolerant outlook in Canada.

Bischoping and Fingerhut (1996) explore several examples of genocide, using the cases of the Mayan people, the Tasmanians, Cambodia, and others, and then linking these examples with the WWII Holocaust. There are many other examples of conflicts between different races, faith communities, and nationalities. The territorial conflict between Israel and Palestine has generated concerns about the living conditions of the Palestinians. David Grossman's *The Yellow Wind* (1988) and Amy Wilentz' *Martyrs' Crossing* (2001) testify to the hatred that festers under occupation, especially the damage to children.

SUMMARY

Conflict between racial groups challenges the validity of what some see as a fictionalized social contract in given societies. This chapter has attempted to show that despite formal measures to ensure racial equality in law and society, scapegoating of minorities, especially visible minorities, has a long tradition in Western societies and elsewhere. The white hegemonic domination of politics has been slow to react to the situation of minorities. The legacy of colonization, and of more modern patterns of immigration in some societies is not easily transformed in modern political economies. Kobayashi (1995) is not optimistic about changes to the refugee determination process, such that female applicants' dire situations might be reconsidered and reframed as gendered victimization. Again, we should stress the importance of a dialectical approach that allows for changes in laws and state policies, along with changes in society. Thus, while legal changes are important in antidiscrimination struggles, changes in culture are also very important as far as racial tolerance, and actual improvements (or worsening of) standards of living for racial groups are concerned.

We should keep in mind that racially-based policies meet with resistance, and that not all members of affected groups are silent or passive. Resistance takes many forms, including boycotts, blockades, and writing. This is true of many racial and ethno-cultural groups, including Indo-Canadians and Indo-Americans (Baldwin 1999, Dulai 1995, Pal 1998), and black writers of African and Caribbean descent (Sarsfield 1997, Woods 1990).

Stereotyping and prejudice have been identified as aspects of racism, and also dislike directed toward identifiable ethno-cultural or national groups who are not regarded as "of colour." Ursula Hegi, for example, chronicles some difficulties of German-Americans living through the legacies of the Holocaust and world wars (1998). The experiences of Italian immigrants to Canada and their descendants have documented racial prejudice and patterns of discrimination, and also resiliency of Italian-Canadians in various communities (Iacovetta 1992; Iuele-Colilli 2000). One of the most criticized legal enactments in Canada in this century was the internment of Japanese Canadians during the Second World War. By 1943, it was estimated that over 12,000 adults and children of Japanese descent were kept in internment camps, officially sugar-coated as "interior settlements" (Adachi 1991). The financial losses and general strain of internment have been well documented in autobiographical accounts and fiction (Miki and Kobayashi 1991, Schipper 1994). In 1988, the Canadian government issued an apology for the internment decision, and financial compensation was offered to those who had endured the evacuation and financial losses.

Contemporary concerns have centred on Canadian immigration policies and reception of first-generation immigrants. Again, there are sharp divisions of opinion here, with some arguing for more controlled immigration policies, reducing the annual number of immigrants, and tightening security and screening procedures. For others, immigration policies are problematic and biased. Jakubowski (1999) brings forward the case-in-point of India. She recounts the tension within the British Empire, between Canadian and Indian authorities in the early twentieth century. This took the form of pressures to allow Indian applicants to immigrate to Canada, and counter-pressures to adhere to a "White Canada" population profile (1999, 100–03). Canadian authorities devised the Continuous Journey

Stipulation (1908) that gave officials discretion to refuse admission to prospective immigrants if they did not take a "continuous journey" to Canada, with what were known as "through tickets" purchased in their country of origin. Jakubowski adds that only the Canadian Pacific Railway Company was able to issue these tickets, and the CPR was instructed by the Canadian government to not sell through tickets (1999, 103). The result was a palpable drop in immigration from India; specifically, from nearly 4,800 immigrants in 1907 and 1908, to only six in 1909 (ibid). Her overall approach is to expose the gap between liberal ideals and political practices in immigration. This involves an appreciation of three interrelated approaches—"capitalism, liberal democracy, and multiculturalism"—that must be considered in securing the state's legitimacy. This is accomplished, in part, by covert official discourses that are presented as just and reasonable, while preserving some discriminatory practices (Jakubowski 1999, 113–14). This disguised approach has also been identified with initiatives to deter American blacks from immigrating to Canada, using such pretexts as medical grounds (Henry et al. 1995, 65–66).

We are witnessing a broad-based movement to achieve equality in law, and in social life generally, by many groups that have long been placed on the margin. Young (1990, 122–23) draws our attention to struggles by disabled people, blacks, Hispanics, Asians, and women to achieve a full measure of legal and social equality. As set out in this chapter, however, there remain many structural barriers—including hiring practices, and limits of legal reforms—that impede these efforts against racial discrimination. Focusing on the issue of racial discrimination and the law allows us to address the key aspects of the ideal liberal-democratic state: equality before the law, equality of opportunity, and fair treatment of people regardless of racial origin.

STUDY QUESTIONS

1. Contrast the perpetrator perspective and the victim perspective, in the context of Freeman's (1982) essay on U.S. antidiscrimination law

2. What parallels can be drawn between legal measures and social policies directed against Aboriginal peoples in Canada (see Chapter Five), Australia, and the South Pacific. How have social movements and legal enactments altered the balance of power between aboriginal and non-aboriginal people? Use specific examples from the course readings and outside sources.

3. Canada is frequently portrayed as a pluralistic country, welcoming different races, faiths, and political beliefs. Discuss ways in which laws have been used to meet this liberal-pluralist ideal, and ways in which laws have contradicted this ideal.

4. Critically discuss the merits of using law to reverse patterns of racial discrimination. Use the Viola Desmond case as a starting point. What other examples—historical or contemporary—can you think of as successful or unsuccessful efforts to address racial discrimination?

REFERENCES

Abella, I., and H. Troper (1983) *None Is Too Many: Canada and the Jews of Europe, 1933–1948*. Toronto: Lester & Orpen Dennys.

Adachi, K. (1991) *The Enemy That Never Was: A History of the Japanese Canadians*. Toronto: McClelland and Stewart.

Angelou, M. (1988) "'There's No Place to Go But Up': A Conversation between Maya Angelou and bell hooks." *Shambhala Sun* 6(3): 16–20.

Appelbaum, I. (1985) "The Keegstra Case." *The Canadian Forum* 65 (749), 7–15.

Backhouse, C. (1999) "'Bitterly Disappointed at the Spread of 'Colour-Bar Tactics': Viola Desmond's Challenge to Racial Segregation, Nova Scotia, 1946." In C. Backhouse, *Colour-Coded: A Legal History of Racism in Canada, 1900–1950*, 226–71. Toronto: University of Toronto Press.

——. (1999a) "Introduction." In C. Backhouse, *Colour-Coded: A Legal History of Racism in Canada, 1900—1950*, 1–17. Toronto: University of Toronto Press.

——. (1999b) "Race Definition Run Amuck: 'Slaying the Dragon of Eskimo Status' in Re Eskimos, 1939." In C. Backhouse, *Colour-Coded: A Legal History of Racism in Canada, 1900–1950*, 18–55. Toronto: University of Toronto Press.

——. (1999c) "White Female Help and Chinese-Canadian Employers: Race, Class, Gender, and Law in the Case of Yee Clun." In *Law in*

Society: Canadian Readings, edited by N. Larsen and B. Burtch, 3–22. Toronto: Harcourt Brace Canada.

Baldwin, S. (1999) *English Lessons and Other Stories*. Fredericton: Goose Lane Editions.

Bales, K. (1999) *Subjugation and Bondage: Critical Essays in Slavery and Social Philosophy*. Lanham: Rowman and Littlefield.

Bauer, Y. (1982). *A History of the Holocaust*. New York: Franklin Watts.

Bercuson, D. (1985) *A Trust Betrayed: The Keegstra Affair*. Toronto: Doubleday.

Bischoping, K. and N. Fingerhut (1996) "Border Lines: Indigenous Peoples in Genocide Studies." *Canadian Review of Sociology and Anthropology* 33: 481–506.

Bolaria, B., and P. Li (1988) *Racial Oppression in Canada* (2nd edition). Toronto: Garamond Press.

Bond, J. (1987) *Eyes on the Prize: America's Civil Rights Years*. New York: Viking.

Cashmore, E. (1994) *Dictionary of Race and Ethnic Relations* (third edition). London: Routledge.

Comack, E. (1986) "'We Will Get Some Good out of This Riot Yet': The Canadian State, Drug Legislation and Class Conflict." In *The Social Basis of Law: Critical Readings in the Sociology of Law*, edited by S. Brickey and E. Comack, 67–89. Toronto: Garamond Press.

Dawidowicz, L. (1986) *The War against the Jews: 1933–1945*. New York: Bantam Books.

Delgado, R., and J. Stefancic, eds. (2000) *Critical Race Theory: The Cutting Edge*. Philadelphia: Temple University Press.

Dulai, P. (1995) *Ragas from the Periphery*. Vancouver: Arsenal Pulp Press.

Edwards, W. (1981) "Civil Rights, Affirmative Action: An Incomplete Agenda." In *Pluralism, Racism, and Public Policy: The Search for Equality*, edited by E. Clausen and J. Bermingham, 83–113. Boston: G.K. Hall.

Ellis, W. (1986) "A Way of Life Lost: Bikini." *National Geographic* (June): 813–34.

Feldman, A. (2000) "Othering Knowledge and Unknowing Law: Oppositional Narratives in the Struggle for American Indian Religious Freedom." *Social and Legal Studies* 9(4): 557–82.

Foley, M. (1984) "Aborigines and the Police." In *Aborigines and the Law*, edited by P. Hanks and B. Keon-Cohen, 160–90. Sydney, Australia: George Allen and Unwin.

Fredrickson, G. (1981) *White Supremacy: A Comparative Study in American and South African History*. Oxford: Oxford University Press.

Freeman, A. (1982) "Legitimizing Racial Discrimination through Antidiscrimination Law: A Critical Review of Supreme Court Doctrine." In *Marxism and Law*, edited by P. Beirne and R. Quinney, 210–35. New York: John Wiley & Sons.

Gould, S. (1981) *The Mismeasure of Man*. New York: W.W. Norton.

Gourevitch, P. (1995) *We wish to inform you that tomorrow we will be killed with our families: Stories from Rwanda*. New York: Farrar Straus & Giroux.

Grossman, D. (1988) *The Yellow Wind*. Translated by Haim Watzman. Toronto: Collins.

Hagan, J., and C. Albonetti (1982) "Race, Class, and the Perception of Criminal Injustice in America." *American Journal of Sociology* 88 (2): 329–55.

Hall, M. (2000) "The Liability of Public Authorities for the Abuse of Children in Institutional Care: Common Law Developments in Canada and the United Kingdom." *International Journal of Law, Policy and the Family* 14(3): 281–301.

Hegi, U. (1998) *Tearing the Silence: On Being German in America*. New York: Touchstone Books.

Henry, F., C. Tator, W. Mattis and T. Rees (1995) *The Colour of Democracy: Racism in Canadian Society*. Toronto: Harcourt Brace & Co. Canada.

Hilberg, R. (1961) *The Destruction of the European Jews*. Chicago: Quadrangle Press.

Hill, L. (2001) *Black Berry, Sweet Juice: On being black and white in Canada*. Toronto: HarperFlamingo Canada.

Iacovetta, F. (1992) *Such Hardworking People: Italian immigrants in postwar Toronto*. Montréal /Kingston: McGill-Queen's University Press.

Iueli-Colilli, D. (2000) *Italian Faces: Images of the Italian Community of Sudbury/Volti italiani: Immagini della comunità di Sudbury*. Welland, Ont.: éditions Soleil publishing inc.

Jakubowski, L.M. (1999) "'Managing' Canadian Immigration: Racism, Ethnic Selectivity, and the Law." In *Locating Law: Race/Class/Gender Connections*, edited by E. Comack, 98–124.

Keeshig-Tobias, L. (1997) "Stop Stealing Native Stories." In B. Ziff and P. Rae (eds.), 71–73. *Borrowed Power: Essays in Cultural Appropriation*. New Brunswick, N.J.: Rutgers University Press.

Kelsey, J. (1995) "Restructuring the Nation: The Decline of the

Colonial Nation-State and Competing Nationalisms in Aotearoa/New Zealand." In *Nationalism, Racism and the Rule of Law,* edited by P. Fitzpatrick, 177–94. Aldershot: Dartmouth Publishing.

Kobayashi, A. (1995) "Challenging the National Dream: Gender Persecution and Canadian Immigration Law." In *Nationalism, Racism and the Rule of Law,* edited by P. Fitzpatrick, 61–73. Aldershot: Dartmouth Publishing

Lanzmann, C. (1985). *Shoah: An Oral History of the Holocaust.* New York: Pantheon Books.

Laqueur, W. (1980). *The Terrible Secret: Suppression of the Truth about Hitler's 'Final Solution.'* New York: Little, Brown and Co.

Lauren, Paul (1996) *Power and Prejudice: The Politics and Diplomacy of Racial Discrimination* (second edition). Boulder: Westview Press.

Li, P. (1988) *The Chinese in Canada.* Toronto: Oxford University Press.

Ligertwood, A. (1984) "Aborigines in the Criminal Courts." In *Aborigines and the Law,* edited by P. Hanks and B. Keon-Cohen, 191–211. Sydney, Australia: George Allen and Unwin.

Lott, J. (1998) *Asian Americans: From Racial Category to Multiple Identities.* Walnut Creek, CA: AltaMira Press.

Lustgarten, L., and J. Edwards (1992) "Racial inequality and the limits of the law." *In Racism and Antiracism: Inequalities, Opportunities and Policies,* edited by P. Braham, A. Rattansi, and R. Skellington, 270–93. London: Sage Publications, in association with The Open University.

Marrus, M. (1987). *The Holocaust in History.* Toronto: Lester & Orpen Dennys.

Miki, R., and C. Kobayashi (1991) *Justice in Our Time: The Japanese*

Canadian Redress Settlement. Vancouver/Winnipeg: Talonbooks and National Association of Japanese Canadians.

Moorehead, A. (1974) *The Fatal Impact: An Account of the Invasion of the South Pacific, 1767–1840.* Harmondsworth: Penguin.

National Bureau of Economic Research (NBER) (1990) "Black Youths Aided by Tight Labor Markets." *The NBER Digest* (December): 1.

Nettheim, G. (1984) "The Relevance of International Law." In *Aborigines and the Law,* edited by P. Hanks and B. Keon-Cohen, 50–73. Sydney, Australia: George Allen and Unwin.

Pal, R. (1998) *pappaji wrote poetry in a language I cannot read.* Toronto: TSAR publications.

Pertschuk, M. (1989) *The People Rising: The Campaign Against the Bork Nomination.* New York: Thunder's Mouth Press.

Porter, J. (1965) *The Vertical Mosaic: An Analysis of Social Class and Power in Canada.* Toronto: University of Toronto Press.

Ranginvi, J.W. (1999) "Maori Sovereignty, Colonial and Post-Colonial Discourses." In *Indigenous Peoples' Rights in Australia, Canada and New Zealand,* edited by P. Havemann, 108–22. Toronto: Oxford University Press.

Postel, D. (2002) "Is Race Real? How Does Identity Matter?" *The Chronicle of Higher Education* 48(30): A10–A12.

Sarat, A., and T. Kearns (1999) "Responding to the Demands of Difference: An Introduction." In *Cultural Pluralism, Identity Politics, and the Law,* edited by A. Sarat and T. Kearns, 1-25. Ann Arbor: The University of Michigan Press.

Sarsfield, M. (1998) *No Crystal Stair.* Toronto: Stoddart.

Schipper, P. (1994) *Assimilation, Loyalty, and the Japanese of Canada, 1931–1948: A Review of the Historical Literature.* Unpublished M.A. Thesis, Department of History, Simon Fraser University.

Slaughter, M.M. (2000) "Contested Identities: The Adoption of American Indian Children and the Liberal State." *Social and Legal Studies* 9(2): 227–48.

Sowell, T. (2001) "Black and White Mischief." *The Sunday Times* (December 16), 10.

Vincent, M. (2001) "Toronto: A Global Village." *Canadian Geographic* 121(1): 54–55.

Walzer, M. (1983) *Spheres of Justice: A Defence of Pluralism and Equality.* New York: Basic Books.

Weimann, G., and C. Winn (1986) *Hate on Trial: The Zundel Affair, the Media, and Public Opinion in Canada.* Oakville: Mosaic Press.

Woods, D. (1990) *Native Song.* Porters Lake: Pottersfield Press.

Worsley, P. (1984) *The Three Worlds: Culture and World Development.* London: Weidenfeld and Nicolson.

Wilentz, A. (2001) *Martyrs' Crossing.* New York: Simon & Schuster.

Young, I. (1990) *Justice and the Politics of Difference.* Princeton: Princeton University Press.

7

Studies of the Judiciary and the Legal Profession

Equality of law has for a long time been narrowly interpreted to mean equality before the judge. In a society emphasizing services, it is inevitable that it should be expanded to mean equality of access to legal aid and advice.

(Aubert 1976, 17)

INTRODUCTION

Aubert's statement speaks directly to the need to ensure more than nominal justice where certain procedures are followed in the legal system. The ideal of equal access to legal information and legal representation has long been questioned. The link between society and the exercise of law is a central focus in the sociology of law. It follows that the profession of lawyering and the nature of the judiciary are important aspects of legal domination and legal reform. In this chapter, we will review several studies of the judiciary and the legal profession. One of our key themes will be the differences and conflicts between lawyering and judging as well as conflicts within the legal profession, including efforts to reverse some elements of professional privilege and to promote a more community-centred approach.

THE JUDICIARY

The courts are an integral, complex part of the justice system. To get a sense of the range of courts, we need only consider the criminal court network in Canada (Verdun-Jones 2002). Verdun-Jones begins with provincial or territorial courts, which are the point of entry for criminal cases. These courts may be divided into more specialized areas to deal with criminal, youth, or family matters (2002, 356). He notes: "All summary conviction offences are dealt with in the provincial or territorial courts, but whether an indictable offence will be tried there depends on the seriousness of the offence and, in some cases, on the choice of the accused person" (2002,

357). There are also provincial and territorial "superior court(s) of criminal jurisdiction," and also appeal courts, including the high-profile Supreme Court of Canada (2002, 357).

The judiciary is often presented as a bulwark against a totalitarian state or a complacent society, accustomed to the various injustices of everyday life. In the democratic tradition, the courts are ideally "above the law" and nonpartisan in deciding a multiplicity of legal cases. The judiciary is bound by requirements that they provide some justification for their decisions, and that they adhere to an objective approach in deciding legal cases (Wróblewski 1992, 13). Accordingly, "The decision, taken together with its justification, is presented as a rational act based on valid legal rules, on the facts accepted as established by a set of proofs, on interpretive agreements, etc." (ibid).

In keeping with the principles of judicial independence and the rule of law, the workings of the courts would seem to be free from outside interference. In his account of the civil courts in Upper Canada in the late eighteenth and early nineteenth centuries, Wylie (1983), however, concludes that the supposedly impartial administration of justice was, in effect, influenced by prominent merchants and by provincial government administrators. These two elites were united in their search for social and economic stability, and in their belief in the importance of British justice in establishing this stability. Both groups favoured the accumulation of wealth through land and trade policies for the elite as well as a stronger legitimation of the social structure of the day. Beyond this, however, Wylie (1983, 4) notes that there were strong differences in strategies to effect accumulation and legitimacy. The government administrators were more likely to rely on British-based administrative structures and policies, while the merchants lobbied against such an importation of structures and policies.

Wylie (1983, 9) documents how judges in Upper Canada dispensed with legal technicalities that were established in Britain. The use of notaries to launch a suit was not always practised in Upper Canada (where there were few notaries). Similarly, the requirement that commercial accounts have the testimony of a third party—usually a clerk—was often waived, since few frontier traders could afford clerks. Even legal terminology commonly used in Britain was altered for the sake of comprehension. Latin words might thus be translated into such phrases as "in debt" or "breach of agreement" (Wylie 1983, 9).

One source of conflict between judges, administrators, and merchants was the problem of delay in legal business. Wylie (1983, 28–35) identifies several sources of delay in legal proceedings. These included provincial geography and weather, the delays in formally entering a verdict, the centralization of procedures at York (now Toronto), a shortage of attorneys to complete the procedural work required for the courts, and so forth. For judges, adherence to proper court procedures, such as ensuring that defendants had been properly served, meant that court proceedings could be delayed. Merchants who acted as plaintiffs in such cases were thus faced with delays. Efforts to expedite court proceedings met with considerable resistance from court administrators who were concerned with maintaining procedural fairness for defendants.

Unlike the English Superior Courts, the Court of King's Bench in Upper Canada relied more extensively on juries to try questions of fact. This situation was further complicated by the limited number of assizes per year in Upper Canada. Only one circuit per year was held in all regions, whereas in England, two to three yearly assizes were common. Wylie (1983, 8) noted that these travelling (circuit) courts were not always relied on in the late eighteenth century in Upper Canada: *"...* the judges failed to take advantage of the provision permitting circuits around the district and met almost exclusively at Kingston. This practice effectively placed the machinery of justice out of reach of most rural settlers and reflected the limited horizons of the prominent residents of Kingston.... *"*

Wylie notes that there were swift calls for reforms to the Court to allow creditors to recover debts and to generally resolve civil matters. Although the efficiency of the King's Bench was eventually improved, it was not completely to the liking of the merchants. Nevertheless, the more influential merchants could survive the court delays, and there were other mechanisms for resolving economic troubles, most notably out-of-court settlements and greater access to credit (Wylie 1983, 36).

O'Malley (1988, 72–74) argues that analyses of judicial decision-making should take contradictions within the capitalist state into account. That is, instead of applying a simplistic theoretical analysis of links between the judiciary and powerful economic interests, it is important to consider the multiplicity of interests at play, including differences among capitalists as a whole. O'Malley stresses the importance of incorporating the concept of the relative autonomy of the state as a factor in judicial reasoning. The concept of historical specificity refers to nuances and variations within particular jurisdictions or locations, during specific historical periods. Historical specificity is used to render a more precise account of historical forces at play, rather than working toward a general theory of law, economy, or society. In capitalist societies, even though judicial procedures and decisions are largely congruent with capitalist economic and political interests, there is nevertheless a measure of autonomy exercised by judges in deciding cases (O'Malley 1988, 74).

Martin (1986) provides a critical assessment of the role of Canadian judges in the context of the Canadian Charter of Rights and Freedoms. The proclamation of the Charter has been hailed as a great advance for citizens' freedoms, and has been tied with "judicial activism" on a variety of social issues. Martin (1986, 210–15) makes a number of points against this celebratory approach to judicial activism, using the American experience of Supreme Court decisions in labour, welfare, and civil liberties cases. He notes that judicial activism in the United States was used against attempts to establish a mixed economy, that is, to balance the private-sector emphasis on individualism and market forces with public resources to fight racial discrimination, to establish a minimum wage and maximum hours of work, and to impose limitations on child labour. Second, Canadian judges are more likely to be influenced by Commonwealth case law and international documents such as the Universal Declaration of Human Rights (1908) than by the Charter. Martin's third point is that further reliance on the judiciary to set social policy only contributes to greater bureaucratization in Canadian society. Individuals become atomized in this process, and personal and traditional methods of conflict resolution are usurped by state authorities (i.e., the judiciary).

Martin (1986, 215–17) adds that the Canadian courts are largely shielded from public criticism and surveillance. The legacy of the courts has been "most dismal" with respect to modern social and political problems. The reasoning of Supreme Court decisions compounds this record: the written reasons are often unintelligible, lacking coherence for both professional lawyers and legislators, let alone the nonspecialist citizen.

Mandel (1989) also provides a critical look at the *realpolitik* of the Charter. His approach challenges romanticized views of the Charter and, more generally, the ostensibly democratic nature of the judiciary and other players in the legal system. Far from restoring a popular basis to legal decision-making in Canada, Mandel argues that the Charter has instead revived many of the inequalities that existed in the years before its enactment. Specifically, reviewing cases that have been brought forward for Charter consideration, Mandel (1989, 4) concludes that it has in fact "undermined" a variety of popular movements: the women's movement, aboriginal rights struggles, the labour movement, and the peace movement, among others.

Mandel also draws attention to the intricacies and the impenetrable logic of a number of Supreme Court decisions. Using the 1988 *Morgentaler* case for illustration, he points out that the course of appeals in this case has resulted in a variety of unanimous and split decisions between the Ontario Court of Appeal and the Supreme Court of Canada (Mandel 1989, 38).

The judiciary in much of the Western world has traditionally been a male preserve. In 1982, Justice Bertha Wilson was the first woman appointed to the Supreme Court of Canada (Martin 1986, 216). McCormick and Greene (1990, 63) estimate that, as of 1990, less than 8 percent of Canadian superior court judges were women; and of the provincially-appointed judges, women made up only 6 percent of the total. McCormick and Greene describe this as a "gross underrepresentation" of women. The history of court appointments confirms critics' charges that certain groups have been excluded from elite positions in the Canadian political structure. Mandel (1989, 43) refers to the survival of "class bias" in the legal profession and the judiciary, professions dominated by white, middle- to upper-middle-class males. McCormick and Greene (1990, 66–68) found that among Alberta judges, only 37 percent had fathers who worked as labourers or in agriculture. In contrast, approximately half of the Alberta judges had fathers who were lawyers, businessmen, or other professionals.

Judges are among the highest-paid public servants. There are approximately 800 provincial judges at the superior, county, and district court levels across Canada. Superior court judges earn over $140,000 annually, while justices with the Supreme Court of Canada earn over $166,000 a year (McCormick and Greene 1990, 14 and 16). It has been estimated that over 90 percent of court cases are heard in the provincial courts (excluding the appellate courts). McCormick and Greene (1990, 18) add that a substantial proportion of these cases involve criminal offences as well as a variety of provincial offences and other actions stemming from the federal Young Offenders Act.

Other commentors take a more optimistic view of the Supreme Court of Canada. Peter McCormick (2000) traces the increased power of the SCC in Canadian social and political life. He credits the court with earning considerable public support for its more influential role, and for its willingness to tackle extremely sensitive questions such as marriage law, abortion, pornography, First Nations issues, and equality rights for persons with disabilities (2000, Ch. 10).

Issues or race continue to surface around the judiciary. For instance, racial imbalance in the appointment of state and federal judges in the United States is a historical fact. In 1852, Robert Morris of Boston was the first black judge to be appointed in the United States. Nonetheless, few black judges were appointed during the next century. This trend was reversed somewhat by the gains of the civil rights movement in the 1960s and 1970s. As of 1990, 500 black judges were active at the state or federal level (Spohn 1990, 1196). At the higher levels of the U.S. judiciary, blacks and women remain underrepresented. Neubauer (1988, 171) shows that, of 300 state Supreme Court judges, only 0.6 percent were black and only 3.1 percent were female. At the federal Appeals Court level, these percentages increased to 16.1 percent black and 19.6 percent female (Neubauer 1988, 171). Neubauer (1988, 170) echoes other reports in his depiction of the homogeneity of the judiciary in Western societies. He finds that judges tend to be upper-middle-class white males with above average education.

Some research tends to contradict the argument that greater judicial representation of blacks is needed to counter discrimination against black defendants. Spohn (1990, 1209) studied sentencing decisions of black and white judges in Detroit and found that black offenders convicted of "violent felonies" tended to receive harsher sentences than white offenders, whether a black judge or a white judge sentenced them. Canadian research suggests that judges from working-class origins may be *less* sympathetic to workers than judges from upper-class or upper-middle-class backgrounds (McCormick and Greene 1990, 67).

Mandel (1989, 44–46) does not adhere to a static analysis of the judiciary. He refers to current changes in the style and objectives of the Supreme Court, including improvements in the writing of judicial opinions and in various means of communicating its decisions to the mass media and the public at large. Mandel (1989, 45) also points to greater access to lawyering and judicial hearings through increased government funding of certain legal challenges. For example, the Women's Legal Education and Action Fund (LEAF) has received $1 million from the Ontario government. LEAF has been involved in the litigation of test cases on behalf of women. These cases have exposed such issues as male bias in the conduct of sexual assault trials, the social context of sexual harassment of women, and employment-related discrimination against pregnant women (see Razack 1991).

Other concerns with the judiciary include the ways in which court structures that are ostensibly oriented toward "grass-roots" people—most notably the small claims courts throughout Canada—actually tend to service disputes brought forward, more often than not, by larger players, including collection agencies, large retail stores, insurance companies, and the like (see Olsen 1980). Hagan (1985) also points out that corporate actors, with their superior economic resources and social power, are more likely to obtain successful results when they initiate prosecutions. Hagan dubs this "the corporate advantage," which has often been applied to defend corporate property interests.

Zander (1980, 204–05) discusses some of the competing studies over the role of judges in lawmaking. While judges in most societies are drawn from a "relatively narrow social class"—primarily from executive, professional, or managerial backgrounds—there is some evidence that judges are not especially biased against workers' organizations, or in favour of management interests, as reflected in civil court actions in England. Zander (1980, 224–25) reports that judges have tended to move away from formalism and inflexibility in interpreting law, and toward a more considered, "active" stance in interpreting law. This shift leads to "a greater flexibility of approach and, in particular, an emphasis on principle rather than the rule and precedent and a noticeably greater inclination to talk about policy" (Zander 1980, 224). Abstract decision-making is thus under question, as social aspects of justice are brought into clearer focus. These aspects include social class, race, and gender but also the discrepancy between offenders' needs and social resources. Recently, the discharge of some offenders without provision for aftercare services has generated controversy in England (see Brindle 1991). Peay (1989, 231) draws our attention to the need to look more deeply into the social impact of judicial and quasi-judicial decision-making (e.g., in tribunals assessing mentally disordered offenders): "... legal safeguards are only likely to be effective in the context of adequate resource provision."

Michael Murphy discusses the reception of aboriginal rights claims in the Canadian courts. He agrees with the argument by First Nations leaders that self-government has not been surrendered, and that their "... normative authority claim is one of the main features which distinguishes the claims of Aboriginal peoples from those of cultural minorities such as new immigrant groups ..." (2001, 115). He refers to the 1990 *Sparrow* decision as a "watershed" in Canadian jurisprudence, including the finding that "... a strong burden is placed on the federal government to justify any legislation whose effect on [aboriginal people] is adverse" (2001, 119). Nevertheless, Murphy is critical of judicial decisions and federal government policies that do not reckon with the impact of colonial and postcolonial forces on Aboriginal life (2001, 128).

In 1991 a claim to Aboriginal right by the Gitksan and Wet'suwet'en of British Columbia was unsuccessful in the B.C. Supreme Court. The case took almost four years to hear, at an estimated cost of $25 million. The judge in this case concluded "... the discovery and occupation of lands of this continent by European nations, or occupation and settlement, gave rise to the right of sovereignty" (quoted in Dickason 1992, 354). Speaking generally of recent Canadian legal decisions concerning Aboriginal title, Bell and Asch predict that there will not be a substantial recognition of autonomy of Aboriginal peoples. Rather conservative judicial decisions help to preserve the status quo; as they put it, such a conservative approach "... allows one to empathize with the discriminatory treatment of Aboriginal people and at the same time declare helpless bondage to fundamental principles firmly established in the common law" (1997, 45). Empirical studies have been undertaken, including critical studies of special provision for sentencing of Aboriginals (see Stenning and Roberts 2001).

Morton and Allen (2001) review 47 appellate rulings linked with 21 cases of interest to feminists. They conclude that the Women's Legal Education and Action Fund (LEAF) was successful, more often than not, in pursuing these cases. Specifically, "Feminist claims prevailed in 72 percent of the cases" (2001, 57). Morton and Allen add that LEAF is the most prominent intervener in Supreme Court of Canada cases, and that it has received the most funding of any group under the Court Challenges program (2001, 56). They found that some cases were more successful than others, especially those involving pornography, family law, and discrimination in the private sector. Speaking of homosexual rights, Morton and Allen agree that the Egan and Nesbit case was a loss for the plaintiffs; however, in some ways it could be seen as a victory, since the Supreme Court of Canada "... unanimously agreed to add sexual orientation to section 15 of the Charter," and more recent cases involving discrimination against homosexuals have used *Egan and Nesbit* successfully (2001, 66). The changing role of the judiciary and the diverse interpretations of the politics of judging are also evident in assessments of the legal profession, to which we now turn.

THE LEGAL PROFESSION

The increased complexity of legal terminology and procedures in Western societies has contributed to the growth of the legal profession. In England, by the thirteenth century, the practice of laypersons representing themselves was gradually replaced by "technical pleading" by "narrators," a practice that in turn led to formal lawyering (Louthan 1979, 80). Worldwide, there is considerable variation in the nature of lawyering, with lawyers playing a less prominent part in business transactions and other work in Japan, for instance, than in North America. Moreover, the number of practising lawyers in Japan is low, compared with North America (Kidder 1983, 214–16).

Today, lawyering is considered one of the most prestigious and well-paid professions. Lawyers are often regarded as especially influential in seeing that justice is done through their legal practices, legal teaching, and involvement in virtually all sectors of political life. They continue to play a pivotal role in American political life, in local constituencies, Congress, state governorships, and even the presidency (Louthan 1979, 83). The overrepresentation of lawyers in government and corporate elites helps to secure their reputation as the most powerful of the professions in North America (Hagan, Huxter, and Parker 1988, 11). A dominant ideology of the legal profession is that it has evolved in the context of a "bargain" with the wider society. Thus, in return for the right to regulate itself as a profession, including restrictions on who may enter the profession and practise as a lawyer, the legal profession agrees to act in a manner consistent with clients' best interests and the good of society as a whole. Observers have criticized the contradictory nature of this ideology, particularly the gulf between social altruism on the one hand and privileged self-interest on the other (Fennell 1980, 10–11). Using the Law Society of B.C. as their focal point, Brockman and McEwen (1990) report that the ideal of professional self-regulation is undermined in practice. In B.C. telephone directories, for example, references to complaint procedures against lawyers were abbreviated in the yellow pages, and deleted in another directory, *The Pink Pages*. Lack of public awareness about the mechanisms for complaining about professional misconduct or incompetence is a large factor in reducing actual formal complaints against lawyers. Furthermore, other people who are regularly in contact with lawyers—other lawyers and paralegals—rarely avail themselves of complaint procedures, except as a last resort (Brockman and McEwen 1990, 10–13). Threatening or launching complaint procedures is often seen as unprofessional or unbecoming conduct within legal and paralegal occupations.

There is tremendous variation among lawyers with respect to income, status, power, and level of specialization. There is a gendered pattern of employment among Canadian lawyers, for example, concerning the kind of practice. Women lawyers are more likely to practice in government settings, while men are more likely to move into private practice. In Joan Brockman's study of 100 British Columbia lawyers, 90 percent of the men and 62 percent of the women were employed in "private firms" (2001, 57). Another gendered difference was the much higher perception of men's advantage over women in terms of career progress. Brockman reported that over 40 percent of women respondents believed men had such an advantage, with only approximately 15 percent of male respondents believing this (Brockman 2001, 59).

Galanter (1983) has coined the terms *mega-law* and *mega-lawyering* to refer to extraordinarily large legal practices. In the United States, for example, the 20 largest law firms in 1979 had, on average, 234 lawyers on their staff. Galanter (1983, 155) carefully traces a broad shift in the United States toward larger "units of practice," with a corresponding decline in small units. He also notes that, while mega-law is frequently linked with corporate clients, the expanding field of public law has also provided substantial work for these elite, large-scale firms. Mega-law firms are distinctive for the wide range of their practices, moving far beyond their headquarters to many regions of the United States, and throughout the world as well. These firms also do highly specialized work and use sophisticated technology for storing and processing information. Mega-law firms use expert advice routinely, whereas many smaller firms cannot afford such highly specialized consultants. Other studies have found differences in legal practices, with corporate lawyers working in a rather uncertain context with their corporate clients, in contrast to "personal plight" lawyers such as divorce lawyers, whose interaction with clients tends to be relatively short-term (Flood 1991, 67–68).

Studies of stratification in the American legal profession also emphasize the relatively narrow composition of elite lawyering. Kidder (1983, 217) notes that the typical elite lawyer is almost invariably male, and usually from a "White, Anglo-Saxon, Protestant background." He adds that most of these lawyers graduated from premier law schools, often with very high standing among their graduating class. Although they make up a small percentage of all practising lawyers, these corporate lawyers "dominate" professional bar associations, which, in turn, are responsible for regulating all lawyers within the state (Kidder 1983, 217). Researchers exploring the nature of lawyers' clientele, including business and professional clients, have questioned the ideal of lawyers' neutrality. For some, professional dominance and survival rested on strategies of exclusion of competing organizations and modifying state control initiatives over the legal profession. Baker's historical analysis of five law offices in nineteenth-century Montreal highlighted many ways in which such practices became dependent on business income for their own survival. Certainly, government-linked work and cases brought by private citizens were evident, but law firms' practices followed what Baker (1998, 175) calls "business ordering."

Porter's classic study of power and social class in Canada, *The Vertical Mosaic* (1965), provides a critical analysis of the structure of the Canadian economic elite. The book underscores the role of lawyers, inasmuch as certain corporate and business lawyers have played a facilitative role in "guiding corporations through the confusion of statute, judicial decision, and legal fiction" (Porter 1965, 277). Economic power was thus co-ordinated by lawyers, in conjunction with the technical and administrative sector of the Canadian economy and the directors of financial institutions. For Porter (1965, 276), the interrelationship of these sectors served to consolidate economic power. Porter (1965, 278) also addressed the links between lawyers, elite economic interests, and political life, noting that elite lawyers were often directly linked with either the Liberal or Conservative parties of the day; some had served as members of parliament or held some other political office. According to Porter (1965, 391–92), lawyers played a "prominent role" in the Canadian political system and had done so at the federal cabinet level since Confederation. Porter (1965, 392) concludes that the increased influence of lawyering represented "a further narrowing in the occupational background of the political directorate."

Gender and Stratification: Law Schools and Lawyering

In the nineteenth century, the practice of law in Canada was the exclusive province of men. Backhouse (1991, 293–94) observes that no women served as magistrates, coroners, or judges during most of the nineteenth century in Canada. The first woman who was called to the bar—Clara Brett Martin, in 1897—was also the "first woman admitted to the profession of law in the British Commonwealth" (Backhouse 1991, 293). The exclusion of women from law school was only a part of this scenario. Women were routinely discouraged from post-secondary education, or were shunted into areas of studies ostensibly more suited to their feminine natures, for example, into the arts and away from the sciences (Backhouse 1991, 299). Law-related matters were clearly seen as off-limits for women. Salvos of ridicule and derision were commonly directed at nineteenth century North American women who sought admission to legal practice or otherwise challenged the "naturalness" of law as a gentleman's profession.

Law schools in North America have seen a dramatic increase in the proportion of female to male students. Of all graduates of American law schools in 1980, about 30 percent were women (Seager and Olson 1986, section 23). Hagan (1989, 835) notes that in Western nations, between 30 and 40 percent of students enrolled in law schools in the 1980s were women. This contrasts with a figure of less than 10 percent a decade earlier. In Canada, women make up approximately half of the student population in law schools. Boyle (1986, 97) notes, however, that even though women are clearly in evidence in contemporary law schools in Canada, there is a tendency to instruct law students "as if women do not matter."

The increased enrolment of women in law schools is evident in data on first-year law school enrolments in Ontario. In the 1977–78 academic year,

31% of such first-year students were female, and this increased to 42.5% in 1986–87 (Mazer 1989, 120). This trend toward greater inclusion of women was leavened, for Mazer, by other concerns. A major concern is the under-representation of Aboriginal people—in 1981, it was estimated that only 70 of the approximately 34,000 lawyers in Canada were "of native ancestry." Mazer adds that law students continued to be recruited primarily from middle or higher socio-economic groups (1989, 122, 128). Returning to the experience of women in law school and legal practice, Mazer cautioned that the continuing masculinist ethos of commitment to the job, or "the firm," often made legal practice untenable for women seeking a more balanced life, e.g., women with family commitments (1989, 121).

Law schools in Canada have traditionally played a key role in legal training, since, almost without exception, those who wish to practise law must graduate from a university baccalaureate program in Canada (Gall 1983, 153). In the early 1980s there were very few part-time programs and no night programs available for those wishing to obtain a law degree (Gall 1983, 153). It has been pointed out that the dominant structure of university education is not well-suited to many women applicants, particularly single mothers. In general, women, more than men, are enrolled in part-time undergraduate studies in Canadian universities, and part-time students are at a "disadvantage" because they are considered for fewer sources of support, in the form of scholarships, bursaries, and fellowships, than full-time students (Dagg and Thompson 1988, 7). Historically, there have also been serious obstacles to women of colour entering the legal profession. The first black woman was admitted to the Ontario bar in 1960; and it was not until 1976 that a Native woman graduated from a Canadian law school (Backhouse 1991, 325–26).

More recent studies have also explored patterns of discrimination with the legal profession. Hagan and Kay (1999) combined two research studies: first, a "panel study" of over 1,000 Toronto-based lawyers in 1985 was conducted, with 815 of these same lawyers resurveyed in 1991; and second, the researchers surveyed over 1,500 lawyers who entered a law practice in Ontario between 1975 and 1990. Hagan and Kay thus base their findings on a relatively large sample, giving special attention to the experiences of women who are active in the legal profession as well as those who have left it. Hagan and Kay found that their women respondents held "a widely based perception" of bias against women with respect to "promotion and partnership" (1995, 80). Many women respondents felt that complaining about sexist discrimination was pointless, partly because it was so embedded and also because it can take quite subtle forms. Often lacking a mentor, and facing subtle and clearcut kinds of sex discrimination, many women become resigned to this scenario or, of course, leave legal practice altogether.

Legal practice often continued to be based on a male breadwinner model, with considerable commitment to the practice of law unencumbered by parental or volunteer responsibilities (Hagan and Kay 1995, 80–81). In keeping with the theme of corporatization of law practice, many respondents reported dissatisfaction with the sheer volume of work required to establish competency and for promotion within firms, especially "mega-firms." An even more common complaint among female lawyers was working within a masculine culture. One female lawyer put it bluntly: "No matter how much you achieve, it is discredited". Yet the most disquieting issue was the balance of "work and family demands" (1995, 161–62), especially when there was mounting pressure at home and at work. While a majority of both men and women surveyed reported fairly strong job satisfaction, and approximately three-quarters of both sexes would stay with their current job—if they had a choice—the 1991 panel of lawyers showed greater job satisfaction among the male respondents (Hagan and Kay 1995, 168–70).

Joan Brockman's recent study of 100 lawyers called to the Bar in British Columbia also explored gender differences and similarities. Exploring reasons why lawyers left positions, she found that both sexes "… gave similar reasons as to why they left their positions. However, the men were more likely to mention a falling-out (or that people were difficult to work with), that they were moving to a better position, or that they wanted more control over their work. The women were more likely to mention that they were looking for less stress (more balance), and the existence of discrimination …." (Brockman 2001, 57).

The teaching of feminist jurisprudence in Canadian law schools has received increased attention in recent years. Although the mandate of legal education goes well beyond ensuring competency among prospective lawyers, it may, in fact, be reproducing sexist patterns of socialization. These patterns are perhaps most visible in the legacy of hiring practices at Canadian law schools. Makin (1989, A1) reported that women constitute only 19 percent of law faculty across Canada. Moreover, the teaching of feminist theory and jurisprudence in Canadian law schools has become a very controversial area. In 1986, Sheila MacIntyre, a law professor at Queen's University, issued a memorandum to all members of the Queen's Law School outlining the disruptions and other forms of resistance by students and faculty toward a feminist perspective in legal training. In direct contrast to the ethos of collegiality among university faculty, the author referred to patterns of isolation, hostility, and discreditation of feminist discourse within law faculties. MacIntyre's memorandum directly addressed gender bias in law schools and the importance of teaching methods that dealt with actual relations of social inequality. The situation at Queen's University has been linked with a general backlash against feminism and the entrenched resistance to critical teaching, particularly in the area of feminist jurisprudence:

Power relations in law school may reinforce the inequality of women. Feminist professors can be targeted for abuse, and can come to believe that their problems are personal rather than institutional (Dagg and Thompson 1988, 71). In 1988, many people protested the decision not to appoint Professor Mary Jean Mossman as dean of Osgoode Hall Law School (Makin 1989). Dagg and Thompson (1988, 60–65) studied the professorate, administration, and student body of Canadian universities. They traced a substantial gap between anti-discrimination rhetoric among university administrations, and implementation of such policies as gender-neutral language and curricula or affirmative hiring practices. The authors found that feminist professors who are openly involved in feminist praxis risk losing tenure and jeopardizing their chances for promotion (Dagg and Thompson 1988, 72–73). The structure of peer review in promotion and tenure decisions can have a chilling effect on academic expression and community service. Dagg and Thompson (1988, 73) note that women are hired for nearly two-thirds of lecturer positions, whereas 93 percent of tenured full professors are men. The net effect of a male-dominated structure that is often hostile to explicit feminist teaching and research is to "jeopardize the career of young scholars who are committed to any but mainstream, conservative ideals" (Dagg and Thompson 1988, 73).

Law professor Christine Boyle describes the atmosphere of intimidation confronting women who wish to incorporate feminist materials into the law school curriculum (or other curricula): "The message is obvious—keep quiet and try to make the fact that you are a woman as inconspicuous as possible. I think more than twice about raising feminist issues in a classroom where there is a danger that I will be accused of incompetence, have my class disrupted by people to whom freedom of speech means their freedom to attack me through pornography, and have to work in a setting in which I cannot post a notice without it being ripped down or defaced" (Boyle 1986, 111). Concern over misogyny in university teaching has, however, resulted in changes that attempt to include feminist content in law schools. Boyle (1986, 106–07) provides several examples of implicit and explicit references to feminist materials in formal teaching situations as well as in more practical situations, such as legal aid clinics, where students must deal with the problems experienced by poor women clients.

McGlynn surveyed 81 law schools in the United Kingdom, with 75 (93%) providing information for her survey. Her findings raise cause for concern on many fronts. Ethnic minorities continue to be underrepresented in university departments generally, including law schools. In 1996—1997, such minorities constituted only 1.6 percent of male staff and 0.6 percent of female staff (1999, 69). Of the nine categories of academic staff surveyed—ranging from Dean and Department Head to fixed-term lecturer—women were in the majority in only one position, the junior position of fixed-term lecturer, and then with a bare majority of 51 percent (1999, 75). McGlynn puts this situation in stark perspective: in approximately three-fifths of institutions responding to her survey, there were *no* female law professors (1997, 76–77). She questions whether female law students can profit from situations where there are few female role models and mentors in research and instructional settings (1997, 87). She notes ongoing concerns over pay inequities and underrepresentation of women in more senior positions. Her research reinforces reports of marginalized status of women in university law schools in Canada, the United States, and Australia (1999, 72–73). Yet, on the other hand, she notes that women have become more prominent in such settings in recent years, and that this positive trend is even more pronounced in newer universities compared with more established ones (McGlynn 1997, 82).

In a thoughtful article, Sam Banks highlights the importance of using diverse examples and materials, both locally and from a cross-cultural perspective. She points out that many categories of people are virtually invisible—"women, women of colour, lesbians or disabled women"—in more abstracted forms of legal instruction. "It is not difficult to contemplate teaching law which integrates differing perspectives and thereby challenges the perception of law as a simple monolithic expression of social rules" (Banks 1999, 467).

Hagan (1989) explores the irony that, while lawyers espouse a doctrine of equal treatment within democratic societies, there are significant differences between male and female lawyers with respect to annual income and other factors. Building on earlier studies that documented substantial disparities in income between male and female lawyers—including Adam and Baer's (1984) research on Ontario lawyers—Hagan (1989) provides a comprehensive examination of a sample of practising lawyers in Toronto. According to the study, male lawyers reported an average income (before taxes) of $86,756, while female lawyers earned $44,210 on average (Hagan 1989, 838). Hagan also discovered that, while increases in specialization status for male lawyers resulted in substantial increments of income, "the comparable gain for women is small and nonsignificant" (Hagan 1989, 846). It was also noted that income varied dramatically with the kind of firm or employer. Male lawyers in managerial or supervisory positions in medium to large firms earned $84,000 on average, while male partners in small firms averaged $53,000. At the lower end of occupational mobility, substantial differences were observed for female lawyers. Hagan (1989, 847) puts it succinctly: "Women suffer most financially at the bottom of the mobility ladder, while men benefit most at the top." He concludes by noting that, while many women lawyers are earning substantially higher incomes than they would in less powerful work settings, these women are also experiencing greater *disparities* in earnings within the legal profession than they would in many other settings (Hagan 1989, 849–50).

In a major study of class structure and the Toronto legal profession, Hagan, Huxter, and Parker (1988, 9) report a tendency for women lawyers to be situated in "a legal working class." This tendency toward stratification between women and men in the profession may reflect the increased number of women in law schools and legal practice, women were still "significantly underrepresented" in more prestigious jobs such as management and supervisory positions, as well as in the role of small employer. The authors (1988, 31) conclude that, at present, "women are about twice as likely as men to be found in this combined 'underclass'."

Hagan, Huxter, and Parker (1988, 36) consider social class and ethnicity in their finding that Jewish lawyers were underrepresented in the capitalist class category of lawyers; that is, lawyers who participated directly in law firm decisions, and who had two or more levels of subordinates over whom they had sanctioning or task powers. The capitalist class lawyers worked in firms with 30 or more lawyers on staff. Less than 1 percent of Jewish lawyers in their sample fell into this category, compared with 8.4 percent of Anglo-Saxon lawyers. This finding corresponds with other studies documenting the underrepresentation of Jewish lawyers in elite firms in New York, Chicago, and Detroit (Hagan, Huxter, and Parker 1988, 36).

Hagan, Huxter, and Parker (1988, 51–52) acknowledge the complexity of these dynamics and traditional patterns of inequality along lines of gender and ethnicity. On the one hand, they assert that legal practice in Toronto continues to be dominated by older, white Anglo-Saxon males who have trained at the larger law schools, such as Osgoode Hall Law School and the University of Toronto Law School. On the other, they point to increased access to positions of power within the legal profession, for both women lawyers and Jewish lawyers. Nevertheless, recent research suggests that women continue to face difficulties in gaining their share of partnerships in the legal profession (see Hagan et al. 1991) and still constitute only a small percentage of professional bar associations (see Brockman, 1992).

Lawyers, Globalization, and Legal Socialization

Globalization may involve the attenuation of state programs and possibly violations of human rights (Halliday and Karpik 1997, 349). The global rearrangement also affects practices and philosophies in the legal profession. Halliday and Karpik (1997, 349–50) lament how studies of the legal profession are often limited to national studies, without little attention to transnational relationships. This national focus is unfortunate, given the historical movement of ideas and people, and the rise of globalization. Global forces may lead lawyers and legal firms to deviate from parochial outlooks and local practices, as they adopt a more standardized corporate outlook. Moreover, lawyers may have to contend with the contradiction of a liberal outlook on legal rights, and the power of market forces and business interests that may erode liberalism (1997, 368).

The value of legal aid services has however been compromised, according to some researchers. Abell's (1995) discussion of legal aid in Saskatchewan underscores the limitations of legal measures. She writes that

"Legal 'victories' are highly individualized and do not readily promote an independent powerbase. Instead, defining the problem legally can depoliti- cize the legal process, promote the idea that experts will solve the problem ... and do little to prevent the particular problem from recurring" (1995, 181). Abell argues that lawyers' socialization often promotes a hierarchy of authority and expertise, and promotes a case-based approach to legal issues rather than "redistributive notions of justice" (ibid). Legal aid was also lim- ited by the relatively low status accorded to legal aid work, high staff turnover, limited opportunities for training, and inadequate funding of legal aid services (Abell 1995, 183).

As law has developed in scope and intensity in modern times, the legal profession has also increased in numbers and diversity of work. Lawyers are often depicted as a monolithic interest group, with essentially similar training, income, work situations, and beliefs. The ideal of a homogeneous community of lawyers does not jibe with the very real stratification that exists within the modern legal profession. In practice, legal practitioners are subject to rivalry and competition from other lawyers; there are variations in the nature of their work (from general practice to highly specialized legal firms); and there are substantial differences in income and prestige, from relatively low-paid lawyers to "elite" lawyers (Cotterrell 1984, 195).

A number of sociological studies have confirmed discrepancies and con- tradictions between lawyers' idealized roles, and the roles they actually take on in advising clients, and in litigation. On the one hand, they are united in their dedication to clients (and the wider community) and their com- mitment to principles of justice; on the other hand, this dedication can easily be undermined by a variety of factors, including sheer economic necessity (Cotterrell 1984, 197), pressures of time, political factors, and so forth. Kidder (1983, 131–32) uses the American situation to illustrate the shortfall of consumer protection law (that is, its limited implementation and effectiveness) and the structural reasons affecting lawyers' unwilling- ness to use existing consumer protection laws. Despite the passage of the Magnuson-Moss Warranty Act in 1975, research in Wisconsin established that many lawyers were unaware of the Act two years after its passage. Moreover, there was often little monetary inducement for lawyers to become familiar with the provisions of this Act or to engage in time-con- suming litigation on behalf of consumers. Kidder (1983, 131) indicates that, under such circumstances, lawyers are likely to take on the role of *mediators* rather than initiate courtroom proceedings. The end result is often either a reluctance to become involved in consumer complaints or a very compro- mised legal approach that emphasizes mediation (Kidder 1983, 131).

Louthan (1979, 84) emphasizes the limits inherent in lawyers' practices. Legal socialization can result in a style of lawyering that is conservative. Pivotal to many decisions regarding public policy and the private sector, the "legal style" characteristically sets formal limits to how issues are framed and how resolutions are formulated. Louthan (1979, 87) is, however, aware of challenges to this conservative style of lawyering. He discusses the emergence of so-called "soft law" curricula including environmental law, Native people and justice, and poverty law. He cautions, however, that environmental law is constrained by a host of "legal niceties" and "legal technicalities," among them the courts' willingness to permit acceptable levels of polluting and the barriers to obtaining "standing" in such matters of public law (Louthan 1979, 90–91; see also Chapter Eight).

SUMMARY

This chapter has examined the nature of law schools, legal practice, and judicial decision-making within the area of sociolegal studies. A number of critical studies adhere to the liberal ideal of altruistically-minded lawyering and the impartial nature of judicial reasoning and judgments. We have noted the complexities of this issue: the variations among professional associations and the differences in the nature of legal practice in various jurisdictions.

The growth of critical legal studies has fostered renewed interest in ways of altering such structures as the curriculum of law schools and the composition of the law faculty so as to include those who have been expressly or tacitly excluded, especially women and racial minorities. This critical approach has generated considerable opposition, but has also led to initiatives such as inquiries into employment equity programs and provision for access to law school for groups who would otherwise be disadvantaged (for example, encouraging Micmacs and blacks to apply to Dalhousie Law School). The legal profession and the judiciary, no less than the structure of law itself, are beset by contradictions between legal operations and the realization of justice.

STUDY QUESTIONS

1. Liberal scholars may welcome the increased involvement of women in the legal profession in Canada. Review the structural barriers that have traditionally faced women aspiring to legal practice. What structural factors might impede women in completing law school, or in establishing a career in law?

2. The judiciary is, according to liberal-pluralist theory, an independent body that resolves competing claims or charges in a neutral, fair manner. Discuss the more critical premise that judges are in effect key players in maintaining unequal power relations in law and society.

REFERENCES

Adam, B., and D. Baer (1984) "The Social Mobility of Women and Men in the Ontario Legal Profession." *Canadian Review of Sociology and Anthropology* 21(1): 22–46.

Abell, Jennie (1995) "Legal Aid in Saskatchewan: Rhetoric and Reality, 1974–82." In *Social Policy and Social Justice: The NDP government in Saskatchewan during the Blakeney Years*, edited by Jim Harding, 173–220. Waterloo: Wilfred Laurier University Press.

Aubert, V. (1976) "The Changing Role of Law and Lawyers in Nineteenth- and Twentieth-Century Norwegian Society." In *Lawyers in Their Social Setting*, edited by D.N. MacCormick, 1–17. Edinburgh: W. Green and Sons Ltd.

Backhouse, C. (1991) *Petticoats and Prejudice: Women and Law in Nineteenth-Century Canada*. Toronto: The Women's Press.

Baker, G.B. (1998) "Ordering the Urban Canadian Law Office and its Entrepreneurial Hinterland, 1825 to 1875." *University of Toronto Law Journal* 38: 174–251.

Banks, N.K. Sam (1999) "Pedagogy and Ideology: teaching law as if it mattered." *Legal Studies* 19(4): 445–67.

Bell, C. and M. Asch (1997). "Challenging Assumptions: The Impact of Precedent in Aboriginal Rights Litigation." In *Aboriginal and Treaty Rights in Canada: Essays on Law, Equality, and Respect for Difference*, edited by M. Asch, 38–74. Vancouver: University of British Columbia Press.

Boyle, C. (1986) "Teaching Law As If Women Really Mattered, or, What About the Washrooms?" *Canadian Journal of Women and the Law* 2: 96–112.

Brindle, D. (1991) "Prison Psychiatric Care Crisis." *The Guardian* (Manchester), December 10: 1.

Brockman, J. (1992) "'Resistance by the Club' to the Feminization of the Legal Profession." *Canadian Journal of Law and Society* 7(2): 47–92.

———. (2001) *Gender in the Legal Profession: Fitting or Breaking the Mould*. Vancouver: University of British Columbia Press.

Brockman, J., and C. McEwen (1990) "Self-Regulation in the Legal Profession: Funnel In, Funnel Out, or Funnel Away?" *Canadian Journal of Law and Society* 5: 1–46.

Cotterrell, R. (1984) *The Sociology of Law: An Introduction*. London: Butterworths.

Dagg, A., and P. Thompson (1988) *MisEducation: Women and Canadian Universities*. Toronto: Ontario Institute for Studies in Education.

Dickason, O. (1992) *Canada's First Nations: A History of Founding Peoples from Earliest Times*. Toronto: McClelland and Stewart.

Fennell, P. (1980) "Solicitors, Their Markets, and Their 'Ignorant Public': The Crisis of the Professional Ideal." In *Essays in Law and Society*, edited by Z. Bankowski and G. Mungham, 7–26. London: Routledge and Kegan Paul.

Flood, J. (1991) "Doing Business: The Management of Uncertainty in Lawyers' Work." *Law and Society Review* 25(1): 41–71.

Galanter, M. (1983) "Mega-Law and Mega-Lawyering in the Contemporary United States." In *The Sociology of the Professions: Lawyers, Doctors and Others*, edited by R. Dingwall and P. Lewis, 152–76. London: Macmillan.

Gall, G. (1983) *The Canadian Legal System* (2nd edition). Toronto: Carswell.

Hagan, J. (1985) "The Corporate Advantage: A Study of the Involvement of Corporate and Individual Victims in a Criminal-Justice System." In *The New Criminologies in Canada: State, Crime, and Control*, edited by T. Fleming, 112–31. Toronto: Oxford University Press.

———. (1989) "The Gender Stratification of Income Inequality Among Lawyers." *Social Forces* 68(3): 835–55.

Hagan, J., M. Huxter, and P. Parker (1988) "Class Structure and Legal Practice: Inequality and Mobility Among Toronto Lawyers." *Law and Society Review* 22(1): 9–55.

Hagan, J., M. Zatz, B. Arnold, and F. Kay (1991) "Cultural Capital, Gender, and the Structural Transformation of Legal Practice." *Law and Society Review* 25(2): 239–62.

Hagan, J., and F. Kay (1995) *Gender in Practice: A Study of Lawyers' Lives.* New York: Oxford University Press.

Halliday, T., and L. Karpik (1997) "Postscript: Lawyers, Political Liberalism, and Globalization." In *Lawyers and the Rise of Western Political Liberalism*, edited by T. Halliday and L. Karpik, 349–70. Oxford: Clarendon Press.

Kidder, R. (1983) *Connecting Law and Society: An Introduction to Research and Theory.* Englewood Cliffs, New Jersey: Prentice-Hall.

Louthan, W. (1979) *The Politics of Justice: A Study in Law, Social Science, and Public Policy.* London: Kennikat Press.

McCormick, P., and I. Greene (1990) *Judges and Judging.* Toronto: James Lorimer.

Makin, K. (1989) "Feminist Content in Courses Stirs Debate at Law Schools." *The Globe and Mail* (December 26): A1–A2.

Mandel, M. (1989) *The Charter of Rights and the Legalization of Politics in Canada.* Toronto: Wall and Thompson.

Martin, R. (1986) "The Judges and the Charter." In *The Social Basis of Law: Readings in the Sociology of Law*, edited by S. Brickey and E. Comack, 207–24. Toronto: Garamond Press.

Mazer, B. (1989) "Access to legal education and the profession in Canada." In *Access to Legal Education and the Legal Profession*, edited by R. Dhavan, N. Kibble, and W. Twining, 114–31. London: Butterworths.

McGlynn, C. (1999) "Women, representation and the legal academy." *Legal Studies* 19(1): 68–92.

Morton, F.L. and A. Allen (2001) "Feminists and the Courts: Measuring Success in Interest Group Litigation in Canada." *Canadian Journal of Political Science,* 34(1): 55–84.

Murphy, M. (2001) "Culture and the Courts: A New Direction in Canadian Jurisprudence on Aboriginal Rights?" *Canadian Journal of Political Science* 34(1): 109–29.

Neubauer, D. (1988) *America's Courts and the Criminal Justice System* (3rd edition). Pacific Grove: Brooks/Cole Publishing Co.

Olsen, D. (1980) *The State Elite.* Toronto: McClelland and Stewart.

O'Malley, P. (1988) "Law Making in Canada: Capitalism and Legislation in a Democratic State." *Canadian Journal of Law and Society* 3: 53–85.

Peay, J. (1989) *Tribunals on Trial: A Study of Decision-Making Under the Mental Health Act 1983.* Oxford: Clarendon Press.

Porter, J. (1965) *The Vertical Mosaic: An Analysis of Social Class and Power in Canada.* Toronto: University of Toronto Press.

Razack, S. (1991) *Canadian Feminism and the Law: The Women's Legal Education and Action Fund and the Pursuit of Equality*. Toronto: Second Story Press.

Seager, J., and A. Olson (1986) *Women in the World*. London: Pluto Press.

Spohn, C. (1990) "The Sentencing Decisions of Black and White Judges: Expected and Unexpected Similarities." *Law and Society Review* 24 (5): 1197–1216.

Stenning, P., and J. Roberts (2001) "Empty promises: Parliament, the Supreme Court, and the sentencing of aboriginal offenders." *Saskatchewan Law Review* 64(1): 137–68.

Verdun-Jones, S.N. (2002) *Criminal Law in Canada: Cases, Questions, and the Code*. Toronto: Harcourt Canada.

Wróblewski, J. (1992) *The Judicial Application of Law*, edited by Zenon Bańkowski and Neil MacCormick. Dordrecht: Kluwer Academic Publishers.

Wylie, W. (1983) "Instruments of Commerce and Authority: The Civil Courts in Upper Canada 1789–1812." In *Essays in the History of Canadian Law*, edited by D. Flaherty, 3–48. Toronto: The Osgoode Society.

Zander, M. (1980) *The Law-Making Process*. London: Weidenfeld and Nicolson.

8

The Criminal Sanction in Canada

Even when a criminal act is certainly harmful to society, it is not true that the amount of harm that it does is regularly related to the intensity of the repression which it calls forth. In the penal law of the most civilized people, murder is universally regarded as the greatest of crimes. However, an economic crisis, a stock-market crash, even a failure, can disorganize the social body more severely than an isolated homicide.

(*Emile Durkheim*, The Division of Labour in Society)

INTRODUCTION

The power of criminal law is often presented as a public resource. As noted in Chapter Two, Durkheim presented repressive law (including the criminal sanction) as indispensable to societal functioning. In contrast to private law—in which specific actors may negotiate or litigate such issues as property rights, torts, and the like—criminal law is the quintessential exercise of state power, executed in the public interest. Criminal law was not always cast in this public light. Beattie (1986) outlines how criminal charges in England were for many years brought by private parties, and prosecution followed similarly private lines. In modern Western countries, however, the evolution of criminal law has meant a tremendous increase in the number of laws, charges, institutions, and officials entrusted with the police, the courts, and the edifice of corrections. There has also been an historical shift from privately initiated prosecution to a public bureaucracy of state officials, and more recently, many governments have taken a neo-liberal tack, privatizing some criminal justice services, including prisons.

Many writers have challenged the conventional definition of criminal law as a neutral, public resource. In general terms, they have argued that the application of criminal sanctions has been class-biased. This means that a variety of acts that cause substantial injury or other damage may be removed from criminal law altogether if such injurious acts are linked with powerful capitalist interests. Historically, this meant that powerful persons

were virtually immune from criminal charges. Chambliss (1982, 169) contends that criminal law in European societies has historically been applied
against the working class and other relatively powerless groups. For
example, police and prosecutors are frequently reluctant to lay criminal
charges (such as criminal negligence) against employers when workers are
injured or killed in the workplace (Reasons, Ross, and Paterson 1981;
Glasbeek and Rowland 1986). Another example of class bias is the use of
regulatory law against large firms for anti-trust violations (Smandych 1991)
or for extensive polluting practices (Schrecker 1989). The reluctance to use
criminal sanctions against these more "respectable" actors contrasts with
the widespread use of prison—or criminal charges in general—for people
who are more publicly visible and less powerful. This has led to the juxtaposition of "suite crime" (corporate crime, which is largely immune from
criminal sanctions) and "street crime" (Goff and Reasons 1978). Street
criminals are subject to greater public and police surveillance and have
fewer resources to contest criminal charges.

Conventional criminal studies examine crime and criminal law at state,
provincial, or national levels. New theoretical work brings in the workings
of globalization and transnational forms of crime. Findlay, for example,
presents globalization as a complex, paradoxical force which simultane-
ously constricts consciousness while allowing for diversity and new forms
of consciousness (1999, 2–3). He outlines many new forms of criminal
activity linked with multinational interests and globalization, and uses the
example of company security forces, including mercenaries, employed by
companies and government in Papua New Guinea (1999, 194).

For some groups, the use of criminal law can become much more of a
certainty. As discussed in Chapter Five, Native people face higher probability of arrest, conviction, and incarceration than the average citizen.
Native people have been much more likely to be incarcerated for public
drunkenness, for example (Hagan 1976), and both male and female Native
people are over represented in many prisons across the country (LaPrairie
1987). In 1991, a speaker at the Women and Law conference in Vancouver
stated that a spate of suicides by Native women at the federal prison for
women in Kingston underscored the discrimination this group experiences. Removed from their communities, they faced not only racism and
sexism, but also profound isolation. Other researchers have explored
degrading and debilitating experiences for women within prison, for
example, the loneliness, isolation, and essential uselessness of being placed
in segregation. Not only does segregation from the general population in a
women's institution carry personal consequences, but it is argued that such
isolation may be a means of silencing women, of blunting political protests
(see Martel 1999).

Significantly, critical theorists have pointed out that, while the use of
the criminal sanction against women warrants attention, changing control
tactics affecting women have permeated the wider society, as social control

becomes "less visible, and more effective" (Davis and Faith 1987, 173). The authors outline how poverty has become "feminized" in the United States, with men's incomes (on average) exceeding incomes for women. Despite a dominant ideology that celebrates women's political, economic, and social gains, Davis and Faith (1987, 175) point out that the majority of jobs women take are insufficient to support their families above the poverty line. Other researchers support this insight into the links between patriarchy, gender, and social inequality. Carlen (1988, 4–5) reports that, in England and Wales, lower-class women have, for decades, been more likely to be incarcerated than middle-class women. Furthermore, poor women from ethnic minorities are more likely to be imprisoned (Carlen 1988, 4).

Work on the sociology of law and gender has emphasized how various legal and cultural practices bolster a patriarchal ideology. Davis and Faith (1987, 176–84) point out that pornography, sexual assault, and prostitution are some of the factors that undermine egalitarian relations between men and women. Specifically, misogynist portrayals of violence against women in mass media are criticized for their "reaffirmation" of men's control over women. The authors also challenge various widely-held beliefs about sexual assault, including the minor nature of sexual assault, the disreputable status of women who are assaulted, and a "no-means-yes" denial by men of women's resistance to unwanted sex (Davis and Faith 1987, 176–79). The authors also suggest that female prostitutes face discrimination from police authorities, especially women of colour, who are most likely to be arrested and sentenced to prison (Davis and Faith 1987, 183). Criticisms of the 1984 Report of the Badgley Committee emphasize the patriarchal structure of our institutions in relation to child sexual abuse. Lowman (1985, 513) interprets the Committee's approach as incomplete, inasmuch as it treats child sexual abuse as an individual problem, and pays insufficient attention to the structural forces underlying sexual abuse of children. The Report is also criticized for failing to put such problems in a context of gender (i.e., most known offenders are male) or to discuss the patriarchal aspects of the supposedly benevolent state intervention in the lives of youth. Efforts to toughen prostitution laws have thus often been criticized, both for ignoring the structural factors that lead to prostitution and the sex trade generally, and for the palpable failure of many recent attempts to better regulate prostitutes (Larsen, 1999).

MURDER, CRIMINAL LAW, AND THE DEATH PENALTY

Murder is at the centre of public controversy over criminal penalties, including the abolition or restoration of the death penalty. Many scholars have confirmed that, while certain crimes are often associated with "the crime problem," especially crimes of violence, the staple of criminal law is the defence of private property. Nevertheless, in media accounts and popular writing, murder remains an object of intense controversy. Neil Boyd (1988) outlines several aspects of the phenomenon of murder, including the doubling of the homicide rate between 1966 and 1975 (1988, 4). He notes that, while some other countries have a higher rate of homicide—approximately four times greater for the United States than Canada—other countries such as Japan and Britain have approximately one-half the rate of murder as Canada (Boyd 1988, 4). Brantingham and Brantingham (1984, 132–33) report that, while homicide was a "rare" crime in Canada, there was a 121 percent increase in the criminal homicide rate between 1962 and 1975.

Even though North America has witnessed an increase in the rate of violent crime, including homicides, Boyd (1988) suggests that the character of these crimes has not changed markedly. In stark contrast to the sensational media images of serial murders or contract killings (in which the killing is premeditated), Boyd (1988, 9) concludes that murder in Canada is primarily unplanned and is prompted by a series of causes: alcohol or other drug use, domestic conflicts, and poverty: "Most murderers are basically ordinary people in socially and economically desperate circumstances. They were fuelled by alcohol or other drugs, and killed family and friends, usually over money or sexual betrayal" (Boyd 1988, 9). Boyd is not only concerned with the particulars of murder cases—he also addresses social policy for murderers. In keeping with other researchers (Fattah 1972; Hagan 1991, 219), Boyd (1988) argues that there is no established general deterrence function associated with the death penalty. Moreover, the use of lengthy sentences—especially the minimum 25-year sentence for first-degree murder—has not proved effective in deterring others or in rehabilitating offenders.

The nature of murder—and of violent crimes in general—is reviewed by Archer and Gartner in their award-winning book, *Violence and Crime in Cross-National Perspective* (1984). Using official measures to produce a Comparative Crime Data File on 110 nations, the authors provide valuable insight into how the nature of violent crimes has changed over time. Archer and Gartner (1984) provide evidence that, despite the popular notion linking high murder rates with cities, there is no convincing historical proof that murder rates have risen as cities grew in size. Reviewing four studies of Buffalo, Boston, and Philadelphia from the 1850s to the 1950s, Archer and Gartner (1984, 100) note that these cities experienced a "consistent decline" not only in murder rates but in rates of other serious crimes as well. A variety of other studies of national rates of murder in Australia, India, France, Germany, Sweden, and England confirm that homicide rates did not automatically increase as the population of major cities grew (Archer and Gartner 1984, 101).

A corollary to these findings is that rural areas—often conceived as low-crime areas—reveal quite high rates of homicide. Archer and Gartner (1984, 103) note that suburban and rural areas in America have higher homicide rates than small cities, and approximately the same rates as those in cities of 50,000 to 100,000 residents. The most important conclusion of the authors' longitudinal study of U.S. cities between 1926 and 1970 is that large cities had consistently higher rates of homicide than the national average for any given year (Archer and Gartner 1984, 108–9).

Social scientists have also explored the merits of the capital punishment debate in Canada and elsewhere. Boyd (1988) provides a clear argument against reinstatement of the death penalty in Canada. Other scholars have used the capital punishment debate to reconsider the value of the death penalty in terms of legal ideologies and social control. Archer and Gartner (1984, 120) note that sentiment in favour of the death penalty has increased in the United States in recent decades. They attribute this phenomenon to the rising crime rate, especially the homicide rate, which has increased dramatically since the mid-1960s (Archer and Gartner 1984, 120). Brantingham and Brantingham (1984, 132) also refer to a significant increase in violent crime in Canada since the 1960s. Between 1962 and 1975, for example, the rate for attempted murder increased by 460 percent; the rate for rape increased by 161 percent. The authors add that, while the rates of violent crime tapered off in the 1970s, they began to increase toward the end of the decade: "The 1980 rates for these crimes were the highest ever recorded" (Brantingham and Brantingham 1984, 132).

Many scholars criticize the argument that capital punishment is an effective deterrent to potential criminals. Research that attempts to show a positive relationship between the death penalty and crime deterrence has been criticized for serious methodological weaknesses (see Archer and Gartner 1984, 125). There is general agreement that the homicide rate does not change dramatically (either increase or decrease) whether the death penalty is abolished or restored (Archer and Gartner 1984, 129). Cross-national studies of 14 countries that have abolished the death penalty indicate that there is "little change" in the homicide rate in the short term after abolition (Archer and Gartner 1984, 132). In fact, these countries generally experienced decreased, rather than increased, rates of homicide (Archer and Gartner 1984, 136).

Comack (1990) takes a critical look at the implications of the capital punishment debate in Canada. Despite a history of Conservative party support for the death penalty, the capital punishment debate in 1987 was structured to defuse a "political crisis" facing the Conservative federal government (Comack 1990, 88–89). Even though the result—the rejection of the reinstatement of the death penalty through a free vote in the House of Commons—appears to be a victory for liberalism, Comack (1990, 94) suggests that such stellar displays of compassion obscure less visible political strategies, especially cutbacks in health and social services and increases in more repressive areas, such as criminal justice.

CORPORATE CRIME AND CRIMINAL SANCTIONS

Studies of the criminal law and criminal sanctions have broadened in scope in the past generation. Growing attention has been paid to the ways in which criminal laws are constructed and applied, with particular attention focused on the relative immunity of corporations and their employees from criminal prosecution. This new emphasis calls into question earlier formulations of the social contract and the social consensus that governs laws.

In Canada, it is well established that the Criminal Code has been enforced selectively. Brannigan (1984, 109) reviews Canadian studies of criminal sanctioning and concludes that the "slant" of laws produces a higher rate of conviction—and relatively severe sentencing patterns—for lower-class Canadians. He adds that the ideology of excusing illegal behaviour by corporations as merely "poor business practices" creates an imbalance in the application of criminal law. Goff and Reasons (1978) offer a critique of the excessive use of the criminal sanction against victimless crimes such as prostitution, gambling, and illicit drug use. They argue that these crimes should be decriminalized, whereas many corporate activities should be brought within the framework of criminal law. Goff and Reasons (1978, 14) note that large corporations, with their enormous concentration of resources and power, have little public accountability. Legislation that ostensibly would govern these corporations—including the first anti-combines legislation, passed in 1899—was weakened by the failure to permanently establish a federal enforcement agency to counteract illegal combines activity (Goff and Reasons 1978, 47). In more modern times, Goff and Reasons (1978, 59) observe that only a limited number of decisions were made against Canada's largest corporations between 1952 and 1972, and that there had been an overall reduction in the number of decisions against these corporations between 1966 and 1972.

In the United States, Edwin Sutherland's classic study, *White Collar Crime* (1949), documents extensive patterns of illegal and unethical conduct on the part of corporations. While more recent studies appear to present illegal and unethical conduct as part and parcel of American business practices, Chambliss (1982) provides a detailed account of corruption at all levels of American society, establishing a clear link between the ostensibly neutral systems of justice and politics and a wide variety of criminal activities. Chambliss (1982, 180) concludes that collusion and corruption are "as much a part of corporate business as they are a part of crime networks everywhere." The explanation for such collaborations among government officials and criminal networks stems from the profitability and efficiency such a network produces. Chambliss contends that crime networks linking "legitimate" businesses and government to such illegal activities as drug trafficking and gambling are evident not only in the United States but throughout Europe and other continents (Chambliss 1982, 183–89).

The use of regulatory and criminal laws to combat corporate crime is seen by many observers to be ineffective. Coleman (1989, 168–69) notes that some government agencies have improved their resources for investigating and prosecuting certain kinds of crimes and offences; however, in many cases, these agencies are simply understaffed. Interestingly, there appears to be a tendency to lay charges against "minor occupational offenders," while large-scale efforts involving complex, costly, and uncertain litigation may be disbanded (Coleman 1989, 169). Even when cases are brought before the courts, it is commonplace for American judges to accept *nolo contendere* ("no contest") pleas by defendants, which tend to reduce the stigma associated with the offence. The general finding is that white-collar criminals receive more lenient sentences than other criminals but some studies indicate mixed findings with respect to occupational status and criminal sentencing for white-collar crimes (see Coleman 1989, 171–72). It is important to bear in mind that few corporate crime cases even reach the point of criminal sentencing. A study in Wisconsin reported that of all sanctions for corporate crimes, only about 4 percent involved criminal proceedings. And for corporate executives who were convicted, "62.5 percent received probation, 21.4 percent had their sentences suspended, and only about one in four (28.6 percent) received short jail sentences" (Coleman 1989, 173). Glazer (1987, 201–03) found that *whistleblowers*—employees who publicly criticize their employers—are often subject to retaliation from their superiors. Promotions may be denied, they may be fired, or blacklisted from other employment.

Although criminal sanctions against white-collar criminals have proved ineffective, there are other options for prosecuting corporate offenders. These options include the civil suit, brought forward by individual victims, or the class-action suit, initiated by persons who share an identical or similar grievance. Coleman (1989, 170–71) outlines several obstacles to realizing these suits, including the considerable delays associated with some suits, recent restrictions that inhibit the impact of class-action suits, and some companies' reliance on technical declarations of bankruptcy to evade liability for dangerous products or working conditions. Coleman adds that while there have been considerable judgments brought against some corporations, civil actions "seldom result in just compensation for all the victims of a dangerous product" (Coleman 1989, 171).

The dreary record of successful prosecutions for corporate criminals has generated considerable interest in new forms of regulation. Some observers favour the use of the criminal sanction against corporate illegality that poses a serious threat to public safety or property. Others recommend a regulatory approach that does not pose excessive restrictions on what Frank and Lombness (1988, 91) call the "good apples," that is, organizations that comply with regulations.

Critical theorists have also explored ways in which licit drugs, including
alcohol, may be marketed. Howard Parker expresses concern over media-gen-
erated moral panics over substance abuse and youth, but also expresses concerns over the marketing of "alcopops"—relatively high alcohol content
"designer drinks" marketed for youth. While this could be seen as simply a
free market strategy, Parker points to underlying imagery "… whereby image,
strength and easy taste are all carefully blended into a blended alcohol
product with youth appeal" (1999, 151). He takes his analysis further, raising
questions of marginalization of youth, social class, and commodification of
products linked with global capitalism (1999, 162).

ENVIRONMENTAL CRIME

One way to approach the topic of corporate power is by examining the
application of environmental law. This is an area that clearly affects all
people worldwide. The Science Council of Canada has stated that fresh-
water pollution is among the most critical environmental issues for
Canadians. The Council (1974, 34–35) singled out serious pollution problems in the Fraser Valley and Lower Mainland areas of British Columbia, as
well as the extensive degradation of the Great Lakes and Gulf of Saint
Lawrence areas in central and eastern Canada, which had "by far the
biggest concentration of pollution problems." A central question in the
environmental debate is whether law can serve as a pivotal force in
resolving disparate economic and political interests. Much of the available
literature—some of which is discussed below—takes a pessimistic outlook
on the supposedly neutral role of lawmaking and law enforcement as idealized by some liberal pluralists.

Socio-legal researchers continue to debunk liberal ideology, insisting
that we examine law in social contexts, not merely as "legal text" (Hutter
1999, 4). This involves an attack on consensus perspectives where environmental law is regarded as an expression of the "public interest." More
critical commentators point to lax enforcement—or non-enforcement—of
laws and regulations, and the massive power of market forces, of corporate
and industrial interests on law-making and law enforcement (Hutter 1999,
10–11). Thus, many of the concepts we have become familiar with—
equality before the law, mystification, and the predominance of special,
powerful interests over the general interest—resurface in analyses of environmental laws. The area of environmental law would appear to be of particular interest to the body politic, given the scale of environmental
damage in highly developed and developing countries. It is noteworthy
that some comprehensive assessments of contemporary ecological damage
indicate that earlier periods were hardly a golden age of pristine practices.
The World Commission on Environment and Development (1989, 242–43)
credits municipal-level innovations for reducing certain kinds of damage in
urban areas. More generally, the Commission concludes that air quality in

"most urban areas" has improved relative to earlier situations in such major centres as London, Paris, and other large cities.

Caputo et al. (1989, 161) contrast growing concern over environmental pollution with earlier standards in Canada. They note, for example, that at the turn of the twentieth century, tidal disposal of sewage was a common practice in municipalities in Nova Scotia. Many others have noted the growing ideological emphasis on technological innovations and burgeoning industrial growth in Canada and worldwide. This developmental ethos was not accompanied by a concern for environmental issues. Caputo et al. (1989, 161) review several major environmental catastrophes of recent years: the nuclear accidents at Three Mile Island and Chernobyl; mercury poisoning in Minimata, Japan and on the Grassy Narrows Reserve (northern Ontario); the leak of poisonous gas from Union Carbide's plant at Bhopal, India (see also Bhullar 1990); and the *Exxon Valdez* oil spill off the coast of Alaska in 1989. It is ironic that despite greater publicity surrounding environmental protection, "governments seem to be unable or unwilling to force polluters to stop their destructive practices" (Caputo et al. 1989, 161).

Once again, the modern controversy over environmental damage must be seen in historical perspective. The network of government officials and key officials in corporations has emerged, over time, as a private resource, in which many decisions are made behind closed doors. This has often been noted with respect to the polluting practices of pulp and paper mills in British Columbia, for example, and to the decision in the 1920s by General Motors and other corporations to promote the use of fossil fuels rather than electricity for public and private transport (see Caputo et al. 1989, 162).

The work of Ted Schrecker is a major contribution to understanding the political and economic context associated with environmental law. In one essay, Schrecker (1989) discusses the *de facto* right of industry to place residues in the natural environment. This practice facilitates production inasmuch as it allows producers to pass on pollution-related costs to "society as a whole," instead of eroding profits (Schrecker 1989, 173). Schrecker (1989, 173) states that, despite earlier common-law protections, there is no established right, in modern times, for people exposed to air pollution to be compensated for related injuries. Schrecker thus develops an argument against law, as it stands, in providing recourse for palpable damages. There is, however, a dialectical element in the creation of such contemporary legislation as environmental laws: while profitability is a key factor in regulating (or failing to regulate) environmental pollution, both the private sector and government ministries must also take other considerations into account (Schrecker 1989, 174). Government legitimacy and the legitimacy of the private sector clearly rest on taking action, or at least the appearance of taking action. Nevertheless, many researchers point to the narrow scope of current government legislation concerning pollution.

For example, Schrecker (1989, 174) states that only five groups of substances are listed under the purview of the Environmental Contaminants Act. Schrecker (1989, 175) adds that provincial legislation is further restricted by its limits on acceptable concentrations of substances (e.g., parts per trillion for dioxin emissions from pulp and paper mills) rather than on total emissions into waterways. He notes that, in Ontario, the development of pollution-related standards "... has historically taken place mainly through the control order process, which is ... secret. Parties outside the charmed industry-government circle ... are typically involved only at the final stage: public meetings where audiences are treated to a defence of a negotiated position previously agreed to by government and the firm in question" (Schrecker 1989, 176). Schrecker (1989, 183) concludes that business interests are "uniquely important" in setting public policy limits.

McLaren (1984) provides a different interpretation of the nature of environmental regulation in his discussion of industrial and commercial development in nineteenth century Ontario. He discusses the case of Antoine Ratté, a small businessman who operated a rowboat rental business on the banks of the Ottawa River. For 18 years, the river area had been fouled by the discharge of the lumber mills about a kilometre upriver. Ratté protested this pollution, alleging that the detritus interfered with his boat operations and generally befouled the area with noxious odours and, occasionally, gas explosions.

Ratté eventually launched an action for damages in 1885, but his action was dismissed. The details of the case need not be recounted here, but essentially the court held that as a riparian owner, Ratté could not claim rights in the water or subsoil, as there had been no legal transfer to him; since his property fronted a water lot, not the river as such, he could not claim riparian rights. Ratté persisted with legal action, successfully appealing the initial decision; after a total of seven appeals (six by the defendants), Ratté finally received damages in 1892. McLaren uses this case study to address the evolution of regulatory mechanisms in Canada. He notes that in the last decade of the nineteenth century, several regulatory and administrative mechanisms were established, which served to mediate economic development in Canada (McLaren 1984, 257). McLaren suggests that these new mechanisms reflected a growing concern over the negative impact of unfettered industrial and commercial growth. Parallel to this growing sensitivity on the part of politicians and civil servants was the emergence of a greater public awareness of the unfortunate consequences of economic growth. It was no longer safe to assume that the environment could forever receive humanity's waste products and assimilate them without permanent injury (McLaren 1984, 255–56).

In environmental law and government regulatory policy, we can see the serious contradictions between the spirit of the law (and its claims of progress in eliminating or minimizing various forms of pollution) and the net effect of continuing pollution in Canada. A renewed awareness of how economic power is translated into legal advantage undermines the argument of law as an arena of conflict, where various groups petition on a more or less equal footing for restrictions or approval with respect to development. As in the area of corporate crime, the environmental movement has taken a critical look at regulatory bodies and their failure to redress environmental accidents. Many critics suggest that not only is current legal regulation inadequate for dealing with the scale of damage to the environment, but short-term gains can be eliminated very easily. Webb (1990, 220), while conceding that courts do serve to limit and guide bureaucratic action with respect to pollution control, provides a note of caution:

> *Often ... there is very little that can be done in law to make the bureaucrat's position more tolerable: political willpower, for example, can disappear with a change in governing party or a downturn in the economy, and no amount of legislation can guard against its disappearance.*

With respect to water management, other observers have noted that the current fragmentation of government functions and poorly-coordinated approaches have greatly hindered efforts to improve the quality of Canada's water supply. For some, the government's ad hoc approach is "completely untenable" (Foster and Sewell 1981, 95).

Webb (1988, 24–33) identifies several difficulties with legislation pertaining to pollution control. In her report to the Law Reform Commission of Canada, she noted that some of the legislation was simply "unrealistic," and if enforced, some industries would not be able to operate and obey the relevant law. Such oversimplified legislation would thus need to be refined in order to give greater guidance to those at risk of pollution-related charges. Webb (1988, 24–33) notes that some jurisdictions have expanded their repertoire of sanctions, going beyond fines or jail terms, and using such options as forcing polluters to compensate victims, publicizing offences, and passing on investigative costs from government authorities to polluters. Webb (1988, 32) recognizes, however, that Canadian courts have "rarely imposed" the full range of penalties against industrial polluters.

Similar concerns have been raised in countries other than Canada. Diana Shelton argues that human rights tribunals are blinkered with respect to environmental claims. "Neither scenic areas, flora and fauna, nor ecological balance are viewed as part of the rights to which humans are entitled, absent explicit recognition of the right to a specific environment"(2001, 256). The norm of regarding nature as an economic resource, as a source of commodities remains a strong barrier for those fighting for environmental protection and/or human rights (2001, 257). She gives an example of a United Nations adjudicated human rights case where mining development was not seen as a human rights violation for reindeer breeders. The UN committee noted that the plaintiffs had been consulted by the Finnish state, and that the mining did not violate their right to culture (2001).

Environmental justice is a growing area within the sociology of law. It has fostered the growth of radical approaches to environmental damage, such as "deep ecology," in which a new ethic of environmental consumerism is developed against the dominant ethic of pleasure, acquisition, and private interests. This new emphasis has attracted interest from the political right, with many free-market proponents exploring how economic factors might be taken into account in reassessing environmental protection (see Block 1989). From this conservative outlook, private economic interests and the public interest are not completely opposed. Ethicists have also explored traditional and evolving frameworks of justice, with some arguing for international cooperation on a global level to regulate energy consumption, and thereby reverse environmental damage. Wenz (1988, 340–43) argues that, since industrialized nations tend to benefit more from current patterns of energy consumption and wealth than do poorer nations, a greater burden would be placed on these more advantaged nations and on the relatively affluent citizens within them. At a local level, seemingly positive initiatives such as noise abatement measures may be undercut by unclear objectives of lawmakers, lack of enforcement personnel (especially during evenings or weekends), and a failure to move beyond limited principles such as establishing nuisance or harm. More effective measures would recognize the prevalence of noise, its harmful impact in many settings, and the importance of more active regulation of excessive noise (see McManus 2000). The point remains that environmental damage, even when repeated and severe, has traditionally been seen as a regulatory problem, not as a crime per se.

CRIMINAL JUSTICE AND SOCIAL ORDERING

Traditional approaches in criminology placed considerable emphasis on the study of criminals as individuals, or on the social context in which crime occurred. More recently, there has been a far greater appreciation among critical scholars of the *political* context of the application of criminal law. Accordingly, emphasis has shifted from the study of criminals as such, to the workings of the state and other disciplinary institutions, especially with respect to how the modern state and related institutions extend their control over people (see Lowman, Menzies, and Palys 1987).

The liberal-pluralist assumption that the criminal law works not only to punish criminals, but to provide strong safeguards for the sake of accused people—the presumption of innocence, due process of law—has been challenged by many scholars concerned with how the state secures compliance and social order. Ericson and Baranek (1982, 1986) present original findings on the status of defendants before criminal law. *The Ordering of Justice: A Study of Accused Persons as Dependants in the Criminal Justice Process* (1982)

focuses on a catchment area outside of Toronto. The authors used partici-
pant-observation techniques, documentary analysis, and interviews to
understand the dynamics of the criminal justice process for a group of
defendants. Their work challenges the premise of legal authority derived
from an authentic social consensus about law. It is also critical of the
applicability of liberal, formal safeguards within the legal structure, especially with respect to defendants' rights. Ericson and Baranek (1982) trace
the social transformation of the accused person (the defendant, with legal
rights and integrity) into a dependant with very limited power within the
criminal justice bureaucracy.

The authors bring forward four major themes with respect to the
ordering process. First, the premise that personal and interpersonal conflicts become "state property" (Ericson and Baranek 1986, 41) is crucial.
This proprietary action represents a "foreclosing" of choices and decisions
by the accused person. Whether innocent or guilty, once charged with an
offence, the accused person is typically able to resolve the charge by
turning his or her fate over to several legal actors. In Canada, these are the
Crown prosecutor, defence attorneys, judges, and others linked with the
formal legal process for criminal cases. Second, individuality—the hallmark
of liberal-democratic ideology—is substantially undermined in this
ordering process. Individual decisions—such as entering a plea of guilty or
not guilty—reflect "submission to pressure from others and to structural
arrangements" (Ericson and Baranek 1986, 42). A third theme is the way in
which the individual accused often rationalizes his or her submission as
just. The elements of mercy and majesty (see Hay 1975 and Chapter Three
of this book) are used to elicit fear and relief in the defendant and thereby
to secure a sense of legitimacy for the criminal justice system. Ericson and
Baranek (1986, 43) put this as follows:

> We find that on the whole the accused expresses satisfaction with the
> process, and especially with the sentencing outcome and the judge who pro-
> nounces it. His satisfaction results from the impact of his appearance in
> court: regardless of what took place up to that point, the order and aura of
> the court serves its mystical function and makes the accused a true believer.

The fourth theme—reform—is discussed extensively by the authors.
The structuring of individual dependency on authorities is set in the wider
context of the social order and how social relations are "re-ordered" by
state agents. Ericson and Baranek (1986) are skeptical of the promises of
reformers: diversion from the formal court process and changing legal rules
to the advantage of the accused are noted, then critiqued in light of
expanding governmental authority in Canada. State discretion, which
translates as state power, remains largely intact, a fact illustrated by the
considerable powers of official discretion even in jurisdictions that seem to
have removed such discretion by the use of "fixed penalties" for criminal
offences (Ericson and Baranek 1986, 44–46).

Ericson (1983) reverses the notion of law's power to reform social arrangements: in effect, legal initiatives and powers really act so as to *reform* existing structures of legal and social inequality. The author thus discounts the ideal of a criminal-law-enforcement apparatus that is being reformed (i.e., improved, made more responsive and democratic). The stated concerns for social equality and social justice are thus often not translated into emancipatory practices by state officials. The Canadian Charter of Rights and Freedoms is singled out by Ericson (1983, 2) as a legal initiative whose "public character" ostensibly is to promote greater equality for Canadians, but whose "social character"—the actions of legislators and other officials—generally has the opposite effect.

The Charter appears as a legal initiative that is imposed on citizens, not a power that was developed from substantial consultation with citizens. Despite this distance between the public and the Charter, proponents of the Charter present it as "a radical enhancement of democracy" (Ericson 1983, 11). Ericson notes, however, that the Charter has, in fact, added to the considerable discretionary powers of state authorities. Thus, illiberal governments are able to embrace high-sounding enactments while using repressive measures against their citizens. Ericson (1983, 20–21) illustrates this paradox by citing how the United Nations Charter of Human Rights has been adopted by totalitarian nations (South Africa and Argentina, for example); in Canada, the passing of the Protection of Privacy Act gave legitimacy to police invasions of citizens' privacy, almost invariably with judicial authorization for requests to wiretap or otherwise monitor private activities of citizens.

The symbolic power of legal ideology works to reinforce the image of a political system that safeguards a "reasonably equal balance" between state powers and citizens' rights (Ericson 1983, 3). Law also strengthens the legitimacy of a control culture, in which police forces are respected and obeyed by much of the public. This image of a decent society, moving toward greater degrees of decency and social equality, is belied by increases in such structured inequalities as homelessness, unemployment, and social isolation (Ericson 1983, 7–9).

In contrast to liberal-democratic ideologies of law, which emphasize the value of citizens' pressure groups in altering legal arrangements, more critical approaches have recognized the power of state agents in deflecting or co-opting grass-roots initiatives. McMahon and Ericson (1987, 38) document how state agents intervene in a variety of ways so as to "convert the property of the outside reform group into its instrumental value for the state." The instance they refer to is the attempt to establish an effective civilian review body of the Toronto police force. McMahon and Ericson (1987) trace the mobilization of protests against two events: the 1979 shooting death of Albert Johnson, who had emigrated from Jamaica to Toronto; and the wide-scale police raid of gay bathhouses in Toronto in 1981. The authors point out that, despite a variety of associations lobbying against police use of deadly force and interference in the lives of gay citizens, the initial protests against police powers were transformed by authorities in the police commission and other official agencies into a more co-operative arrangement between state officials and citizens. Opportunities to openly criticize state agendas are limited by various structures, including the practice of appointing officials to the police commission and the use of closed-door meetings, which limit public scrutiny or commentary (McMahon and Ericson 1987, 56–57). Such gatekeeping measures, in conjunction with processes that marginalize radical critics of policing procedures (and less visible minorities, such as gay activists), thus provide for concrete accountability to other state officials, with nominal accountability to the citizenry at large. Ironically, attempts to reform the police may be followed by a "solidification" of police and state control (McMahon and Ericson 1987, 65).

Taylor (1981) has argued for alternate solutions to crime than those forwarded by the political right (among them, right-wing criminologists). Using England and Canada as examples, Taylor (1980, 1981) challenges the conservative ideology that crime stems from a lack of discipline, and that law-and-order powers must be increased to instil "social discipline." Taylor (1981, 210–12) points to how social antagonisms and inequality are, in fact, social products, and how, without a genuine "community of interest" for citizens, the right-wing agenda of greater police powers, more severe prison sentences, the death penalty, and incapacitation of offenders will continue as social policy. Taylor (1981, 210) notes that crime rates have likely increased in the past decade, including crimes that threaten women and people of colour (predatory crimes, racist attacks by white supremacists, and so forth). Taylor's work coincides with other arguments for socialist transformation of the alienating political and economic arrangements in Britain (see, for example, Benn 1980). Significantly, such work combines a critical, theoretical outlook on the capitalist state and society with practical changes to the objectives and structure of social institutions such as work, law, and political life. For groups that have traditionally been managed by the state—people of colour, renters, women, and welfare recipients—Taylor envisions a community-based approach that would strengthen them, not only in terms of criminal law, but also of social justice:

> Such an enfranchising, for example, of women's organizations in relation to local police committees, would significantly transform the character and function of particular aspects of the police and the local state (Taylor 1981, 205; emphasis in original).

THE PENAL SANCTION IN CANADA

The wry observation that "the rich get richer, the poor get prison" (Reiman 1989) underscores the general theme in the sociology of criminal law:

inequalities in society are often translated into incarceration of those who are economically disadvantaged. Reiman's work deals with the now familiar theme of how powerful interest groups, who have been implicated in causing severe harm to health and the environment, are virtually exempt from criminal prosecution. He also documents the overrepresenta-tion of economically marginal people in U.S. prisons. Gosselin (1982) uses Marxist-based theory to reassess the evolution of the prison in Canada. He challenges the orthodox view of the prison as a necessary last resort in defence of public safety. For Gosselin (1982, 17), the prison is part of a wider pattern of the "repressive apparatus of the state" in Canada.

At the inception of the prison institution, prior to Confederation, prison regimes were very harsh, with corporal punishment and other sanc-tions given for a variety of breaches of prison regulations (Gosselin 1982, 72). The first penitentiary—Kingston Penitentiary—was still under con-struction when its first prisoners were admitted in 1835 (Gosselin 1982, 71). In 1873, a second penal institution—the St. Vincent de Paul Penitentiary—was established in Quebec. Gosselin reviews the expansion in the number of penal institutions, noting that, in over a century of exper-imentation with the prison system, this system has been adapted "to the ever-expanding needs of the capitalist system which gives it life" (Gosselin 1982, 81).

Claire Culhane (1985) wrote extensively about prisoners' rights in Canada and elsewhere, and translated her concerns into social action. Culhane (1985, 57–58) notes how many Canadian prisoners and their sup-porters have observed National Prison Justice Day—August 10 of each year—-since its inception in 1976. Culhane's work appreciates the different form of prisoners' struggles against the rather monolithic and unrespon-sive apparatus of prison bureaucracy and the justice system in general.

Sociological factors also come into play in the discussion of the legal realities facing many prisoners. There has been a longstanding critique of the ways in which legal resources and safeguards have not been extended to prisoners, as evidenced by the practice of granting them privileges rather than extending them rights. It has also been noted that prison conditions are often not corrected, and even such practices as placing prisoners in punitive or administrative segregation (i.e., solitary confinement) are largely under the discretionary control of prison authorities, with little external review (Jackson 1983). Critics also charge that prison officials give a greater priority to prison security—including prevention of escapes— than to life-saving measures (Burtch and Ericson, 1979). Once again, there is a growing interest in gender in various settings, including prisons. Grossman (2000) reviews deaths of female inmates, beginning with the deaths of six prisoners over a two-year span in the 1990s (2000, 160). She argues that aboriginal women, including those in prison, are more disad-vantaged than other Canadian women in terms of formal education, employment and income, and exposure to violence. For example, a study of aboriginal women sentenced to federal institutions revealed that about 9 in 10 women had been physically assaulted, and nearly two-thirds reported being sexually assaulted (2000, 162–64). Moreover, aboriginal female prisoners are at a higher suicide risk than non-aboriginal prisoners. Grossman favours substantial change in aboriginal women's lives, including reduced exposure to violence and improved access to education, work, and other resources (2000, 166).

Steve Duguid (2000) offers a critical, philosophical look at prisons in his recent book, *Can Prisons Work?* His work is a far cry from the denunciation of prisoners and the call for more prisons with greater security and longer sentences. Duguid traces many successes associated with prison education programs. Resisting a simple cause-and-effect scenario of greater education empowering prisoners, he nonetheless claims that "For some individuals the mere completion of high school, learning to read, or completing college courses might be a sufficiently influential mechanism that would cause a rethinking of career options, attitude, and social life" (2000, 256). He also discusses the tension between prisons as punitive organizations and the nature of university-level courses. He argues, as have many other researchers and activists reviewed in earlier chapters, that initiatives from within prisons or other institutions must have outside support from professions, organizations, and the wider public (Duguid 2000, 250–51). Hardly naïve about the opposition to or lack of interest in prison issues, he nevertheless suggests that society might well "look to its interests rather than its passions" and explore more creative ways of dealing with prisoners (2000, 260).

Many modern studies of crime control have called into question not only agents' practices, such as arrest, prosecution, and sentencing, but also the wider context of social control. Ericson, Baranek, and Chan (1987, 1989), for example, have written a number of critical works on how the media are used to create an overarching ideology that re-establishes political authority. At the same time, Ericson (1991, 242) is sensitive to contradictions in media coverage of crime, law, and justice. He notes that the mass media are more pluralistic than some writers allow: "While mass communications are hierarchical and structured by power, so that particular institutions, people, topics, and formats predominate, they still provide an appreciably open terrain for struggles for justice."

Ericson is certainly not alone in exploring possibilities for making institutions such as law and media more responsive to struggles for justice. Sargent (1989, 60–61), for example, discusses corporate crime and law, concluding that the traditional hegemony of the legal system is being challenged, and to some extent influenced, by consumer groups and many other groups seeking to transform law. Herman and Chomsky (1988, 306) portray the American mass-media network as serving to induce conformist beliefs and behaviours that are largely congruent with the needs of the privileged and powerful. The authors conclude that, with this media network, the state has succeeded in inculcating conformity and deference in Americans without resorting to sheer repression or other kinds of coercion. They acknowledge that this is not a total system, inasmuch as media have at times served other interests than state propaganda. Mathiesen (1987, 71) notes that modern media have served to present communications in a way that essentially preserves or extends "the power of groups which are already in power." He notes, however, that future media may provide a more interactive potential between the telecast information and the viewer. Mathiesen (1987, 75) stresses that political struggles against media messages that promote deference and subordination involve the creation of "alternative communication networks." Nevertheless, Mathiesen is well aware of the danger of co-optation through the media. Ericson, Baranek, and Chan (1987, 358–59) note that journalists, among other media workers, must establish some degree of legitimacy with their readerships and sources.

SUMMARY

The idealistic image of criminal law as reflecting a clear consensus of morality and social defence has been eclipsed by more critical approaches to criminal sanctioning. These approaches focus on the power relations among various groups—along lines of gender, race, and social class—and how the use of criminal law maintains these relations. The renewed interest in crime as an index of social conflict is paramount among the recent developments in criminology. Marxist-based criminology, for example, documents the economic factors that underlie patterns of crime control in capitalist societies. There has also been a shift in scholarly interest away from studies of criminals and deviants as problems in their own right toward a more critical assessment of criminal justice officials and other state agents. The power of media construction of what constitutes "dangerousness" has also been challenged, with many writers critiquing mass-media constructions of crime and authority, and some offering alternative approaches. Concurrent with these developments, a number of critical theories derived from feminism and ecological concerns have redirected scholarly interest away from narrow interpretations of Criminal Code sanctions to more general approaches to punitive measures.

Scholarly opinion, not surprisingly, is divided on the topic of the criminal sanction. Some favour extensions of state powers in the interests of order and justice; others are extremely skeptical of the political agenda of crime control agencies and their potential for reform from within or from outside pressures. The example of corporate crime seems to evoke mixed opinions, perhaps corresponding to the mixed evidence on state regulation of the private sector. Cullen, Maakestad, and Cavender (1987) suggest that many actions—civil actions, for example, as well as government-initiated regulatory actions—serve a largely symbolic purpose. Thus, they find some importance in the symbolic movement against corporate illegalities. Even with the legacy of leniency toward these offences, Cullen, Maakestad, and Cavender (1987, 27) detect a popular movement that is more aware of the effects of white-collar crime and motivated to redirect legal actions that had previously been tolerated or excused by legal officials and many members of the public.

STUDY QUESTIONS

1. Discuss the phenomenon of murder, with particular attention to how murder is socially defined. Discuss Boyd's (1988) premise that such social definitions serve to apply severe sanctions (such as long-term imprisonment) to a relatively powerless group of marginalized persons.

2. Review the debate over criminalization of certain corporate wrongdoings, including environmental pollution. How do legal ideology and government practice serve to excuse or tolerate what might be seen as "crimes"? In what ways is legal policy *dialectical*, that is, reflecting contradictions in society and in the legal apparatus?

3. What regulations are in place with respect to environmental protection in Canada? What strategies are used in "resisting regulation" (Schrecker 1989, 178–83)? How might Schrecker's analysis of these regulations be applied in your neighbourhood?

4. The mass media are clearly one of the more important sources of information in modern societies. Critically assess the ways in which media representations of crime and law-breaking generally are portrayed (or distorted) by media sources. To what extent do media programs contribute to social ordering?

REFERENCES

Archer, D., and R. Gartner (1984) *Violence and Crime in Cross-National Perspective*. New Haven: Yale University Press.

Beattie, J. (1986) *Crime and the Courts in England, 1660–1800*. Princeton: Princeton University Press.

Benn, T. (1980) *Arguments for Socialism*. Harmondsworth: Penguin.

Bhullar, B. (1990) "Union Carbide and the Bhopal Disaster: A Case Study in the Causes of Corporate Crime." In *Studies in Corporate Crime*, edited by R. Gordon, 123–51. Burnaby, British Columbia: School of Criminology, Simon Fraser University.

Block, W., ed. (1989) *Economics and the Environment: A Reconciliation*. Vancouver: Fraser Institute.

Boyd, N. (1988) *The Last Dance: Murder in Canada*. Toronto: Prentice-Hall.

Brannigan, A. (1984) *Crimes, Courts, and Corrections: An Introduction to Crime and Social Control in Canada*. Toronto: Holt, Rinehart and Winston.

Brantingham, P., and P. Brantingham (1984) *Patterns in Crime*. New York: Macmillan.

Burtch, B., and R. Ericson (1979) *The Silent System: An Inquiry into Prisoners Who Suicide*. Toronto: Centre of Criminology.

Caputo, T., M. Kennedy, C. Reasons, and A. Brannigan, eds. (1989) *Law and Society: A Critical Perspective*. Toronto: Harcourt Brace Jovanovich.

Carlen, P. (1988) *Women, Crime and Poverty*. Milton Keynes: Open University Press.

Chambliss, W. (1982) *On the Take: From Petty Crooks to Presidents*. Bloomington: Indiana University Press.

Coleman, J. (1989) *The Criminal Elite: The Sociology of White Collar Crime*. New York: St. Martin's Press.

Comack, E. (1990) "Law and Order Issues in the Canadian Context: The Case of Capital Punishment." *Social Justice* 17(1): 70–97.

Culhane, C. (1985) *Still Barred from Prison: Social Injustice in Canada*. Montreal: Black Rose Books.

Cullen, F., W. Maakestad, and G. Cavender (1987) *Corporate Crime Under Attack: The Ford Pinto Case and Beyond*. Cincinnati: Anderson Publishing Company.

Davis, N., and K. Faith (1987) "Women and the State: Changing Models of Social Control." In *Transcarceration: Essays in the Sociology of Social Control*, edited by J. Lowman, R. Menzies, and T. Palys, 170–87. London: Gower Books.

Duguid, S. (2000) *Can Prisons Work? The Prisoner as Object and Subject in Modern Corrections*. Toronto: University of Toronto Press.

Durkheim, E. (1965) *The Division of Labour in Society*, translated by George Simpson. New York: The Free Press.

Ericson, R. (1983) "The Constitution of Legal Inequality." John Porter Memorial Address. Ottawa: Carleton University Press.

———. (1991) "Mass Media, Crime, Law, and Justice: An Institutional Approach." *British Journal of Criminology* 31(3): 219–49.

Ericson, R., and P. Baranek (1982) *The Ordering of Justice: A Study of Accused Persons as Dependants in the Criminal Justice Process*. Toronto: University of Toronto Press.

———. (1986) "The Reordering of Justice." In *The Social Dimensions of Law*, edited by N. Boyd, 41–65. Toronto: Prentice-Hall.

Ericson, R., P. Baranek, and J. Chan (1987) *Visualizing Deviance: A Study of News Organization*. Toronto: University of Toronto Press.

———. (1989) *Negotiating Control: A Study of News Sources*. Toronto: University of Toronto Press.

Fattah, E. (1972) *A Study of the Deterrent Effect of Capital Punishment with Special Reference to the Canadian Situation*. Ottawa: Information Canada.

Findlay, M. (1999) *The Globalisation of Crime: Understanding Transitional Relationships in Context*. Cambridge: Cambridge University Press.

Foster, H., and W. Sewell (1981) *Water: The Emerging Crisis in Canada*. Toronto: Canadian Institute for Economic Policy.

Frank, N., and M. Lombness (1988) *Controlling Corporate Illegality: The Regulatory Justice System*. Cincinnati: Anderson Publishing Company.

Glasbeek, H., and S. Rowland (1986) "Are Injuring and Killing in the Workplace Crimes?" In *The Social Dimensions of Law*, edited by N. Boyd, 66–85. Toronto: Prentice-Hall.

Glazer, M. (1987) "Whistleblowers." In *Corporate and Governmental Deviance: Problems of Organizational Behavior in Contemporary Society,* edited by M. Ermann and R. Lundman, 187–208. Oxford: Oxford University Press.

Goff, C., and C. Reasons (1978) *Corporate Crime in Canada: A Critical Analysis of Anti-Combines Legislation.* Toronto: Prentice-Hall.

Gosselin, L. (1982) *Prisons in Canada.* Montreal: Black Rose Books.

Grossman, M. (2000) "Two Perspectives on Aboriginal Female Suicides in Custody." In *Criminal Justice in Canada: A Reader,* edited by J. Roberts, 160-168. Toronto: Harcourt Canada.

Hagan, J. (1976) "Locking up the Indians: A Case for Law Reform." *Canadian Forum* 55 (658): 16–18.

———. (1991) *The Disreputable Pleasures: Crime and Deviance in Canada* (third edition). Toronto: McGraw-Hill Ryerson.

Hay, D. (1975) "Property, Authority and the Criminal Law." In *Albion's Fatal Tree: Crime and Society in Eighteenth Century England,* edited by D. Hay, P. Linebaugh, J. Rule, E.P. Thompson, and C. Winslow, 17–63. New York: Pantheon Books.

Herman, E., and N. Chomsky (1988) *Manufacturing Consent: The Political Economy of the Mass Media.* New York: Pantheon Books.

Hutter, B. (1999) "Socio-Legal Perspectives on Environmental Law: An Overview." In *A Reader in Environmental Law,* edited by B. Hutter, 3–47. Oxford: Oxford University Press.

Jackson, M. (1983) *Prisoners of Isolation: Solitary Confinement in Canada.* Toronto: University of Toronto Press.

LaPrairie, C. (1987) "Native Women and Crime in Canada: A Theoretical Model." In *Too Few to Count: Canadian Women in Conflict with the Law,* edited by E. Adelberg and C. Currie, 103–12. Vancouver: Press Gang.

Larsen, N. (1999) "The Politics of Law Reform: Prostitution Policy in Canada, 1985–1995." In *Law in Society: Canadian Readings,* edited by N. Larsen and B. Burtch, 60–74. Toronto: Nelson Thomson Canada.

Lowman, J. (1985) "Child Saving, Legal Panaceas, and the Individualization of Family Problems: Some Comments on the Findings and Recommendations of the Badgley Report." *Canadian Journal of Family Law* 4 (4): 508–14.

Lowman, J., R. Menzies, and T. Palys, eds. (1987) *Transcarceration: Essays in the Sociology of Social Control.* London: Gower Books.

Martel, J. (1999) *Solitude and Cold Storage: Women's Journeys of Endurance in Segregation.* Edmonton: Elizabeth Fry Society of Edmonton.

Mathiesen, T. (1987) "The Eagle and the Sun: On Panoptical Systems and Mass Media in Modern Society." In *Transcarceration: Essays in the Sociology of Social Control,* edited by J. Lowman, R. Menzies, and T. Palys, 59–75. London: Gower Books.

McLaren, J. (1984) "The Tribulations of Antoine Ratté: A Case Study of the Environmental Regulation of the Canadian Lumbering Industry in the Nineteenth Century." *University of New Brunswick Law Journal* 33: 203–59.

McMahon, M., and R. Ericson (1987) "Reforming the Police and Policing Reform." In *State Control: Criminal Justice Politics in Canada,* edited by R. Ratner and J. McMullan, 38–68. Vancouver: University of British Columbia Press.

McManus, F. (2000) "Noise law in the United Kingdom—a very British solution?" *Legal Studies* 20(2): 264–90.

Parker, H. (1999) "Illegal Leisure: Alcohol, Drugs and the Regulation of Modern Youth." In *Crime Unlimited: Questions for the 21st Century*, edited by P. Carlen and R. Morgan, 144–65. London: MacMillan Press.

Reasons, C., L. Ross, and C. Paterson (1981) *Assault on the Worker: Occupational Health and Safety in Canada*. Toronto: Butterworths.

Reiman, J. (1989) *The Rich Get Richer and the Poor Get Prison*. New York: John Wiley & Sons.

Sargent, N. (1989) "Law, Ideology, and Corporate Crime: A Critique of Instrumentalism." *Canadian Journal of Law and Society* 4: 39–75.

Schrecker, T. (1989) "The Political Context and Content of Environmental Law." In *Law and Society: A Critical Perspective*, edited by T. Caputo, M. Kennedy, C. Reasons, and A. Brannigan, 173–204. Toronto: Harcourt Brace Jovanovich.

Science Council of Canada (1974) "The Quality of Natural Environment." In *Protecting the Environment: Issues and Choices—Canadian Perspectives*, edited by O. Dwivendi, 21–37. Toronto: Copp Clark.

Shelton, D. (2001) "Environmental Rights." In *People's Rights*, edited by P. Alston, 185—258. Oxford: Oxford University Press.

Smandych, R. (1991) "The Origins of Canadian Anti-Combines Legislation, 1890–1910." In *The Social Basis of Law: Critical Readings in the Sociology of Law*, edited by E. Comack and S. Brickey, 35–47. Toronto: Garamond Press.

Sutherland, E. (1949) *White Collar Crime*. New York: Dryden Press.

Taylor, I. (1980) "The Law and Order Issue in the British General Election and Canadian Federal Election of 1979: Crime, Population and the State." *Canadian Journal of Sociology* 5(3): 285–311.

——. (1981) *Law and Order: Arguments for Socialism*. London: Macmillan.

Webb, K. (1988) *Pollution Control in Canada: The Regulatory Approach in the 1980s*. Ottawa: Law Reform Commission of Canada.

——. (1990) "Between Rocks and Hard Places: Bureaucrats, Law and Pollution Control." In *Managing Leviathan: Environmental Politics and the Administrative State*, edited by R. Paehlke and D. Torgenson, 201–27. Peterborough, Ontario: Broadview Press.

Wenz, P. (1988) *Environmental Justice*. Albany: State University of New York.

World Commission on Environment and Population (1989) *Our Common Future*. Oxford: Oxford University Press.

9
Reproduction and Law: Family Law, Abortion, and Midwifery

In the little world in which children have their existence, whosoever brings them up, there is nothing so finely perceived and so finely felt, as injustice.

(Charles Dickens, Great Expectations)

INTRODUCTION

This chapter addresses family law reform, the abortion debate, and the midwifery movement in Canada. These topics illustrate how political and social movements seek to influence existing laws and public opinion. For some, legal reform is often forestalled, or implemented in ways that restrict women's access to reproductive care, therapeutic abortion, or adequate childrearing after separation. For others, liberalized laws and state policies undermine fundamental values and create their own forms of injustice for men and women. This chapter brings us directly into a discussion of the limits of law, as well as the extent to which particular groups are denied full participation in the social contract.

A central theme of this chapter is the way in which the Canadian legal structure has been used to translate law into power and to secure social order in the family, the economy, and the regulation of such private decisions as reproduction. Beginning with family law, followed by the abortion debate, and finally the midwifery movement's efforts to legalize midwifery practice in Canada, we will see how the politics underlying law and social policies suggest the difficulties that certain interest groups face in challenging existing legislation and services. The following discussion also outlines various contradictions in legal policies, including the difficult process by which marginalized groups gain a legitimate status in law.

FAMILY LAW REFORM

family. *basic kinship unit, in its minimal form consisting of a husband, wife, and children. In its widest sense it refers to all relatives living together or recognized as a* *social unit, including adopted persons. The U.S. Census defines a family as two or more persons living together who are related to each other by blood, marriage, or adoption. Thus by this definition a husband and wife, or two sisters living together, would be considered a family. The family is often called "the basic social institution" because of its important functions of procreation and socialization, and because it is found, in some form, in all societies.*

(Theodorson and Theodorson 1979, 146)

This quotation might evoke considerable emotion for many of us. What is it like to live in a joyous family, or a hateful, unhappy family, or more likely, a family that oscillates between these two extremes? What does it mean to be cast out of a family, or to be embroiled in the legal processes of separation and divorce? And if love sets us off, how do we cope with both the death of love and the obligations that survive the ending of a relationship? Family law is one of the most emotionally charged areas of law. Discussions of families and family law are often deeply-felt, whether it is of our family of origin (parents and, usually, siblings) or families we create. Some people lament the loss of a parent, grandparent, or aunt or uncle for the rest of their lives; others may regret the lack of feeling, the absence of grief, especially if they have felt unloved or even grossly abused by a family member. In this section, we review some social class, race, and gender considerations in Canada, and move to a consideration of legal arguments for and against granting family status or an analogous status to gays and lesbians.

Family law is concerned with the rights and responsibilities associated with marriage, childrearing, separation, and divorce. The following section pursues the major theme of this book—the social context of law and the link between the living law and the law in action—in a discussion of the politics of marriage and the legal processes following marital breakup. This section provides examples of a macrosocial approach to legal reform. This macrosocial approach goes far beyond particular cases in family law and concentrates on wider patterns of stratification, patriarchy, and ideology and how these patterns influence legal processes. Reference is also made to sociological work that is based on qualitative research, specifically, studies of lawyer-client interactions.

Changing Family Forms

Statistics from 1986 reveal that significant portions of Canadian families are single-parent families, 82 percent of which were headed by women. Common-law families amounted to 7 percent of families. Increasingly, "... more and more women are marrying late in life or not marrying at all. Between 1971 and 1986, the mean age of brides at first marriage has increased from 22.2 to 24.6 [years] ... the proportion of women married in the age group 20–24 decreased from .592 to .391 ..." (Balakrishnan et al. 1993, 105). Divorce rates increased from 169 per 100,000 marriages in 1960–1962 to 1,129 divorces in 1982. Balakrishnan et al. (1993, 105) note that this rate decreased to 1,062 in 1984. Some predict that 38 percent of marriages will result in divorce (Mandell and Duffy 1995). In 1985, 30 percent of marriages in Canada were remarriages. Along with marriage and divorce trends, trends in childbearing are important. In 1971, 29% of families were childless—in 1986, this was 33 percent. In 1986, single parent families were "the third largest family type" and it was predicted that half of all Canadian children would be raised at some time by a single-parent family (Conway, in Hovius 1992, 8–9).

Cohabitation outside of marriage has also increased. There have also been pressures on legislators and the courts to amend legislation governing separation and divorce. These have led to a liberalization of divorce, generally welcomed by the Canadian public, but also subject to criticism from some religious quarters for undermining family structures and contributing to various social problems, particularly for children of divorce. Historically, few nineteenth-century women in Canada were encouraged to divorce. Women were exhorted to preserve the original marriage and to endure a situation that frequently involved serious physical abuse. Women were often unable, for economic and geographic reasons, to avail themselves of legal protection (Backhouse 1991, 198–99).

Family Ideologies

Structural-functionalists often present the family as a fundamental social institution. The family is seen as a primary source of attachment for children, parents, and extended kin, and through its socializing functions and transfer of property, as a major force of social equilibrium. Historical functions of livelihood, religious instruction waned in modern times, with focus on socialization of children and intimacy. Immense structural changes took place in the 1960s with reduced barriers to divorce, and changing ideologies of cohabitation and lifelong marriage. Images of family life are extremely mixed, with some presenting family life as a "haven in a heartless world" with others seeing families as oppressive institutions for family members.

Patterns in family law are influenced by the clash of competing ideologies. Bob Simpson (1998, 160) identifies the powerful ideology of familism, requiring parental commitment and considerable sacrifice, and also an ideology of individualism and acquisition. He adds that contemporary family life rests precariously on a nostalgic view of family as panacea: Using the metaphor of an electrical circuit he claims that families "... increasingly took on the character of a delicate and overcharged circuit. As people fed more and more emotional voltage into this circuit in the form of potent desires for love, fulfilment, happiness, security and well-being, the fuses began to blow" (Simpson 1998, 161). Simpson acknowledges gendered patterns of divorce, including a greater tendency for estranged wives to report concerns over familial and monetary issues, whereas estranged husbands are more likely to cite concerns "over the loss of home and family" (1998, 92). Simpson points out that these are not cut-and-dried distinctions: there is considerable overlap between divorcing and divorced men and women, not least of all in the highly stressful process of divorcing (1998, 126). Even so, feminists' criticisms of unfair legal decisions and social policies hold fast. For example, in a study based in Newcastle, England, the researchers found that women receiving family maintenance rarely reported increased sums over time (only 4 percent of the sample). It was much more likely for maintenance sums to be frozen, or to be reduced or simply not paid at all (1998, 112–13).

Jane Pulkingham explores key issues of child custody, child support (or spousal support), and division of matrimonial property in Canada. She draws on feminist theory throughout this article, and presents criticisms of and support for some tenets of feminism. She begins with a critique of some precepts in family law: (1) the "feminization of poverty" assumption, where women are seen as profoundly disadvantaged economically after separation and divorce; and (2) perceived threats to women receiving custody of children, due to litigious husbands or partners (p. 277). Pulkingham insists that sweeping statements about mass impoverishment of divorced mothers should be supported by evidence (1999, 279). Taking a broader outlook, the author contends that divorce is not the signal event that leads to women's disadvantaged position. Rather, there has been "a decrease in the incidence of poverty in the general population" (p. 281). Increases in the divorce rate in Canada have played a part in women's worsened economic status, yet as Pulkingham notes, there have also been state-sponsored efforts to ensure that child support obligations are met (overwhelmingly, it is fathers who are obliged to pay child support to custodial mothers). These initiatives include tables for calculating adequate support levels, using the estranged parents' income as a basis, and also stepped-up enforcement efforts for parents who fail to support children. Pulkingham, building on Eichler's formulation, identifies three key models: (1) individual responsibility model, (2) social responsibility model, and (3) patriarchal model. She contends that the ideology of individuality remains very strong in family law matters. Family law policy rests on the assumption that ex-husbands/ex-partners will be responsible for child care and at times, for spousal support too (1999, 282).

Moving to child custody, the practice of maternal preference is identified as standard practice in Western jurisdictions in the twentieth century and arguably, in the twenty-first century. This preference is not entrenched in statutes but rather in judicial practice (1999, 284–85). Pulkingham is concerned with small, unrepresentative samples that cannot be used to generalize about all women in separation or divorce proceedings (p. 286). For those fearing a sharp increase in men receiving custody of dependent children, she cautions that less than 15 percent of fathers receive sole custody [ibid]. Pulkingham notes that formal legal protections often fall short in practice. For example, many child support orders are not paid in full over the life of the order, and some people (almost always fathers) build up considerable arrears despite enforcement efforts.

Parenthetically, one point rarely addressed in this area is the need to take a longitudinal approach to the adjustment of women and men following separation. Typically, divorce is presented in a fairly static way, as if there are no remarriages or other alliances, no financial or emotional support from extended families or friends. We rarely see studies of satisfaction levels of men or women some years after separation. This reflects a tendency to treat family law and a myriad of other legal and social phenomena as "social problems" with an emphasis on misuse of power and injustice. There is also little attention to new, intimate relationships that might be formed after—or even before—separation. In future, it would be prudent to see more detailed studies of the ways in which people cope not only with family law, but also the process of uncoupling and possibly moving into stepfamilies or analogous relationships.

Pulkingham considers material circumstances of spouses (income, assets, etc.) and also ideologies associated with family formation and family breakup. These ideologies can include a belief in lifelong marriage, pronatalism, in egalitarian (or non-egalitarian) relationships, or in marriage as a battleground or a sanctuary. Depending on which ideologies are in place, we can expect quite different forms of legislation and law enforcement. She concludes, "… as long as it is individual women's (maternal) rights that remain the objection of attention for reform, rather than societal responsibility and paternal obligations and responsibilities within and beyond marriage, paternal rights will be fortified" (1999, 290).

Generic discussion of divorce and family structure are increasingly tied with race and racism. In many parts of the world there is a relaxing of taboos against intermarriage, yet stigmatization and retribution survive even in these liberal times. Breger and Hill write of "… the daily courage necessary for such couples and their children to face the smaller-scale, casual racism and discrimination—not only from majority White people, but also from the minority groups, such as Blacks, Indians and Chinese in Britain—that abounds in everyday life" (1998, 28). In a case study from Guyana, Yoshiko Shibata traces interracial conflicts to colonization with its slavery and "plantation economies" and the relegation of "Indians" (from the sub-continent of India) to a lower social and economic status than "Blacks" (linked to Africa) (1998, 85). She introduces gender in her discussion of race and racialization, documenting how, for instance, Afro-Guyanese/Black women are often stereotyped as homely, immoral and aggressive (1998, 89). Shibata also lists many punishments meted out to people who trespass "racialized boundaries" such as ostracism and even direct physical threats (1998, 87).

It is important to contrast these varied images of the family—as the *sine non qua* of coherent societies, and as a structure that ought to include intermarriage, common-law relationships, and gays and lesbians and to recognize pluralistic family-forms including single-parent families and stepfamilies. There has been a liberalizing trend in family law in many Western jurisdictions. Ignatieff notes that "[t]he only distinctive aspect of the Canadian pattern has been the speed with which courts and legislatures have responded to demands for children's rights, easier divorce, abortion rights, the equation of marriage and co-habitation, and the full entrenchment of rights to sexual difference" (Ignatieff 2000, 85). He portrays conservative views on the family as of limited value, primarily taking the form of backlash and even a "reactionary" spirit, using legislation and social policy to penalize certain people, e.g., single mothers. Ignatieff attacks narrow definitions of "family values" as despotic, arguing that family values must be truly pluralistic. Thus, "… the essential moral needs of any child can be met by family arrangements that run the gamut from arranged marriages right through to same-sex parenting" (see Ignatieff 2000, 100–03).

The application of family law principles has generated tremendous controversy within the legal profession and with respect to social policy generally. For some advocates of a liberal approach, marriage and family law should serve to mediate conflicting interests between estranged spouses so as to achieve a resolution for all parties. This process could involve reconciliation—in which the spouses agree to sort out their differences and continue living together—or mediated settlements—in which court services (or related services) enable the ex-spouses to resolve such issues as child custody, child support, and division of assets and property. A settlement may be imposed by the court in cases where parties cannot resolve their differences. This is perhaps most dramatic in cases in which both parties seek child custody.

The benign, commonsensical face of liberal reform has again been criticized in the context of divorce mediation. Critics express concern over the unwillingness of many mediators to address family violence. A study of 10 agencies in the United Kingdom found that mediators were often reluctant to delve into allegations of abuse, or to refer victims to other resources (Greatbach and Dingwall, 1999). This finding matches that of an American study of community mediation in 30 agencies. Sara Cobb (1997) concluded that mediation is part of a "… discursive process in which victims and victimizers are erased, rights are reframed as needs, and relationships are constructed as economic arrangements." Sarat and Felsteiner (1986) observed and tape-recorded 115 lawyer-client conferences in Massachusetts and California. The researchers also attended court and mediation sessions and conducted extended interviews with lawyers and clients. The research largely confirmed the disadvantage that many clients face in the restructuring of divorce actions by legal experts. Knowledge of legal terminology and legal strategies is very limited for most clients. Specialized terminology used by lawyers means that law and legal processes are often "impenetrable," even for well-educated clients (Sarat and Felstiner 1986, 103). This study raises concerns over the notion that conciliation activities offer advantages to clients.

On the other hand, lawyers may also be helpful in advocating for disadvantaged clients hemmed in by tradition. A study of family law mediation proceedings in Japan suggested that legal representation was generally an advantage for both husbands and wives. Murayama (1999) reported that there are strong cultural pressures to be conciliatory in such situations. Once again, there may be cultural and financial barriers to acquiring legal representation. Thus, while lawyers may be useful in such proceedings, they are retained in only 14 percent of Japanese divorce proceedings. Moreover, Japan has a relatively sparse legal aid budget compared with North American and European nations (1999, 60). That weaker parties may be at risk of unfair settlements calls into question the positive image of mediation; that is, as an impartial process rooted in goodwill and geared to establishing a fair consensus among the parties.

In keeping with the law-society connection, family law is linked with community-based family services and the issue of diversity in such services. We again encounter established patterns of underrepresentation of certain groups. Henry et al. (1995, 158–59) identify several barriers to obtaining family services for such people who are not fluent in the English language, or whose ethno-cultural communities do not adhere to (for lack of a better phrase) a mainstream, Anglo-Saxon outlook on family matters. Henry et al. (1995) document other patterns of discrimination, such as lack of representation of visible minorities on boards of directors for human-services agencies, and relatively poor hiring experiences of visible minority graduates seeking work in the human services field, including family services (Henry et al. 1995, 156–57).

The description of marriage and family law as a means of resolving family or spousal conflicts is often presented in a liberal framework. That is, law is seen as above the interests of any one party and as acting in a fair, impartial manner in the interests of justice. Many feminist scholars challenge this liberal-pluralist concept. They point to the patriarchal basis of marriage laws and the ways in which modern legal processes place women at a disadvantage. As we will show in the following section, it is often argued that, despite the liberalization of family law (for example, easier access to divorce) and general concessions to women, marriage law and family law serve in many respects to consolidate the power of men over women, economically, socially, and politically. Freeman (1984, 2–3), for example, attacks complacent myths of the dramatic improvement in women's situations. Using studies from the United Kingdom and the United States, he concludes that the norm is for mothers and dependent children to suffer more than ex-husbands (and, where applicable, their new spouses). Freeman (1984, 2–3) also notes that many women are forced onto social security programs following marital breakup.

Morton (1988) assesses the reform of family law in Ontario. Her assessment strengthens the view that legal reforms often conform to power relations, and that such reforms often perpetuate legal and economic inequalities. Morton provides a strong argument that women remain disadvantaged through their attention to domestic matters and discriminated against in the paid work force. This disadvantaged position is structurally rooted in a complex mix of capitalism and patriarchy. The weaker position of women is often intensified after marital dissolution, for "the female spouse is likely to have a more poorly paid job and also to bear the primary responsibility for childcare costs" (Morton 1988, 261). Law reflects a predominantly male perspective, and feminist jurisprudence is developed to understand the material interests of women and dependent children. Other researchers shift the focus to better include men's interests, alongside feminists' concerns with women and children. Seel, for example, suggests that men are sometimes targets of sexist thinking and practices: "It is not until they become fathers that most men experience sexism directly ... But once a man embarks on fatherhood for the first time he will be lucky to escape it. Firstly, there is institutional prejudice: in the antenatal clinic where he may be matronized, in the labour room where he may be treated as an irrelevance, and in the postnatal ward where he may be treated as an inconvenience ..." (Seel 1987, 129). Support for greater involvement of fathers in childrearing is evident in other forms and in explicit protests of courtroom bias against fathers seeking greater involvement with their children (Weber 2002, 6).

Family law provides considerable support for a major theme in this book: the gap between legal ideals and actual implementation of rights. This implementation becomes complex and controversial. There have been efforts by the courts to provide a more considered approach to child custody, such that estranged parents might agree to co-parent their children. Ideally, this would provide more continuity for children and both parents, and may result in a more cordial divorce. Feminists have quickly countered, however, that efforts to reach joint custody can be used strategically to undermine the power of the primary parent (most often, the mother), and to impose a parenting arrangement that serves neither the children nor the mother. At another level, there are ongoing problems for many women in receiving adequate child support, a situation that can pose substantial hardships after separation. Finally, lest we become complacent with formal legal victories in areas of reproductive choice or in family law, it is important to note that victories can be undone. There is evidence of a backlash against feminism (Menzies and Chunn 1991, 63–67), for example, trivializing expressions of violence against women (Ahluwalia 1991, 56). Laws can be reversed, or policies established that undermine the spirit of formal legal equality. The issue remains whether legal advances in these areas will be consolidated or weakened in future.

Gay and Lesbian Rights

Much hinges on what we mean by "family." Douglas Sanders states that despite progress on many fronts, Canadian homosexuals remain "stigmatized minorities," presumably in all societies (1999, 158). Nevertheless, there has been increased public acceptance of cohabitation outside of marriage and of homosexuality. Sanders cautions that there have been countervailing pressures as well, especially conservative efforts to curtail rights of gays and lesbians. Nevertheless, gay and lesbian issues have become part of a wider "public human rights discourse" (p. 158). Sanders' focus is on ways in which lesbian and gay rights are framed, and the implications of legal actions for gays and lesbians, and for society-at-large. His work covers key facets such as privacy, victimization, and equality claims. He begins with a review of the privacy doctrine, where consensual activity between homosexual adults has been decriminalized in many jurisdictions in Europe, North America, and Australia (p. 159). While decisions have not been uniform—drawing on the American context, Sanders highlights a Supreme Court rejection of the privacy argument, for example—in Canada the trend has been toward greater legal recognition of gay and lesbian rights. Sanders argues "equality, not privacy" is the cornerstone of gay and lesbian rights (p. 160). In fact, the seemingly positive value of privacy "is linked to invisibility and silence" (p. 160) not to affirmation and extended benefits such as spousal benefits.

Sanders next raises the issue of violence against homosexuals and some successful examples of including gay and lesbian related victimization as part of hate crimes (see Shaffer 1999). Quite accurately, Sanders cannot say definitively if the incidence of violence against homosexuals is increasing, but he acknowledges that reports of gay-bashing are on the rise. Research conducted in Vancouver revealed high levels of self-reported victimization among gay men and lesbians (Samis 1995). The discussion of equality claims is a vital part of this exploration. There is a clear argument that discrimination can have a negative impact on homosexuals, and that the courts have not had a uniform outlook on such equality claims. Sanders raises some fundamental questions about choice and determination of sexual orientation. Sanders refuses to settle for a simplistic discussion of gays versus straights, for instance, incorporating issues of feminism and bisexuality in this debate. The growth of federal and provincial human rights legislation and offices had not been accompanied by a focus on gays and lesbians. After considerable pressure, most human rights offices now include "sexual orientation" as a prohibited ground with respect to discrimination (page 164). While there are jurisdictions where homosexuals are not protected from discrimination, Sanders establishes several Canadian and non-Canadian bailiwicks where protection has taken root.

The watershed for recognizing gay and lesbian rights is set at 1985, when then Minister of Justice John Crosbie stated in the House of

Commons that section 15 of the *Charter* includes sexual orientation (page 165). Subsequent court cases affirmed this position (pages 165–66). We can also consider an inside look at gay activism in Canada, recently chronicled in a documentary film, *Jim Loves Jack*. This film traces the political work of Jim Egan, beginning with his anonymous letters to the editor. These letters tried to counter the dominant images of homosexuals as criminal, psychologically disturbed, and sinful. As such, Jim Egan and some of his contemporaries jousted with powerful institutions of criminal law, mental health, and religious denominations, all of which decried some aspects of homosexuality. Egan is part of Canadian legal history, with his attempt to have his long-term partner, Nesbit, regarded as a "spouse" and thus eligible for spousal benefits under the Old Age Security provision. Sanders is critical of the reproductive assumption built into some legal decisions, including *Egan*. Mothers and fathers may shift from heterosexual to homosexual (or bisexual) relationships, for example, or there are options of artificial insemination or adoption. And, of course, many heterosexual couples do not have children.

ABORTION AND LAW

The divisive abortion debate in Canada shows no sign of abating. At the extremes, interest groups have argued for pro-life or pro-choice social policies, sometimes relabelling each other as anti-choice and anti-life. In this battle, reproductive rights have been established and then dismantled, with no clear direction for the development of legal and social issues surrounding abortion. Recent opinion studies indicate that two-thirds of Canadians polled express support for a right to abortion (O'Neil 2000). At the same time, few people favour either a complete ban on all abortions or, at the other extreme, abortion "on demand," that is, as a personal right of every woman throughout the entire pregnancy. It has been noted that religious denomination is often correlated with outlook on abortion. Hartnagel, Creechan, and Silverman (1985, 415) report that Catholics and "more fundamental Protestants" are most opposed to legalization of abortion, whereas those with no religious affiliation, along with Jews, Unitarians, and atheists, are the most liberal with respect to abortion. Members of dominant status groups—older, male, well-educated, affluent, of British ancestry—were more likely to hold a liberal outlook on abortion law, other variables such as church attendance and religiosity were necessary in explaining abortion approval or disapproval (Hartnagel et al. 1985, 417 and 423; see also Clarke 1987).

The right to abortion involves struggles by women to gain access not only to abortion for unwanted pregnancies but also to contraceptive information and devices. In 1969, the use of contraceptive devices became legal in Canada, and abortion was permissible under certain conditions. The decision to grant and perform a therapeutic abortion rested with therapeutic abortion committees composed of physicians, and with those physicians who were willing to perform the operation. Historically, reproduction has been aligned with political power. Different interests vied for influence over contraception and abortion policy in Canada during the nineteenth and twentieth centuries. For example, some socialists encouraged the use of contraceptive devices to emancipate women from the demands of large families, while others opposed contraception, believing that a socialist society could support large families (McLaren and McLaren 1986, 140–41). Consider also the *revanche des berceaux* ("revenge of the cradle" in Québec, in which French-Canadians maintained a majority of the population in New France, then Quebec, through a high birth rate), and fears of "race suicide" (whereby the numbers of the dominant culture shrink in the face of a decline in birth rate and of an increase in immigration) in Canada, Britain, and the United States (see McLaren and McLaren 1986, 17). Historians have offered a critical examination of abortion practices. Professor Angus McLaren used archival materials concerning abortion practices and law in Vancouver between 1886 and 1939.

Professor McLaren begins with the case of Sarah Robins. Mrs. Robins, a mother of three, died in Vancouver General Hospital in 1919, after complications of an illegal, botched abortion (McLaren 1999, 22). This case is a point of departure for a wider discussion of efforts to regulate women's fertility during this time period. He uses 100 actual cases of inquests or trials in B.C. to explore patterns of social control in British Columbia. McLaren cautions that these cases are not representative of all abortion efforts or reactions to them. He emphasizes that legal actions tended to focus on the women concerned, less so on husbands' or boyfriends' involvement in these incidents, or the complicity of physicians (p. 24). Professor McLaren qualifies this point later in the essay: he mentions that bachelors were more likely to face legal sanctions than married men, and that some might be faced with charges of arranging an abortion or even "seduction" (see p. 29). Many women were desperate to gain control over conception and childbearing. This might stem from poverty, or as McLaren points out, for pregnant single women, their reputation was often severely jeopardized if they conceived out of wedlock (p. 25). On this same page, McLaren argues that the foremost reason for abortion for married women was economic necessity. Despite its criminal status, abortion efforts included self-induced efforts by women, procedures by other people, and there was a wide range of substances available—to different degrees—for women wishing to end pregnancy (pages 26–27).

Without readily available medical services or approval (or tolerance) through the courts, women with unwanted pregnancies might rely on the unregulated, "underground" remedies and procedures in Canada or the United States. Such resources proliferated despite the criminalization of abortion, with physicians liable to prosecution not only for performing abortions, but also for not reporting abortion-related deaths (p. 30).

Nevertheless, in practice few physicians faced the stigma and formal penalties of criminal prosecution; instead, non-physicians—"midwives, masseuses, and herbalists"—were more common targets of legal action (p. 35). Husbands were rarely charged under the Criminal Code (pages 29–30).

Significantly, physicians accused of abortion-related activities were often successful in avoiding conviction or censures from professional medical bodies (i.e., being prohibited from practicing medicine, see pages 31–32). In practice, these formal sanctions were not always applied, and if they were, they might be removed on appeal. Moreover, the reluctance of witnesses to testify in legal proceedings and over barriers to obtaining evidence often meant that no formal charges were made. McLaren found that only 34 of the 100 cases he studied resulted in filing of charges (p. 33). This essay brings forward the issue of power in society, including its application or misapplication against fairly vulnerable individuals or groups. Keep in mind that punitive actions could be seen as desirable, reinforcing a common morality or common objectives such as increasing family size (pronatalism), preserving the power of Church officials, or protecting private property rights. Professor McLaren believes that "almost everyone was victimized by an inequitable and unenforceable law" (p. 34). Opinion was deeply divided about the implications of birth control, abortion, and childrearing at this time, and certainly it remains contentious today.

Dr. Henry Morgentaler and his supporters have been involved in the establishment of abortion clinics in Quebec, Ontario, and elsewhere. His legal battles included a prison sentence, and a series of appeals to the Supreme Court of Canada. In January 1988, in *Morgentaler et al.*, the Supreme Court of Canada struck down a statute in the Criminal Code that legalized abortion in accredited hospitals, provided that it was certified—by committees of doctors—that pregnancy endangered a woman's life, or physical or mental health. The Supreme Court decision hardly resolved the deep divisions in the abortion debate. There have been ongoing efforts to regulate protests against abortion clinics, such as injunctions against pro-life protesters and creation of "bubble zones" outside abortion clinics. The protests and lobbying continue, along with fatal and non-fatal attacks on abortion clinics and their employees (Dunphy 1996, 425). Advocates of legalized abortion frequently mention injury to women denied access to safe abortion services. It is estimated that from 1926–1947, several thousand Canadian women died following illegal abortions. Deaths were attributed chiefly to infection, as well as hemorrhage, poisoning, and embolisms (see Childbirth by Choice Trust 1998; McLaren and McLaren 1986).

In another case, in the summer of 1989, the Québec Court of Appeal upheld an injunction on behalf of Jean-Guy Tremblay that prohibited his ex-girlfriend, Chantal Daigle, from getting an abortion. This injunction, which would have strengthened efforts by males to veto women's reproductive choices (see Gavigan 1986), was not upheld. By the time the Court of Appeal decided against the injunction, however, Daigle had defied the injunction, having had an abortion in the United States even before the court's decision was handed down. Currently, Canada is still without an abortion law, since a recent proposal for an amended law failed to gain majority approval by the Canadian Senate. Moreover, old problems have resurfaced, such as regional disparities in women's access to abortion, and unwillingness of some medical and nursing staff to assist in abortion procedures (see Gavigan 1987, 276–77).

Gavigan (1986) examines the contradictory nature of the criminal law and abortion policy in Canada. Although she is sensitive to the myriad ways in which women have been discriminated against in law, she does not accept the perspective that sees laws as simply reflecting the interests of men; law may, indeed, afford some protections for women. For example, Canadian legislation has been interpreted to deny biological fathers a veto right in a legal abortion. Gavigan also argues that, while women remain "substantively unequal," they have achieved a measure of formal equality (Gavigan 1987, 266–67). The achievement of formal equality for women in this century is not a hollow victory: it reflects ongoing struggles by women, not merely concessions from the dominant classes or the goodwill evolving from a maturing society. Gavigan (1987, 268) notes that because women can no longer be portrayed as mere property, or "objects of exchange," they have various rights—among them the right to vote, to hold public office, and to own property. As such, women are now "legal subjects," and are able to form strategies to create a "radical restructuring" of society and gender relations (Gavigan 1987, 264).

Gavigan notes, however, that there have been general efforts to limit women's access to legal abortion (Gavigan 1987, 276–77). These efforts stem from the constituencies that are legally able to restrict women's access to abortion, including government officials and medical practitioners. Under Canadian constitutional arrangements, the administration of health care falls within provincial jurisdictions. Thus, despite the observation that not all Canadian women enjoy ready access to hospitals (or clinics) with accredited therapeutic abortion committees, or other provisions for therapeutic abortions, most hospitals do not offer such services (Gavigan 1987, 270–77). Medical practitioners, under the previous liberalized abortion policies, could recommend or reject a woman's request for a therapeutic abortion. Thus, the power to decide whether or not to continue a pregnancy rested not with women but with government agencies and medical practitioners. Building on the feminist critique of formal protections for women, Gavigan (1986, 117) notes that the intersection of law and medicine, while inhibiting men's prerogatives (specifically, claims for veto power over abortion decisions), has reproduced "the subordinate position of women."

Davis (1987, 373) refers to a "crisis" with respect to women's freedom to obtain therapeutic abortions. What appears to have been a liberalization of American abortion law has been recast in the form of continued constraints on women's options in reproduction. Like Gavigan, Davis believes that control over abortion has been transferred from police authorities to physicians, resulting in a new form of state power over women: "A stronger alliance now exists between state and medical groups with certain negative implications for women's autonomy" (Davis 1987, 373). Davis's approach, in keeping with other critical theoretical approaches, challenges the validity of liberal-consensus theory. Conflicts such as the abortion debate are seen as emerging not from widely shared customs or general features of social harmony, but rather from struggles for dominance among opposing groups. Law, like social relations generally, assumes an essential position in power relations, especially with respect to social inequalities and social domination (Davis 1987, 373–74).

An example of this struggle among groups is the criminalization of abortion in the United States. Davis (1987, 376–77) notes that prior to the 1870s, abortion was "a relatively common practice," with approximately one abortion per five to six live births between 1840 and 1870. The criminalization of abortion was linked with movements protesting against vice (including abortion and obscenity). One such movement was led by Anthony Comstock, described by Davis (1987, 394) as "an American morals crusader," in the late nineteenth and early twentieth centuries. Another factor in the decreased use of abortion was the declining birth rate, especially among American-born, white Protestants. Davis (1987, 378) adds that there was also concern over patient deaths following abortion attempts; significantly, the American Medical Association began to lobby against the "evil" of abortion. Davis (1987, 378) thus places the changes in abortion law in a social context, contending that outlawing abortions served to promote an ideology of feminine domesticity (placing women as full-time mothers and homemakers) and to allay fears of a decrease in white, Protestant citizens.

Davis describes later changes in abortion law, including decriminalization policies in many American states in the 1960s and 1970s, and the landmark Supreme Court decision in *Roe v. Wade* in 1973. Gavigan (1987, 280) notes that this ruling "held that the constitutionally protected right to privacy extended to freedom in decisions regarding abortion." Furthermore, state legislation limiting women's rights in this regard had to be based on "compelling state interest." Gavigan (1987, 280) notes that very shortly after the decision, state legislatures implemented laws restricting women's choices, including waiting periods prior to abortion, cuts in Medicaid funds, and enactment of various processes surrounding spousal or parental consent and notification. Davis (1987, 385) refers to nearly 200 abortion bills brought forward within four months of the 1973 *Roe* decision. She notes that, while many bills raised issues of safeguarding women's health, other aspects, such as protection of hospitals that did not permit abortions and bans on second-trimester abortions in clinics, were essentially "hostile to women's reproductive rights" (Davis 1987, 385). As was the case in Canada, physicians became more prominent, serving as gatekeepers in approving or denying abortion requests. This situation thus empowered medical interests, while "severely diluting" (Davis 1987, 383) women's power to decide whether or not to terminate pregnancies. The fragmented nature of state policies, extensive litigation on a case-by-case basis, and contradictory approaches to women's integrity in abortion choices resulted in a "crazy-quilt pattern" (Davis 1987, 383), in which women's access to an abortion varied considerably from state to state, and likely within particular states.

Similar findings were made with respect to abortion practices in Canada. The *Report of the Committee on the Operation of the Abortion Law* (Canada 1977, 238–40) commented on variations in consent requirements pertaining to the age of the woman requesting the abortion. The Committee (Canada 1977, 140–41) also noted "sharp regional disparities" in women's access to abortion, due in part to a lack of (then necessary) therapeutic abortion committees in many hospitals, and compounded by physicians' decisions not to perform therapeutic abortions. The Committee (Canada 1977, 140–41) found that nearly half of the obstetrician-gynecologists surveyed did not perform abortions. The net effect was that, despite the formal procedures then in effect under the Criminal Code, "obtaining therapeutic abortion is in practice illusory for many Canadian women" (Canada 1977, 140–41). Nevertheless, since the *Roe* decision, the net effect has been that more low-cost, safe therapeutic abortions were permitted than at any time prior to the Supreme Court ruling (Davis 1987, 387).

Eisenstein (1988, 186–87) observes that the United States Supreme Court has confirmed its 1973 abortion ruling in more recent times. In a 1986 case *(Thornburgh v. American College of Obstetricians and Gynaecologists)*, the court did uphold a Pennsylvania law that would have interfered with women seeking abortions (Eisenstein 1988, 186–87). Eisenstein notes that the court was divided on this case—the ruling was 5 to 4—but that the result was an affirmation of the privacy doctrine. Eisenstein adds that, while the privacy doctrine has been useful strategically in preserving some degree of reproductive autonomy for women, the overall effect of such rulings is to obscure "the political nature of the private realm" of sexuality (Eisenstein 1988, 187).

Davis (1987, 391) contends that abortion laws and policies have served to consolidate the "medicalization" of abortion, allowing more for the convenience and empowerment of professional objectives than for the convenience of women. MacKinnon (1987, 101) concludes that in the United States, "every ounce of control that women won out of this legalization has gone directly into the hands of men—husbands, doctors, or fathers—or is now in the process of attempts to reclaim it through regulation." She adds that abortion reforms have been recast as a "private privilege" rather than a "public right." In this process, she notes that a strong measure of oppression concerning women's sexuality remains intact—an everyday pervasive power in which the political and personal spheres are inseparable. Access to abortion is a central issue in the North American debate. Such provisions as enabling physicians or hospitals to refuse abortions helped to undermine access to abortions. Davis (1987, 392) notes that in 1981, two-thirds of counties in the United States had no one to provide abortions to women. Moreover, low-income women were rendered particularly dependent due to underfunding of abortion services and subsequent amendments that have centred on fetal rights.

In the wake of *Roe*, Davis (1987, 393–94) concludes that the feminist goal of using abortion rights as a point of departure for securing a wider range of "social, political, and economic rights" has been substantially undermined. The end result of this situation is to alienate women thorough legalization of abortion, a process that does not redress social class divisions in the United States or substantially enhance women's rights as citizens. This alienating process has been especially severe for welfare-dependent women. The abortion debate remains vital, with considerable lobbying for legal change—to restrict, eliminate, or broaden access to abortion—and difficulties faced by "both sides" of this divisive issue. It is important to recognize, however, that despite variations in services and in governing laws, many feminist writers see logic—a "continuity"—within these diverse practices. Eisenstein (1988, 18–19) observes that relations of power surrounding reproduction (among other areas) retain coherence. This includes ways in which male bodies maintain a "gendered privilege," and inequalities between women and men are partly reinforced by the agency of the state. Abortion laws, and social policies surrounding abortion, vary considerably across jurisdictions. The polarized outlook on abortion (pro-life vs. pro-choice) was not as evident in European countries, where a compromise between access to abortion and the sanctity of life was the norm (Glendon 1989, 473).

MIDWIFERY AND LAW

Love set you going like a fat gold watch.
The midwife slopped your footsoles, and your bald cry
Took its place among the elements

(Sylvia Plath, "Morning Song" 1965)

"Midwife" refers to a woman who assists other women in childbirth. While midwives are active worldwide, Canadian midwives have only recently been granted legal and professional recognition. In the 1970s, lay midwives began attending women throughout pregnancy and at delivery. High rates of Caesarean section, forceps delivery, induction of birth, and the unnecessary use of medication and fetal monitoring were seen as unjustifiable interference with normal labour and delivery. This "midwifery challenge" (Kitzinger 1988) has been met with a mixture of support and resistance. Midwives seek to assert their own autonomous status as experts in the management of normal obstetrics, separate from obstetrical nursing, general practice, and specialty obstetrics. Midwives seek self-regulation through a college of midwives and believe in greater recognition of parental rights in birth and continuity of care for expectant mothers through pregnancy, labour, delivery, and into the postpartum period.

In Canada, childbirth was increasingly defined as a medical event, properly supervised by medical practitioners in hospital settings. This ideology of medical control was reinforced by legislation forbidding midwifery practice (Burtch 1994). Restrictive laws and ideologies surrounding birth established medicalized birth as a desirable norm that was in the interests of birthing women and the public at large. The sphere of practice for nurses was circumscribed, with male physicians now "presiding" over birth. Medicalization of birth thus involved the transformation of women into receptive clients or assistants to physicians. Women were no longer active in understanding and influencing their own well-being. One woman describes her experiences of childbirth in Canada in the 1950s:

> *I had my first baby in the mid-50s and it was very impersonal and very terrifying. You went to the hospital and your husband just dropped you off ... You went into the delivery room and you were with strangers. You didn't know anybody. I think the most terrifying part for me was delivering when you were lying on your back. Your legs were strapped in stirrups, and then he strapped your hands down, so you were completely strapped down and that's how you delivered. Just before the baby was born, they put you under again and when you woke up this is when you were told if it was a boy or a girl, and then you never saw your child again, usually until the next day ... It was lonely, very lonely ... I found all three births a terrifying experience ...." (Gerrie White, quoted in* Midwifery and the Law *1991).*

White contrasts her own experiences with the birth of her first granddaughter, born at home in Vancouver in 1976. She describes the birth as "a very loving experience," much different from the way women were delivered a generation before. Although White raised three children, she had never experienced delivery, due to the 1950s practice of forceps delivery with the mother unconscious.

The state is responsible for enacting and enforcing legislation governing birth attendance; moreover, provision of childbirth services—medical insurance plans, hospital services, and so forth—is largely administered through provincial or federal bureaucracies or agencies that depend on government payments for their operations. Second, pregnancy has been interpreted as a medical event, although it is not inherently a disease state. Pregnancy and delivery tend to be viewed as pathological, or potentially pathological, states that require medical supervision and control. Third, there has been renewed interest in the role of economic and political factors in structuring health care. Doyal (1981) emphasizes the political economy of health care, in which health is treated as a commodity, and profit becomes a consideration in the formation of maternity and infant services. A hierarchy is perpetuated within medical and nursing spheres, such that nurses are less influential and less rewarded than physicians. And in contrast to the liberal ideal of equal treatment for all people, social class, gender, and race remain important variables in the composition of health care services (Shroff 1997).

More recent studies have also questioned the limits of liberal ideology in midwifery practice. Once again, there are concerns over fiscal cutbacks in health care, and increased competition and decreased resources in Canadian higher education. There are also trends that undermine midwifery principles such as being assigned to a midwife rather than choosing a midwife (see James 1997, 189–91). More recent work has concentrated on conflicts between aboriginal midwives and the movement toward professionalization, and under-representation of minority women in midwifery education and midwifery practice in Canada (Couchie and Nabigon 1997a). Sheryl Nestle (1996–97) found that visible and racial minority women are under-represented among practicing midwives in Ontario, and concludes that privilege and exclusion survive within the woman-centred profession of midwifery and its educational institutions. Sheila Kitzinger (2000, 139) cautions that North American midwives run the risk of serving more affluent clients while paying less attention to poor women. In North America, midwives face the danger of being co-opted by the dominant medical and nursing professions. If midwives are integrated into the health care system, it has been argued that they may no longer be able to provide the same level of intimate, noninterventionist service to women. Yet, if midwifery remains on the margin, without legal status, its clientele will be limited to those who can afford private fees, and midwives will not necessarily follow guidelines for safer practice (Kilthei 2002). Other researchers document global disparities in maternity care, including the estimated half million women who die, usually unnecessarily, of "childbirth-related causes." Most of these women are in poorer countries and suffer from contaminated water, lack of access to qualified personnel and health care resources (Hird and Burtch 1997).

Coroners' Inquests and Inquiries

Midwifery receives substantial media coverage when a midwife-attended birth results in an infant's death or injury. Often, a coroner's inquest or inquiry may be held to determine the cause of death and the circumstances surrounding the birth. Recommendations from coroner's juries in Ontario support the establishment of midwifery as a separate profession, with specific guidelines for midwifery practice. A 1982 inquest recommended "The College of Physicians and Surgeons of Ontario and the College of Nurses of Ontario together should set up standards for and establish a program of study in midwifery leading to a licence to practise midwifery in the province of Ontario" (Burtch 1992, 166). The inquests stressed the importance of public education about the risks and benefits of various birthing settings. The complementary roles of physicians and midwives were emphasized. Differences of opinion over coroners' inquests are evident. For example, Kaufman (1989, 2) cautions that inquests are expensive and "inherently reactive" in addressing health-related problems, while James (1997, 185) suggests that coroners' recommendations in British Columbia and Ontario may have played a key role in the implementation of midwifery regulations and legislation.

Few midwives are willing to continue practice without an assurance that the law will not be invoked against them. Criminal prosecution, coroner's investigations, or prosecution for practising medicine without a licence are ever present threats for community midwives. In the mid-1980s in Vancouver, B.C., following an infant's death after an attempted home birth, two midwives—Gloria LeMay and Mary Sullivan—were found guilty of criminal negligence causing death. The conviction was appealed and the appellants were found guilty on a new charge of criminal negligence causing bodily harm (to the mother), a charge that had been substituted for the original one. In 1991, six years after the first conviction, the Supreme Court of Canada acquitted both midwives. This was in keeping with the general trend in Canada of acquitting midwives facing formal charges under criminal or quasi-criminal law. Other midwives have been subject to coroner's inquests or inquiries, and in at least one case in B.C., criminal prosecution was seriously considered, following an infant death. In Alberta, in 1990, a longstanding community midwife, Noreen Walker, was charged with practising medicine without a licence, even though the delivery was successful, and no complaint was registered by the parents (Jimenez 1990). On June 5, 1991, a trial judge directed an acquittal without calling for defence witnesses (Burtch 1994).

Midwifery has been legalized in a number of provinces, including Alberta, Ontario, and British Columbia. Even so, there has been considerable discussion over the merits of legalization and professionalization. Farah Shroff (1997) reviews concerns over the replacement of a woman-friendly midwifery model with a "medical model" of birth that reduces women's choices as mothers, and unnecessarily restricts midwives in certain activities. DeVries (1985) examines how the violation of regulatory law by American midwives raises serious questions about the value of legal regulation of practice. The value of self-regulation is not entirely positive. Once subject to a licensing law, midwives' practices are not reviewed by peers alone, but by "a legal code that defines acceptable and unacceptable behavior" (DeVries 1985, 120). Where midwives are not subject to regulatory laws, several factors can operate in their favour: (1) few charges brought by clients against midwives and reluctance of clients to testify against midwives; (2) positive publicity about alternative birth practices; (3) mobilization of financial and other support from other midwives; and (4) "hesitancy on the part of the courts to penalize unlicensed midwives" (DeVries 1985, 121).

Once licensed, midwives are subject to the scrutiny of medical personnel and disciplinary proceedings. DeVries's work highlights the dilemma of using state law to regulate parental choices and midwifery practice. While the use of repressive law, such as criminal prosecution, has traditionally not resulted in conviction of unlicensed midwives, legal costs are high, and the adversarial nature of such actions can widen the gulf between midwives and physicians. Yet where licensing is established, midwives face loss of the right to practise as a midwife and possibly loss or suspension of a nursing licence. As such, the once-blurred legal status of midwives practising outside the system is sharpened by legalization, but in a manner that retains an edge of punitiveness (1985, 136–37). It has also been pointed out that legalization in itself does not guarantee adequate midwifery services. Midwifery can be established but it can also be whittled away or removed.

The reappearance of community-based, independent midwifery practice in Canada in the mid-1970s challenged the medicalization of childbirth. As a countercultural movement in Canada and elsewhere, midwifery offered an alternative to hospital-based, professionally directed management of birth. The appropriation of childbirth by the (predominantly male) medical profession and the cultural definition of women as incapable of managing birth were strongly contested in theory and practice by midwives. Many positive developments have strengthened the solidarity of Canadian midwives. Securing the 1993 International Congress of Midwifery in Vancouver was a major coup. The *realpolitik* of professional resistance as well as limited resources among pro-midwifery groups has led to broader alliances among activist groups. As the conflicting evidence is weighed, it is clear that there are no convincing arguments against the implementation of midwifery services as part of Canadian social policy. Opponents of midwifery seem to keep midwives in the backcourt by means of expensive litigation and fallacious arguments concerning women's preferences in childbirth and the costs of establishing midwifery training and practices. Midwives are moving to the forecourt, however, and now have international support, a growing research base, and a history of promoting safe, pluralistic birth attendance. The political will of government officials, legislators, and the medical and nursing professions is likely to be decisive in determining the future of midwifery in Canada. As Carol Smart (1989) has cautioned, it is crucial that we recognize that new forms of legal control may create substantial gaps between what women seek by way of freedoms, and what is offered to them in policies.

SUMMARY

The three general areas discussed in this chapter—family law, abortion, and childbirth options—provide considerable support for a major theme in this book: the gap between legal ideals and actual implementation of rights. This implementation becomes complex and controversial. There have been efforts by the courts to provide a more considered approach to child custody, such that estranged parents might agree to co-parent their children. Ideally, this would provide more continuity for children and both parents, and may result in a more cordial divorce. Feminists have quickly countered, however, that efforts to reach joint custody can be used strategically to undermine the power of the primary parent (most often, the mother), and to impose a parenting arrangement that serves neither the children nor the mother. The importance of feminist studies on family, abortion, and childbirth has been well-established in recent research and theorizing. We should keep in mind that access to legal services and other resources varies throughout Canada, whether this is lack of access to state-subsidized midwifery services or fragmented abortion services across Canada. At another level, there are ongoing problems for many women in receiving adequate child support, a situation that can pose substantial hardships after separation. Finally, lest we become complacent with formal legal victories in areas of reproductive choice or in family law, it is important to note that these victories can be undone. Laws can be reversed, or policies established that undermine the spirit of formal legal equality.

STUDY QUESTIONS

1. The status of Canadian midwives illustrates how social conflicts reach into the legal sphere. Summarize the key argument for and against the legalization of midwifery in the Canadian provinces. How has the course of legal cases affected the status of midwives?

2. Mary Morton (1988) observes of family law reform in Ontario that, while women's status has been altered through legal enactments and changing policies, it is essentially unimproved. Assess whether family law reforms provide a fairer basis for separation and divorce in your province or territory.

3. Compose a position statement on reforms you believe are warranted in family law legislation and procedures. Identify which specific reforms are necessary, in your opinion, and articulate a rationale for these reforms. Make reference to available studies, statistics, and theoretical positions to support your suggestions.

4. Select two Canadian legal cases involving (a) child custody, (b) property settlement, or (c) child/spousal maintenance and discuss how Professor Pulkingham's outlook might bear on arguments and outcomes in these two cases. You should give a clear indication where these cases might be found, and if on-line, the exact URL for the marker's reference.

WEB SITES

http://www.lexum.umontreal.ca/csc-scc/en/pub/1995/vol2/html/1995scr2_0513.html (*Egan v Canada* case, from the Supreme Court of Canada site at the University of Montreal)

REFERENCES

Ahluwalia, S. (1991) "Currents in British Feminist Thought: The Study of Male Violence." In *New Directions in Critical Criminology*, edited by B. MacLean and D. Milovanovic, 55–62. Vancouver: The Collective Press.

Backhouse, C. (1991) *Petticoats and Prejudice: Women and Law in Nineteenth-Century Canada*. Toronto: The Women's Press.

Balakrishnan, T.R., Evelyne Lapierre-Adamczyk, and Karol Frótki (1993) *Family and Childbearing in Canada: A Demographic Analysis*. Toronto: University of Toronto Press.

Breger, R., and R. Hill (1998) "Introducing Mixed Marriages." In *Cross-Cultural Marriage: Identity and Change*, edited by R. Breger and R. Hill, 1–32. Oxford: Berg.

Burtch, B. (1994) *Trials of Labour: The Re-emergence of Midwifery*. Montréal: McGill-Queen's University Press.

Canada (1977) *Report of the Committee on the Operation of the Abortion Law*. Ottawa: Supply and Services Canada.

Childbirth by Choice Trust (1998) *No Choice: Canadian Women Tell Their Stories of Illegal Abortion*. Toronto: The Childbirth by Choice Trust.

Clarke, A. (1987) "Moral Protest, Status Defence and the Anti-Abortion Campaign." *British Journal of Sociology* 38(2): 235–53.

Cobb, S. (1997) "The Domestication of Violence in Mediation: Patrolling the Perimeters of Law's Disciplinary Power." *Law and Society Review* 31(3): 397–441.

Couchie, C., and H. Nabigon (1997) "A Path towards Reclaiming Nishnawbe Birth Culture: Can the Midwifery Exemption Clause for Aboriginal Midwives Make a Difference?" In *The New Midwifery: Reflections on Renaissance and Regulation*, edited by F. Shroff, 41–50. Toronto: The Women's Press.

Davis, N. (1987) "Abortion and Legal Policy." *Contemporary Crises* 10: 373–97.

DeVries, R. (1985) *Regulating Birth: Midwives, Medicine, and the Law*. Philadelphia: Temple University Press.

Dickens, C. (1995) *Great Expectations* [ed. Tim Seward]. Cambridge, New York: Cambridge University Press [originally published 1861]

Doyal, L., with I. Pennell (1981) *The Political Economy of Health.* Boston: South End Press.

Dunphy, C. (1996) *Morgentaler: A Difficult Hero.* Toronto: Random House of Canada.

Eisenstein, Z. (1988) *The Female Body and the Law.* Berkeley: University of California Press.

Freeman, D. (1984) "Introduction: Rethinking Family Law." In *State, Law, and the Family: Critical Perspectives,* edited by D. Freeman, 1–6. London: Tavistock.

Gavigan, S. (1986) "Women, Law and Patriarchial Relations: Perspectives in the Sociology of Law." In *The Social Dimensions of Law,* edited by N. Boyd, 101–24. Toronto: Prentice-Hall.

——. (1987) "Women and Abortion in Canada: What's Law Got to Do With It?" In *Feminism and Political Economy: Women's Work, Women's Struggles,* edited by H. Maroney and M. Luxton, 263–84. Toronto: Methuen.

Glendon, M. (1989) "On Abortion and Divorce in the Western World." In *A World of Ideas,* edited by B. Flowers, 470–83. New York: Doubleday.

Greatbach, D. and R. Dingwall (1999) "The Marginalization of Domestic Violence in Divorce Mediation." *International Journal of Law, Policy and the Family* 13(2): 174–90.

Hartnagel, T., J. Creechan, and R. Silverman (1985) "Public Opinion and the Legalization of Abortion." *Canadian Review of Sociology and Anthropology* 22(3): 411–30.

Henry, F., C. Tator, W. Mattis, and T. Rees (1995). *The Colour of Democracy: Racism in Canadian Society.* Toronto: Harcourt Brace and Company.

Hird, C. and B. Burtch (1997) "Midwives and Safe Motherhood: International Perspectives." In *The New Midwifery: Reflections on Renaissance and Regulation,* edited by F. Shroff, 115–45. Toronto: The Women's Press.

Hovius, B., (1992) *Family Law: Cases, Notes, and Materials* (3rd edition).Toronto: Carswell.

Ignatieff, M. (2000) *The Rights Revolution.* Toronto: House of Anansi Press

James, S. (1997) "Regulation: Changing The Face of Midwifery?" In *The New Midwifery: Reflections on Renaissance and Regulation,* edited by F. Shroff, 181–200. Toronto: The Women's Press.

Jimenez, M. (1990) "Midwife Must Stand Trial, Judge Decides." *The Globe and Mail* (November 10).

Kaufman, K. (1989) "Midwifery on Trial." *The Midwifery Task Force Journal* 2(1): 1–2.

Kilthei, J. (2002) "Letter to the Editor: *Today's Parent.*" March 22 (sent to *Today's Parent* magazine).

Kitzinger, S., ed. (1988) *The Midwife Challenge.* London: Pandora Books.

——. (2000) *Rediscovering Birth.* Boston: Little, Brown.

MacKinnon, C. (1987) *Feminism Unmodified: Discourses on Life and Law.* Cambridge: Harvard University Press.

Mandel, M. (1989) *The Charter of Rights and the Legalization of Politics in Canada.* Toronto: Wall and Thompson.

McLaren, A., and A. McLaren (1986) *The Bedroom and the State: The Changing Practices and Policies of Contraception and Abortion in Canada, 1880–1980.* Toronto: McClelland and Stewart.

McLaren, A. (1999) "Illegal Operations: Women, Doctors, and Abortion, 1886-1939." In *Law and Society: Canadian Readings,* edited by N. Larsen and B. Burtch, 22–38. Toronto: Nelson.

Menzies, R. and D. Chunn (1991) "Kicking Against the Pricks: The Dilemmas of Feminist Teaching in Criminology." In *New Directions in Critical Criminology,* edited by B. MacLean and D. Milovanovic, 63–70. Vancouver: The Collective Press.

Midwifery and the Law (1991) Educational videotape. Directed by Keet Neville and Michael Doherty and produced by Brian Burtch. Simon Fraser University (Continuing Studies) and the Knowledge Network. 30 minutes.

Morgentaler, Smoling and Scott v. The Queen (1988), 37 C.C.C. (3d) 449 (S.C.C.).

Morton, M. (1988) "Dividing the Wealth, Sharing the Poverty: The (Re)formation of 'Family' in Law in Ontario." *Canadian Review of Sociology and Anthropology* 25 (2): 254–75.

Murayama, M. (1999) "Does a Lawyer Make a Difference? Effects of a Lawyer on Mediation Outcomes in Japan." *International Journal of Law, Policy and the Family* 13(1): 52–77.

Nestle, S. (1996/97) "A New Profession to the White Population in Canada: Ontario Midwifery and the Politics of Race." *Health and Canadian Society* 4(2): 315–41.

O'Neil, P. (2000) "66% are pro-choice, poll finds: Majority of Alliance members also say they support right to abortion, Environics finds." *The Vancouver Sun* August 31, p. A1.

Plath, S. (1965) "Morning Song." In *Ariel,* p. 11. London: Faber and Faber Ltd.

Pulkingham (1999) "Private Troubles, Private Solutions: Poverty among Divorced Women and the Politic of Support Enforcement and Child Custody Determination." In Larsen and Burtch, 277–96.

Registered Nurses' Association of B.C. (rnabc) (1987) "Position Statement: Midwifery." *rnabc News* (July/August): 22.

Samis, S. (1995) *"An Injury to One is an Injury to All": Heterosexism, Homophobia, and anti-gay/lesbian violence in Greater Vancouver.* Unpublished M.A. Thesis, Department of Sociology and Anthropology, Simon Fraser University.

Sanders, D. (1999) "Constructing Lesbian and Gay Rights" In *Law in Society: Canadian Perspectives,* edited by N. Larsen and B. Burtch, 158–94. Toronto: Harcourt Brace Canada.

Sarat, A., and W. Felstiner (1986) "Law and Strategy in the Divorce Lawyer's Office." *Law and Society Review* 10(1): 93–134.

Seel, R. (1987) *The Uncertain Father: Exploring Modern Fatherhood.* Bath, England: Gateway Books.

Shaffer, M. (1999) "Criminal Responses to Hate-Motivated Violence: Is Bill C-41 Tough Enough?" In *Law in Society: Canadian Perspectives,* edited by N. Larsen and B. Burtch, 302–32. Toronto: Harcourt Brace Canada.

Shibata, Y. (1998) "Crossing Racialized Boundaries: Intermarriage between 'Africans' and 'Indians' in Contemporary Guyana." In *Cross-Cultural Marriage: Identity and*

Change, edited by R. Breger and R. Hill, 83–100. Oxford: Berg.

Shroff, F. (1997) "Introduction: Midwifery—from Rebellion to Regulation: The Rebirth of an Ancient Calling." In *The New Midwifery: Reflections on Renaissance and Regulation,* edited by F. Shroff, 15–37. Toronto: The Women's Press.

——. (1997) "All Petals of the Flower: Celebrating the Diversity of Ontario's Birthing Women within First-Year Midwifery Curriculum." In *The New Midwifery: Reflections on Renaissance and Regulation,* edited

by F. Shroff, 261–310. Toronto: The Women's Press.

Simpson, B. (1998) *Changing Families: An Ethnographic Approach to Divorce and Separation.* Oxford: Berg.

Smart, C. (1989) *Feminism and the Power of Law.* London: Routledge and Kegan Paul.

Theodorson, G. and A. Theodorson (1979) *A Modern Dictionary of Sociology.* New York: Barnes and Noble.

Weber, M. (2002) "Dad passes judgement on system." [letter to the Editor] *The North Shore News* April 14, p. 6.

10
New Directions in Law and Society Studies

From 1948's Universal Declaration of Human Rights onward, the history of the past half-century has been the struggle of colonial peoples for their freedom, the struggle of minorities of colour and women for full civil rights, and the struggle of aboriginal peoples to achieve self-government.

(Ignatieff 2000, 3)

Law has two contrasting faces. On one face, the rule of law represents a crucial means whereby the dominant rules and values in a society are applied and enforced. On the other, law represents a place where, sometimes, those rules and values are challenged and new ways of understanding may emerge.

(Asch, 1997)

INTRODUCTION

This concluding chapter examines possibilities for changing the nature of law. We reconsider the relation of law-in-theory to the "living law" and the often vexing, ambiguous responses to legal authority. As anthropologist Robin Fox puts it, "… a fascination with the law penetrates all sectors of society. We are all touched by it, scared of it, sometimes glad of it, and always baffled by it" (p. 356). On the other hand, our understanding of law is, in my opinion, much less cloudy than in past eras. There has been a resurgence of interest in socio-legal matters, moving past a self-enclosed jurisprudential approach to embrace ever-growing, multiple outlooks.

The roots of modern and postmodern social movements lie in earlier perspectives on the nature of legal and political authority. Classical works in the sociology of law have clearly outlined the important role of law in modernizing societies, and traced numerous contradictions between the ideal of legal authority as a legitimate arbiter of these conflicts and the reality of law as a powerful interest in its own right. The postmodern spirit, along with many other perspectives outlined in earlier chapters, demonstrates how law and other social institutions are continually challenged.

For example, citing Lyotard, Ward contends that postmodernism is "... ultimately, an exercise dedicated to social and political reform" (1998, 175). Postmodernists object to efforts to promote "universal moral theories" ill-suited to a world of "... irreducible particulars, of differences between individuals [and] situations ..." (ibid). The task is to discover justice not in universal moral or legal frameworks, but "in the particular" (Ward 1998, 179). For example, the issue of race is important in postmodern discourse. Postmodernism offers a means of breaking down the hegemony of law and narrow (primarily Anglo-Saxon) representations. Some critical race theorists honour gains such as the civil rights movement that demonstrate solidarity among Afro-Americans, and establish rights for Afro-Americans and other visible minorities (see Handler 1992, 707–08).

The critics' challenge to legal formalism and legal positivism has been enhanced by a wide range of works on struggles by groups facing discrimination in law and society. These works stem from feminism and feminist critiques of jurisprudence (McDaniel 1991; Tomm and Hamilton 1988). Feminist scholars/activists, advocates for persons with disabilities, visible minorities and aboriginal people, and peace and environmental groups collectively challenge traditional legal structures and government policies (Young 1990). Many modern efforts to transform (or reform) legal powers reveal a tendency toward activism among social scientists and legal scholars. Many would agree with the spirit of Roscoe Pound's interest in combining a *social control* perspective with pragmatism. Pound argued that legal scholars should not assume a strict detachment from issues of the day, and seek to act as if they were "legal monks" (Milovanovic 1988, 91). Pound also formulated a set of *jural postulates*:

1. no intentional harm to others

2. personal control over discoveries and acquisitions

3. good faith in contractual dealings

4. responsible control of potentially dangerous elements (Milovanovic 1988, 92)

While Pound has been criticized for not attending to structured inequalities in American justice and society, he nonetheless provides a critical approach to legal politics. He also maintains the importance of preserving legal authority. Pound described law as "a highly specialized form of social control, carried on in accordance with a body of authoritative precepts, applied in a judicial and administrative process" (cited in Milovanovic 1988, 91). As we consider new directions in sociolegal studies, it is important to note that there are strong disagreements over the nature of law and the appropriate role of social scientists and legal scholars/practitioners. These disagreements emerge even within particular schools of thought. Legal realists, for example, show considerable differences of opinion and approach in their work. As noted in Chapter Four on feminism and law, there appears to be less emphasis on abstract analysis, and more attention to grounded work that investigates the actual results of decision-making (see Milovanovic 1988, 94).

The establishment of critical legal studies in recent decades reflects a growing interest in Marxist-based, feminist studies of law. Class, race, gender, and the perdurable concepts of discrimination, hegemony, and legal domination are at the forefront of critical legal studies. The critical legal studies approach, as it has matured, retains an interest in the role of legal ideology, including the process of *reification* (inflation of the law, thereby expanding its power of domination) and *hegemony* (use of ideology and other resources to secure the consent of oppressed people to the rule of an elite).

The critical legal studies approach offers not only a critique of significant disparities between legal ideals and law in practice, but also an analysis of how power is conveyed through socialization in law school. Power is seen as conveyed through patterns of dependency, hierarchy, and legal terminology (Kelman 1987, 103). The approach also affords a viewpoint on contradictions in legal training: Kelman (1987, 184–85) observes that many law students appear receptive to progressive objectives, yet can also argue convincingly for "right-wing" economic policies, retaining some faith in the free market and propertied relations. One measure of changes in law school training will be the extent to which feminist jurisprudence and other equally progressive approaches are incorporated into curricula. These other approaches would include labour law (examining the dynamics of power between workers and owners) and critical approaches to anti-discrimination law and limits to affirmative action (see Milovanovic 1988, 103–05).

Critical legal studies provides an important critique of ways in which individuals are made dependent on legal officialdom and many other forms of power, for example, in social services (see Handler 1990). The critical legal studies approach also offers a careful look at the scale of devastation that can be brought to cultures in what are now seen as developing nations. Historical examples include the European influence in the South Seas in the eighteenth and nineteenth centuries (Moorehead 1974), culminating in the relocations and ruined economies of South Seas residents with the advent of nuclear testing. Closer to home, there is overwhelming evidence of genocidal and paternalistic policies by Euro-Canadians toward aboriginal peoples. The decimation and resurgence of First Nations peoples, their forced removal onto reserves and into residential schools, and the imposition of Western systems of criminal law all underscored these control-oriented policies (see York 1990).

This critical legacy is rapidly moving toward a more holistic approach, incorporating key variables of social class, race, ethnicity, and gender (e.g., Comack 1999). New directions treat these variables as interactive, recasting patterns of social stratification and legal decision-making. For example, Barak, Flavin and Leighton (2001, Ch. 5) detail embedded patterns of inequality and privilege in American society. They document women's lower average income than men's, the clustering of many women in lower-paid, less secure service work, and under-representation of women in colour in better-paid positions vis-à-vis "white" counterparts (2001, 194–95). Feminist scholars also explore strategies of resistance to patriarchal structures and market-based, neo-liberal ideologies. Dorothy Chunn, for example, contests arguments of gender equality in work, family matters, and family law, identifies new forms of disadvantage for women and children, and argues for a far-reaching "social responsibility model" in Canada (1999, 256–59). Similarly, Joan Brockman's study of gender and the legal profession offers a detailed analysis of ways of "breaking the mould," in her words. This includes recognition of some common ground for male and female lawyers—the benefits and drawbacks of legal practice, for example—and recommendations for transforming law schools and legal practices (Brockman 2001).

Current thinking in political science, law, and sociology includes the argument that there should be a right to secede, under certain circumstances. The image of social contract can be invoked here. Kai Nielsen argues for a limited right of secession within larger political bodies such as a nation-state. In his own words, he favours a "... presumptive moral right of a nation to secede from a larger multination state or centralized state should the majority of the members wish to do so" (1998, 253). People seeking a distinct status of a nation should however demonstrate a "common history," "common culture," and "historical attachment to a particular territory" (1998, 255). Nielsen draws a distinction between those aspiring to separate nationhood and other groups such as immigrants who cannot make such compelling claims to distinct nationhood.

This chapter reviews a few examples of works that fit with the more progressive, critical character of sociolegal studies. Mandel (1989) provides a critical look at the effects of the Charter of Rights and Freedoms, particularly its regressive character with respect to popular, democratic expressions. Brickey and Comack (1987) review instrumental Marxism vis-à-vis structural Marxism, with a view to reassessing the place of law in social transformation. Next, Elizabeth Comack (1988) disputes the ideal of "justice for all," based on the limited reforms in criminal law processes for battered women. Finally, Young (1990) examines the struggles of various social movements against oppression.

MANDEL: RULE OF LAW AND CANADIAN POLITICS

Mandel, currently a professor of law at Osgoode Hall, provides a critical assessment of the Charter of Rights and Freedoms. Mandel (1989) notes that the enactment of the Charter generated various reactions from socialist and Marxist scholars. Mandel (1989) defines his own response as "negative."

Before addressing the implications of the Charter for Canadian politics, Mandel (1989) reviews the central debate between structural Marxists (exemplified by the late E.B. Pashukanis) and the English social historian E.P. Thompson. Mandel (1989) relates how interest in Pashukanis's class writings on law and the state was revived along with a renewed interest in Marxist and socialist approaches to law. In particular, the legal precept of the *rule of law* was criticized. The rule of law rests on the realization of a legal sphere that is "autonomous and egalitarian." This idealized sphere was, according to its critics, nullified by the everyday oppression of the social relations of production under capitalism (Mandel 1989, 305). Mandel recaps the range of this critique, including the base-superstructure relationship and the less economically oriented approach that sees law as serving a legitimizing function under capitalism.

Mandel takes seriously the issue of the rule of law and whether or not the traditional *devaluation* (Mandel 1989, 306) of the rule of law is correct. One factor in such an assessment is the implementation of lawless, repressive policies under the Stalinist regime. These policies have been interpreted as a form of mass "terror." A second factor is the implication of devaluing the rule of law at a *theoretical* level, while acknowledging the importance of the rule of law as a *pragmatic* aspect of ongoing struggles about law (Mandel 1989, 306).

Mandel then moves to an appreciation of Thompson's classic work, *Whigs and Hunters* (1977). This book deals with the implementation of the Black Act in England in 1723, and especially the great number of offences that became capital offences. Clearly, the Black Act was a form of terror, one that established the importance of protecting private property. As a piece of "class legislation" (Thompson, cited in Mandel 1989, 306), however, the Black Act was not complete or all-powerful. Thompson outlines how the Black Act was resisted, undermined, and eventually repealed. Here, Thompson points out that the ideological power of law is contested, and that some concessions to interests other than the dominant class must be made. Otherwise, the legitimacy of law becomes fragile and possibly insupportable, except by repressive measures.

We ought to expose the shams and inequities which may be concealed beneath this law. But the rule of law itself, the imposing of effective inhibitions upon power and the defence of the citizen from power's all-intrusive claims, seems to me to be an unqualified human good. To deny or belittle this good is, in this dangerous century when the resources and pretentions of power continue to enlarge, a desperate error of intellectual abstraction. More than this, it is a self-fulfilling error, which encourages us to give up the struggle against bad laws and class-bound procedures, and to disarm ourselves before power. It is to throw away a whole inheritance of struggle about law, and within the forms of law, whose continuity can never be fractured without bringing men and women into immediate danger (Thompson 1977, 266, emphasis in original).

The experience of repression is symbolized by the totalitarian regimes of Nazism and Stalinism in the twentieth century (see Mandel 1989, 307). Thus, despite the inequities of modern legal rule, Thompson still aligns himself with the democratic possibilities within the rule of law but not, as he humorously puts it, "the rule of the people by any old codger in a wig" (Mandel 1989, 308). Aware of the sham aspects of modern legal power, Thompson is nevertheless not prepared to abandon legality, with its protections and its possibilities for checking the absolute powers of the state or other sectors.

BRICKEY AND COMACK: LAW AND SOCIAL TRANSFORMATION

Brickey and Comack (1987) make the valuable point that Marxist perspectives on law have tended to focus on a critique of Western legal systems. As such, the strategic use of law in promoting socialism has been underemphasized or, in some cases, disregarded altogether. There has nonetheless been stronger emphasis in critical legal scholarship on developing practical strategies for overturning oppression, including practical legal strategies. Brickey and Comack (1987) shift the focus from theorizing about law to considering the practical uses of law in the interests of social justice. The authors' discussion builds on the rule of law as a political doctrine that legitimates and constrains political, economic, and social activities. The key point that formal equality does not reach into the stratified sphere of economics is well taken (Brickey and Comack 1987, 100). Nevertheless, the state under capitalism is not entirely wedded to the interests of the dominant class, but mediates the conflicting interests of class, gender, race, age, and so forth, through its relative autonomy, which allows it to act semi-independently from any particular class.

Brickey and Comack voice their concern over the skepticism of structuralists regarding the value of law as "a vehicle for social transformation" (Brickey and Comack 1987, 101). The structuralist perspective is thus criticized for its failure to appreciate the influence of class consciousness, an influence that may curb state activities and the workings of the private sector. Such an accomplishment would include engaging in legal struggles and struggles over rights, and accepting that, in the modern world of capitalist democracy, societies are "unavoidably legalistic" (Brickey and Comack 1987, 103). Law can thus be a fulcrum for progressive social movements. Brickey and Comack (1987, 103) caution that if legal struggles are not launched, current law-and-order campaigns may prevail in shaping law and social policies. They note that several groups are already active in formulating what they wish in terms of social justice: women, Native peoples, prisoners, and other "subordinated" groups (Brickey and Comack 1987, 103). Belliotti (1995) admits that there is not a Marxian theory of law; rather, a primary contribution of this perspective is its debunking of liberal perspectives on law and capitalism. Specifically, law is not seen as "inevitable" and there is an argument for non-legal forms of cultural and social relations. Similarly, law is not seen as autonomous from specific interests, but in fact legal authority is "complicit" in the protection or extension of capitalist interests (1995, 11–12). Even though explicitly Marxist approaches to law and society are widely criticized, Belliotti credits this tradition with informing emerging critical frameworks, including contemporary feminist and critical race perspectives (1995).

COMACK: BATTERED WOMEN AND SOCIAL JUSTICE

Once a taboo subject, only cryptically referred to in academic and popular literature, violence against women has recently come out into the open. It is now acknowledged that such violence is widespread, either as direct acts of injury or as threats against women. The study of "date rape" has likewise confirmed that such assaultive behaviour is far from rare. One contentious area in the discussion of domestic violence has been the availability of legal defences for women who retaliate against their abusers, especially in cases of homicide of husbands or common-law husbands. Comack (1988) reviews two legal decisions concerning wife-battering in Manitoba, using these cases as a background for the wider issue of wife-battering and the concept of the "battered-wife syndrome" (see the earlier discussion in Chapter Four).

Comack (1988, 10–11) links the continuing phenomenon of wife assault with *structural* conditions that limit women's choices. Comack does not imply that all women are powerless or that the legal reaction is entirely unhelpful to all women who have been abused. Nevertheless, the play of male bias and misunderstanding remains central to Comack's analysis. It is also important to bear in mind that abused women often find that the police and prosecutors are far from effective in deterring batterers from injuring or harassing them. Comack's work is clearly pertinent and informative and leads us to ask how her approach might be extended to account for violence by men against men. A wider approach to male violence and gender socialization is needed to trace and explain such variations in violent behaviour. Greater attention could be given to the overall victimization associated with violent crimes. It appears that not only have Americans been exposed to a substantial increase in the likelihood that they will be assaulted, murdered, or sexually assaulted, but, as Davis and Stasz (1990, 298) note, there are no indications that patterns of violence are easing. They add that this victimization is not spread evenly though American society: youths, and particularly black youths, are disproportionately victimized by violent crime.

Beyond assessments of victimization, an understanding of how physical abuse affects women could include legal strategies for victims of violence. Parallel to Comack's interest in the battered-wife syndrome as a legal defence, Goldberg-Ambrose (1989, 954–55) recommends that rape-trauma syndrome be employed in rape prosecutions. This emphasis on the physical and psychological impact of rape on the victim could be used to overcome conflicting testimonies or the cultural emphasis on women-blaming, in which women are held "responsible for controlling both sexes' sexuality" (Goldberg-Ambrose 1989, 954–55). Goldberg-Ambrose (1989, 954) concludes that such research could serve to reshape legal perceptions of the act of rape and its impact, and could thus hold the potential for transforming current legal practices surrounding rape.

YOUNG: ON JUSTICE AND THE POLITICS OF DIFFERENCE

Much of the contemporary writing and research in the sociology of law emerges from disenchantment with liberal ideals of harmony and shared interests. This disenchantment has given rise to new social movements that challenge existing premises and structures of law. These new social movements include the women's movement, gay liberation, and struggles by people of colour (including blacks, Hispanics, Native peoples) and disabled persons (Young 1990, 3). For Young (1990, 9), it is crucial to appreciate the diversity of these groups, rather than impose an artificial consensus as a guiding point for their aspirations and needs.

Young insists that the concept of *oppression* is crucial in any legal philosophy purporting to address these movements. Oppression takes several aspects: marginalization, exploitation, powerlessness, cultural imperialism (referring to the superiority or inferiority attributed to certain groups), and violence (Young 1990, 9). Young (1990, 179) thus cautions against using such overly general concepts as "the public": there is no homogeneous public, as many understand it, and efforts to establish this reified public in legal policy can be devastating for minorities. Young cites the "English-only" movement in the United States as a case in point—an example that also applies to the Canadian context, given the efforts to establish primacy of the English language or the French language in Quebec. Such one-dimensional approaches, embedded in law and social policy, would obscure linguistic differences in both countries. Another example of the inappropriateness of this concept of a universal public is available in studies of municipal politics in New England. Young (1990, 184) notes that, while all citizens are invited to participate in town meetings, some groups are underrepresented: disabled people, mothers, racial minorities, and the elderly. At such meetings it is often "white middle-class men [who] assume authority more than others" (Young 1990, 184).

Young's emphasis on oppression leads her to make provocative statements about "right" and "wrong," an approach that raises as many questions as it answers. In the face of white male hegemony, for instance, she concludes that it is now improper to maintain or establish all-male clubs (thus excluding women), but all-women's associations are acceptable, and likely preferable. The point for Young (1990, 197) is to strategically combat oppression generated and "embedded" in social institutions. This approach certainly places the abstract nature of much legal discourse over "rights" in a political context. Young's work thus takes seriously the embedded nature of privilege, and argues for wider mobilization of social movements concerned with social justice.

Another difficulty with Young's analysis is overgeneralization. Young (1990, 197) refers to the "priority of the point of view of white heterosexual men." Clearly, this generalization obscures differences among men, not only in opinions or values, but also in social power. This tendency to group people is ironic, given Young's emphasis on diversity and struggling against stereotyping. The strength of her work, however, is her insight into how law, cultural practices, and state policies have often been implemented so as to exclude or silence various groups, and how it will take more than a liberal reshuffling of programs and opportunities to implement substantive change.

NEW DIRECTIONS IN THE SOCIOLOGY OF LAW

One of the most promising directions in sociological research on law has been the incorporation of rigorous qualitative and/or quantitative research in addressing legal issues. Scholars could take note of the artificial divisions between qualitative and quantitative methods, and work toward a more integrated approach in exploring what Palys (1997) calls "research questions". Hagan (1986, 57) favours a pluralistic approach to sociolegal research. As issues become more complex, and attention turns from formal legal rules to informal processes underlying legal decision-making, for instance, it becomes important to develop theories that are empirically grounded and attentive to less formal negotiations. These less formal processes include negotiated settlements via arbitration and mediation, and plea bargaining in criminal law (Hagan 1986, 48). Sociological research that combines theorizing with rigorous statistical analyses is a particularly promising approach to understanding legal issues. One example of this is Arnold's (1991) study of professional deviance among Ontario lawyers and disciplinary actions against them. Arnold (1991) provides a framework that examines why lawyers may become involved in unethical or illegal practices, and variations in sanctions for those in violation of professional standards of conduct.

Research of a more qualitative nature also helps us understand the power and limitations of law, dramatizing the gulf between legal rhetoric and legal practice. MacKinnon (1979, 192–93) uses the example of sexual harassment of working women to underline ways in which harassment has not been taken seriously, even when formal complaints have been made. For MacKinnon, sexual harassment is not merely inappropriate behaviour by an individual against employees or co-workers. Rather, it stems from and strengthens sexist values concerning women. It also places limits on women's position within the occupational structure. Sexual harassment "singles out a gender-defined group, women, for special treatment in a way which adversely affects and burdens their status as employees. Sexual harassment limits women in ways men are not limited. It deprives them of opportunities that are available to male employees without sexual conditions. In so doing, it creates two employment standards: one for women that includes sexual requirements, one for men that does not."

MacKinnon (1979, 192) thus challenges the usefulness of assuming equality of the sexes before the law or in social life generally. She recommends adopting a "differences approach," one that appreciates gender (or race, class, or other extra-legal factors), since "most sexually harassed people are women" (MacKinnon 1979, 193; see also Ahluwalia 1991, 58–61; Young 1990).

Anthropological studies of law and custom will no doubt continue to enhance our understanding of law and society. A collection of essays edited by Olivia Harris (1996), for example, offers many critical insights into such issues as globalization, land use, and resistance by indigenous people to Westernized systems of law, including formal court adjudication of conflicts. This collection of essays underscores another theme that will no doubt characterize new work in this area: a reluctance to treat law or society as simple, easily understood constructs, and a willingness to appreciate nuance and contradiction rather than cut-and-dried theoretical explanations. Struggles by First Nations, Métis, and Inuit people in Canada, and by indigenous people in other countries reestablishes a new benchmark in discussions of sovereignty, difference, and justice.

Grace Skogstad (2001) emphasizes the historical fact of Canada's vulnerability to international forces (2001, 805). She defines four facets of globalization: economic, political, cultural, and ideological. The economic facet includes greater movement of capital across borders and a "deepening integration of markets ..." while the ideological factor is manifested in the rise of "... market liberalism, deregulation and privatization" (2001, 808). She defines this neo-liberal spirit as focused on budget deficit reduction and a "retreat" in "expenditure and regulatory policy areas" (2001, 826). Again, the power of global capitalism, like that of law and other social institutions, is contested. Orford also contends that globalization forces are being resisted and that globalization, whether economic, cultural, or political, is not a fait accompli. Cuts in social expenditures have become commonplace in more conservative governments in Canada and elsewhere. Dismantling the liberal welfare state can be a boon for those with capital and property, and a cascade of social problems for the disabled and unemployed, for example (Allen 2000, 13–14). Blaming individuals for their immorality and inadequacies has become a staple in retrenchment politics, with less attention paid to systemic disadvantage and efforts to redistribute social justice and other benefits (Allen 2000, Ch. 4).

Habermas (1996) provides a complex analysis of the legitimacy of law and ways in which legal power can be destabilized and reconstructed in complex societies. Changes in legal rules and thinking reflect not only an effort to achieve fairness and solidarity in a given jurisdiction, but also "money and administrative power" (1996, 39–40). There is an ongoing interest in cultural studies and law, with deconstruction of texts, discourses, and efforts to extract identities and experiences out of media and state-mediated constructions. Alison Young's *Imagining Crime* (1996) exemplifies a postmodern approach to social control measures and new ways of interpreting crime and reactions to it. She reconsiders gender, especially ways in which women have become "criminology's secret," both managed and yet resistant (1996, 47).

The growth of coalitions is another new direction in the sociology of law. For example, specific interest groups have lobbied for greater access to abortion services, and in British Columbia and other provinces some of their efforts have been fostered by the work of provincial and national civil liberties associations (see Russell 1989). In this example, we see the potential for moving beyond traditional libertarian critiques of abuse of state authority to an appreciation of state measures that can be made more compatible with expressions of freedom (McKercher 1989, 245).

Communitarianism has also become a prominent aspect of social movements and appeals to law. On the one hand, this approach can be seen as regenerating communities and aiding marginalized people. On the other hand, it can also be a more conservative, property-oriented force. Communitarianism has been criticized for a romantic, even myopic view of individuals leaving their "private places" and using more public settings for walking, socializing, and other leisure pursuits. Jeremy Waldron points out that for homeless people, there is no private space to leave (2000, 394–95). Moreover, not all public interest, pressure groups are working for social justice in the sense of greater inclusion of marginalized people. Waldron uses the American Alliance for Rights and Responsibilities (AARR) as a case-in-point. The AARR has expressed concern over the occupation of public spaces by the homeless, listing specific concerns such as illicit drug sales and use, begging, and poor hygiene (Waldron 2000, 373). Again, the communitarian spirit may cloak the specific interests of well-heeled people who, in Waldron's view, cling to a sentimentalized image of city and family life in spite of widespread structural disadvantage (2000, 404–05).

New approaches to law and society often rest on a stronger appreciation of the legacy of colonialism on international development and human rights. The myths of equal opportunity and equal protection of law come clearly into focus when we consider global disparities and the uneven application of legal and quasi-level powers. Doris Buss contends that colonialism must be taken into account for such key areas as environmental degradation and violations of human rights. Moreover, we should be aware of negative stereotyping, for example, of people in what is variously called the Third World, developing countries, or the South (Buss 2000, 468 and 484).

There is a distinct trend to include international law and human rights issues in socio-legal studies. This sometimes takes the form of persecuted religious minorities and other groups who seek legal protection and co-existence with other, more dominant groups (Robertson 2000, 142). The twentieth century witnessed a number of efforts to foster minority rights, including the 1948 Convention on the Prevention and Punishment of Genocide, three years later, a declaration from the International Court of Justice that genocide was "… a crime under customary international law, confirming that such groups had at least a right to exist, maintainable against states which sought to splinter or extinguish them by physical force" (Robertson 2000, 143). The norm, however, is to link the concept of "peoples" with state citizens, reinforcing the linkage between nation-states and peoples. Accordingly, ethno-cultural minority groups other than First Nations may be subsumed as part of a larger sense of a people (see Robertson 2000, 150). This distinction can be quite profound, evidenced in the Human Rights Commission's refusal to hear a Mikmaq effort to secure "independent state" status or to adjudicate the "Indonesian invasion of East Timor" (Robertson 2000, 150–51).

Theorists who regard nation states as sovereign and as the ultimate arbiters of economic, social, and political matters may have to soften this position when we consider the power of transnational corporations (TNCs). As of the mid-1990s, only six nations generated larger revenues that the most powerful TNCs. These nations, in order, are the United States, Germany, Japan, the United Kingdom, Italy, and France (Forsythe 2000, 191–92). To put this in a Canadian perspective, with revenues of approximately $90 billion, Canada was sandwiched between two TNCs: ranked just below Wal-Mart, just above Hitachi (Forsythe 2000, 192). Forsythe warns of the unimpressive record of International law in dealing with human rights violations, giving the example of the suppression of protests against oil extraction in Nigeria, and the execution of activist Ken Saro-Wiwa (2000, 197). Once again, however, this is not a static situation. Human rights activists have been aided by many social movements and sometimes, mass media, in forwarding their concerns over profit-based activities that violate human rights (2000, 198–201).

Criminological research has also followed new, critical contours that move beyond local or national concerns. Ian Taylor took a broad theoretical approach to crime and social exclusion in *Crime in Context* (1999). He dealt directly with the impact of globalization on social, economic, and political life, pointing out that government cutbacks and private sector decisions in the last two decades of the twentieth century generated unemployment not only for many visible minorities but also for working-class "white" populations (1999, 30). Rather than focusing on individual pathology or even national policies, Taylor argued for an international approach that accounts for "… the demise of national Keynesian welfare states and the emergence of their successor, the post-Fordist market society" (1999, 64). Here again, we see a realist outlook that does not fall into pessimism but, like some other observers, the importance of resisting globalization and other forces is accentuated (see also Khor 2001).

The longstanding debate about the value of legal rights will also persist, as will "rights struggles" on many levels. As Ignatieff notes, struggles over rights in Canada have moved well beyond the "bilateral" negotiations between Québec and federal politicians, or the issue of Aboriginal treaty rights and self-government. Ignatieff contends that these important developments are part of a "multi-dimensional chess game" that for some weakens social cohesion and government authority. For others, this proliferation of rights struggles can be a democratizing force, where more and more people and groups are identified and recognized, as society becomes somewhat less hierarchal (Ignatieff 2000, 116–17).

Restorative justice initiatives have also attracted attention, ranging from the laudatory to the very pessimistic. The debate continues over the wisdom of devising alternative means of conflict-resolution and justice. Some praise efforts to move beyond the strictures of formal adjudication of conflicts. The truth commissions in South Africa and Chile are seen as means of relaxing certain evidentiary rules and of allowing victims to "tell their stories" and sometimes to be compensated for their losses and suffering. On the other hand, critics express concern over impediments to civil or criminal courts, and some question whether diluting or abolishing more retributive models is commendable (see Llewellyn and Howse 1999, 355–56, 369).

Delgado (2000) takes a less sanguine view of restorative justice. He combines a critique of the U.S. criminal justice system (for its racist underpinnings and activities) with strong misgivings over the seemingly progressive restorative justice movement. Many restorative justice measures sacrifice "procedural rights," worsen social inequalities, and narrow rather than widen the scope of disputing processes. Moreover, he warns of enhanced state control through net-widening and, in some cases, a lack of punishment/retribution (Delgado 2000, 758–71).

Alternative justice initiatives have also been criticized for an overly benign presentation. Findlay (1999, 198) points out the ironies of putting youth through restorative-style measures linked with substance abuse, while the wider community itself may be conflicted over alcohol consumption and other drug use. He also notes that such restorative measures may conceal corruption and malfeasance among officials (ibid).

The article begins with a short review of "positive law" and its premises of formal authority and a set of rules to guide human conduct (p. 132). In partial contrast, "tribal societies" without formal positive law arrangements often resolved disputes through community-wide participation and a sense of justice aiming at "[r]estoring peace" (p. 133). Barsh and Marlor use these two outlooks to identify different ways of approaching conflict and establishing a sense of justice. The former paradigm—dubbed the "power paradigm" (p. 133)—is attractive in its insistence on articulation of rules and balancing set or standardized expectations with individual freedoms. This idealized paradigm has garnered considerable criticism, including deep concerns about the limitations of punishment in assuring public safety and also protests the targeting of specific groups for punishment, e.g., poor people, and First Nations (p. 134, see also ICOPA web page).

The *process paradigm* contrasts with the power paradigm through its emphasis on more flexible, decentralized interactions designed to reach a satisfactory resolution to the concerned parties (p. 134). Proponents of this process-based framework contend that it is an advance over more constricted avenues of prosecution and sentencing through the state. Barsh and Marlor move toward a rather searching critique of negotiated justice principles and programmes. These criticisms include:

a) lack of evidence that such processes are truly restorative or transformative

b) inability of such programmes to correct serious imbalances of power in all quarters of society

c) absence of longitudinal studies of programme effectiveness, using a wider range of variables

d) failure to distinguish between the "symbolic" effects of process-based measures and actual outcomes, such as crime rate reduction

Barsh and Marlor dedicate one section to "Indigenous Initiatives" (pages 142–48). Rather than simply accepting such initiatives as distinctive and legitimate, they caution that there is great diversity within the First Nations in Canada, for example, and we should be cautious of overgeneralizing, as if all communities were identical (p. 143). They also point out that in some indigenous communities, women have worked with external agencies to ensure protection that might not be available within their particular communities (ibid). Lest this be seen as some kind of backlash against First Nations traditions and initiatives, the authors argue that "expecting healing circles to heal oppressed communities is not only unrealistic, it trivializes the oppression" (p. 144). Furthermore, they argue that there may be benefits to healing circles and alternative dispute resolution, but question whether these positive aspects might not fade when, for example, prisoners return to largely unchanged social and economic milieux after release (p. 147).

Angela Harris extends theorizing about racism, gender, and criminal justice to include "Men dispossessed by racial or class status ..." (2000, 780). Rather than treating men as a monolithic group, Harris explores patterns of power and brutality among men. Clearly, some men are singled out for hateful crimes, such as the gross sexual violation of a Haitian immigrant man by a New York City police officer in 1997, and the 1998 murder of Matthew

Shepard, a gay, University of Wyoming student (2000, 778 and 806). For Harris, an appreciation of how gender and power interact means much more than punishing culpable individuals—the clichéd "rotten apples." It involves a much deeper transformation of, for example, "... the entire gendered culture of policing" (2000, 804). Zillah Eisenstein echoes this forward-thinking approach in her insistence that our understanding of race, of racist thinking and behaviour, are changeable. She sees politics as "... the struggle to define racialized meanings, which are cultural, economic, and historical ... The system of racism should therefore be understood as dynamic and in flux ... The racism of legalized slavery was significantly different from the racism of the 1990s. However, the changes do not bespeak the demise of slavery but rather its reformulation" (1994, 44).

RESEARCH APPROACHES

Simon and Lynch (1989) offer a number of suggestions concerning the development of research in the sociology of law. They report that such research has had a greater impact on criminal law policy than policies associated with civil law. They favour more venues for research on civil law in order to circulate recent research findings and to translate more of these findings into civil law areas. Even where solid sociolegal research is completed—for example, on the nature of the American legal profession— Simon and Lynch (1989, 835) comment that policy implications are not always sufficiently drawn. The social organization of professions such as law is interesting not only in its own right, but also in terms of how "non-elite" lawyers and legal services might be protected. This would seem especially pertinent as corporate power (and public-interest advocacy) continues to grow.

New research approaches will likely also be directed more toward the experiences and "voice" of those affected by law. Rather than simply treating entire collections of people as subject matter to be coded, analyzed, and reanalyzed as patterns, researchers will make efforts to hear of their experiences in the justice system. This need not only apply to victims and offenders, to plaintiffs and respondents, but to lawmakers, lawyers, judges, and to the wider public. It is also likely that groups that have traditionally not spoken for themselves, or at least have not been nearly as vocal as professional, mainstream researchers, will articulate their own standpoints and recommendations for change. This is perhaps most evident in resistance to appropriation of voice among indigenous peoples and persons of colour, but also applies to gender and sexual orientation and the entire array of people dealing with legal regulation or lack of legal protections.

SUMMARY

Another dimension to the sociology of law is the importance of restoring a greater sense of democracy at the community level. Some local organizations can reflect citizens' interests and possibly offset the interventionist, politically-motivated initiatives of more conservative political parties and governments (see Taylor 1981, 1983).

Roger Cotterrell, in *Law's Community* (1995), contemplates the nature of community and law's standing as a community unto itself, and in relation to other communities. He concludes that community is strengthened through trust and reciprocity, and that particular power relationships are at the core of community. Far from being overseen and regulated by elites or state regulatory bodies, communities are enhanced by "discussion and debate" and through mechanisms that include members (1995, 330–31). In complex ways, this may mean that some state controls are relaxed, while others are strengthened. Cotterrell thus expects that individuals pressured or displaced from certain communities "… should be able to appeal to the law of the nation state for a guarantee of certain minimum principles of collective participation and public altruism …" (1995, 334).

Another area of struggle involves legal protection for workers, along with other aspects of democratic politics, including expansion of individual liberties, strengthening of the democratic framework of politics, and consideration of the value of institutions like private property (see Fine 1984, 211–12). Again, there is a persistent spirit of resistance against what could be seen as an indomitable legal colossus and an indelibly stratified society. The numerous but selective cases and concepts we have discussed in this text have hopefully pointed out past struggles around law and justice, and helped to formulate new paths for social and legal research, policy, and political action.

STUDY QUESTIONS

1. Discuss the likely direction of law and society research and teaching in Canada. Which theoretical frameworks or research strategies do you think will become most prominent in the near future? Give specific examples.

2. What groups might successfully adopt the *collective* and *political* strategies recommended by Brickey and Comack (1987, 325–29)? What constraints are these groups likely to encounter in their legal struggles? Ultimately, how important are legal struggles for specific groups, vis-à-vis other than legal strategies (e.g., political lobbying, social and cultural resources)

3. The battered-wife syndrome, as discussed by Comack (1988), illustrates one aspect of criminal law: the use of psychological expert testimony in

criminal trials. What concerns does Comack (1988, 9–10) voice with respect to the battered-wife syndrome, especially its use as a strategy for realizing justice for battered women? Do you agree with her emphasis on *structural* conditions affecting women, made concrete by their "lack of choice" (Comack 1988, 10)?

4. Review barriers and possible solutions linked with litigation and with lobbying legislators to change existing laws. Which issues are most amenable to legal change; which ones are least amenable? Use specific examples such as abortion, affirmative action, immigration, domestic violence, for example.

NOTES

1. E. P. Thompson, *Whigs and Hunters: The Origin of the Black Act.* Harmondsworth: Penguin, 1977, p. 266. Reproduced by permission of Penguin Books Ltd.

REFERENCES

Asch, Michael (1997). "Introduction." In M. Asch (ed.), *Aboriginal and Treaty Rights in Canada: Essays on Law, Equality, and Respect for Difference,* ix–xv. Vancouver: University of British Columbia Press.

Ahluwalia, S. (1991) "Currents in British Feminist Thought: The Study of Male Violence." *In New Directions in Critical Criminology,* edited by B. MacLean and D. Milovanovic, 55–62. Vancouver: The Collective Press.

Allen, T. (2000) *Someone To Talk To: Care and Control of the Homeless.* Halifax: Fernwood Books.

Arnold, B. (1991) *A Life Course Dynamics Approach to Professional Deviance and Self-Regulation: The Case of Ontario Lawyers.* Unpublished Ph.D. thesis, Department of Sociology, University of Toronto.

Barak, G., J. Flavin, and P. Leighton (2001). *Class, Race, Gender, and Crime: Social Realities of Justice in America.* Los Angeles: Roxbury Publishing.

Barsh, R. and C. Marlor (1999) "Alternative Paradigms: Law as Power, Law as Process." In *Law in Society: Canadian Readings,* edited by N. Larsen and B. Burtch, 132–57. Toronto: Harcourt Brace Canada.

Belliotti, R. (1995) "The Legacy of Marxist Jurisprudence." In *Radical Philosophy of Law: Contemporary Challenges to Mainstream Legal Theory and Practice,* edited by D. Caudill and S. Gold, 3–33. New Jersey: Humanities Press.

Brickey, S., and E. Comack (1987) "The Role of Law in Social Transformation: Is a Jurisprudence of Insurgency Possible?" *Canadian Journal of Law and Society* 2: 97–119.

Brockman, J. (2001) *Gender in the Legal Profession: Fitting or Breaking the Mould.* Vancouver: University of British Columbia Press.

Buss, D. (2000) "Racing populations, sexing environments: the challenges of a feminist politics in international law." *Legal Studies* 20(4): 463–89.

Chunn, D. (1999) "Feminism, Law, and 'the Family'." In *Locating Law: Race/Class/Gender Connections*, edited by E. Comack, 236–59. Halifax: Fernwood Books.

Comack, E. (1988) "Justice for Battered Women? The Courts and the 'Battered Wife Syndrome.'" *Canadian Dimension* 22(3): 8–11.

——. (ed.) (1999) *Locating Law: Race/Class/Gender Connections*.

Cotterrell, R. (1995) *Law's Community: Legal Theory in Sociological Perspective*. Oxford: Clarendon Press.

Davis, N., and C. Stasz (1990) *Social Control of Deviance: A Critical Perspective*. New York: McGraw-Hill.

Delgado, R. (2000) "Goodbye to Hammurabi: Analyzing the Atavistic Appeal of Restorative Justice." *Stanford Law Review* 52: 751–75.

Eisenstein, Z. (1994) *The Color of Gender: Reimaging Democracy*. Berkeley: University of California Press.

Findlay, M. (1999) *The Globalisation of Crime: Understanding Transitional Relationships in Context*. Cambridge: Cambridge University Press.

Fine, B. (1984) *Democracy and the Rule of Law: Liberal Ideals and Marxist Critiques*. London: Pluto Press.

Forsythe, D. (2000) *Human Rights in International Relations*. Cambridge: Cambridge University Press.

Fox, R. (1995) *The Challenge of Anthropology: Old Encounters and New Excursions*. New Brunswick, N.J.: Transaction Publishers.

Goldberg-Ambrose, C. (1989) "Theory, Practice, and Perception in Rape

Law Reform." *Law and Society Review* 23(5): 949–55.

Habermas, J. (1996) *Between Facts and Norms: Contributions to a Discourse Theory of Law and Democracy*, translated by W. Rehg. Cambridge, UK: Polity Press.

Hagan, J. (1986) "The New Legal Scholarship: Problems and Prospects." *Canadian Journal of Law and Society* 1: 35–56.

Handler, J. (1990) *Law and the Search for Community*. Philadelphia: University of Pennsylvania Press.

——. (1992) Presidential Address, *Law and Society Review*.

Harris, A. (2000) "Gender, Violence, Race, and Criminal Justice." *Stanford Law Review* 52: 777–807.

Harris, O., ed. (1996) *Inside and Outside the Law: Anthropological studies of authority and ambiguity*. London: Routledge.

Ignatieff, M. (2000) *The Rights Revolution*. Toronto: House of Anansi Press

Kelman, M. (1987) *A Guide to Critical Legal Studies*. Cambridge: Harvard University Press.

Khor, M. (2001) *Rethinking Globalization: Critical Issues and Policy Choices*. Halifax: Fernwood Books.

Llewellyn, J., and R. Howse (1999) "Institutions for Restorative Justice: The South African Truth and Reconciliation Commission." *University of Toronto Law Journal* 49: 355–88.

MacKinnon, C. (1979) *Sexual Harassment of Working Women*. New Haven: Yale University Press.

Mandel, M. (1989) "The Rule of Law and the Legalization of Politics in Canada." *In Law and Society: A Critical Perspective*, edited by T. Caputo, M. Kennedy, C. Reasons,

A. Brannigan, 305–15. Toronto: Harcourt Brace Jovanovich.

McDaniel, S. (1991) "Feminist Scholarship in Sociology: Transformation from Within?" *Canadian Journal of Sociology* 16(3): 303–12.

McKercher, W. (1989) *Freedom and Authority.* Montreal: Black Rose Books.

Milovanovic, D. (1988) *A Primer in the Sociology of Law.* New York: Harrow and Heston.

Moorehead, A. (1974) *The Fatal Impact: An Account of the Invasion of the South Pacific, 1767–1840.* Harmondsworth: Penguin.

Nielsen, K. (1998) "Liberal Nationalism, Liberal Democracies, and Secession." *University of Toronto Law Journal* 48: 253–95.

Palys, T. (1997) *Research Decisions: Quantitative and Qualitative Perspectives* (second edition). Toronto: Harcourt Brace Canada.

Robertson, G. (2000) *Crimes Against Humanity: The Struggle for Global Justice.* London: Penguin Books.

Russell, J. (1989) *Liberties.* Vancouver: New Star Books.

Simon, R., and J. Lynch (1989) "The Sociology of Law: Where We Have Been and Where We Might Be Going." *Law and Society Review* 23 (5): 825–47.

Skogstad, G. (2001) "Globalization and Public Policy: Situating Canadian Analyses." *Canadian Journal of Political Science* 33(4): 805–28.

Taylor, I. (1981) *Law and Order: Arguments for Socialism.* London: Macmillan.

——.(1983) *Crime, Capitalism, and Community.* Toronto: Butterworths.

——. (1999) *Crime in Context: A Critical Criminology of Market Societies.* Oxford: Polity Press/Blackwell Publishers.

Thompson, E.P. (1977) *Whigs and Hunters: The Origin of the Black Act.* Harmondsworth: Penguin.

Tomm, W., and G. Hamilton, eds. (1988) *Gender Bias in Scholarship: The Pervasive Prejudice.* Waterloo, Ontario: Wilfrid Laurier University Press.

Waldron, J. (2000) "Homelessness and Community." *University of Toronto Law Journal* 50: 371–406.

Ward, I. (1998) *An Introduction to Critical Legal Theory.* London: Cavendish Publishing. York, G. (1990) *The Dispossessed: Life and Death in Native Canada.* London: Vintage.

York G. (1990) *The Dispossessed: Life and Death in Native Canada.* London: Vintage.

Young, A. (1996) *Imagining Crime: Textual Outlaws and Criminal Conversations.* London: SAGE Publications.

Young, I. (1990) *Justice and the Politics of Difference.* Princeton: Princeton University Press.

INDEX